NEW ZEALAND'S
CHINA
EXPERIENCE

ITS GENESIS, TRIUMPHS, AND
OCCASIONAL MOMENTS OF
LESS THAN COMPLETE SUCCESS

EDITED BY CHRIS ELDER

VICTORIA UNIVERSITY PRESS

VICTORIA UNIVERSITY PRESS
Victoria University of Wellington
PO Box 600 Wellington
http://www.victoria.ac.nz/vup

National Library of New Zealand Cataloguing-in-Publication Data

New Zealand's China experience : its genesis, triumphs, and
occasional moments of less than complete success / edited by
Chris Elder.
Includes bibliographical references.
ISBN 978-0-86473-837-0
1. China—In literature. 2. New Zealanders—Travel.
3. China—Description and travel. I. Elder, Chris, 1947-
808.803251—dc 23

Published with the assistance of the Ministry of Foreign Affairs
and Trade to mark the fortieth anniversary of the establishment
of diplomatic relations between New Zealand and the People's
Republic of China

Printed in China by 1010 Printing International Ltd

CONTENTS

The map reproduced here is taken from the Chinese geographical treatise *Yue Liu Kuang 1*, published in 1602. It is based on a map drawn by the Jesuit priest Matteo Ricci, incorporating the most up-to-date European knowledge (but tactfully altering the projection to place China in the centre). Where New Zealand will later find a place in the Chinese world there is shown a large, irregular continent, with the comment that 'Few people have been to this place in the South, and no one knows what things are there'.

INTRODUCTION

In 1956, Ormond Wilson, the civil libertarian and former Labour Member of Parliament, led a small delegation of New Zealand 'cultural representatives' on a fact-finding visit to China. In the course of their visit, they were invited to a reception hosted by the Chinese Premier, Zhou Enlai. Finding themselves in conversation with the Premier, members of the group took the opportunity to express the hope that New Zealand would soon establish diplomatic relations with China. 'Well,' responded Zhou reassuringly, 'I think that China can wait.'

China did wait. It was another sixteen years before New Zealand formally recognised the People's Republic, one of the phalanx of countries that shifted their position after Beijing took up China's seat at the United Nations in 1971. That act cleared the way for a substantive political relationship, which has grown closer over the years, and which has provided the bedrock for developing links in many other spheres of activity.

It would be a mistake, nonetheless, to think that it was only with the establishment of diplomatic relations that dealings between the two countries acquired any real substance, or that the official relationship has crowded out everything else since. Interaction between New Zealand and China had its beginnings in the earliest days of New Zealand's dealings with the outside world. It has seen contact in both directions that has developed beyond early prejudice and misunderstandings. And it has given rise to interchanges—of goods, of people, of thought and literary expression—that have contributed materially to New Zealand's development as an economy, as a society, and as a culture.

It was in 1792 that Captain William Raven landed a sealing gang at Dusky Sound to procure skins for the China market, then the most lucrative in the world. Others followed. There is something poignant in the image of Manchu grandees protecting themselves against the North China winter with the products of New Zealand's desolate southern coastline. Sadly, however, New Zealand's first export trade did not last long. The unchecked depletion of the stocks of seals soon made their exploitation uneconomic. Other brief enthusiasms, such as the export of greenstone (pounamu) to Eastern lapidary markets, followed. But it was with the discovery of gold in the mid-nineteenth century that the first substantial contact with China had its beginnings.

Chinese had travelled to New Zealand before the gold rushes. The country's first Chinese immigrant very nearly predated the Treaty of Waitangi. Appo Hocton disembarked (or possibly jumped ship) at Nelson on 25 October 1842. He went on to become a naturalised New Zealander and a substantial property owner, some of whose solidly-built houses survive in Nelson to this day. It was the gold discoveries of the 1860s, however, that led to the first large-scale influx of Chinese to New Zealand. They came first from the Victoria diggings in Australia, and then directly from Southern China, to take up claims too poor or too difficult for the European miners. Only men came, and they did not see themselves as long-term migrants: their objective was to win a sufficient amount from the goldfields and then return home. This many did. Others went from the goldfields to enterprises such as market gardening and operating laundries and fruitshops. They formed a cohesive, distinctive and different group in the community, and they were not made welcome by colonial society. Over time, measures were set in place to limit the numbers of Chinese entering New Zealand.

By the late nineteenth century, the stream of travel was not all one way. The church missionary societies had scarcely ceased civilising New Zealand before they set in place a reverse flow, sending missionaries from New Zealand to help in the evangelisation of China. The Presbyterian Church, indeed, adopted a two-pronged attack, appointing Alexander Don to minister to the Chinese miners on the goldfields, and later establishing a mission station, together with a hospital, in the miners' home districts in Guangdong Province.

By the time China became a republic, New Zealanders were beginning to arrive with secular rather than religious motives: the economists J. B. Cundliffe and Brian Low, Agnes Moncrieff with the YWCA, Rewi Alley pursuing a variety of humanitarian objectives. Not all of these did much to promote knowledge of New Zealand in China (James Bertram, for instance, remains a 'British journalist' throughout) but it is apparent that through their reporting and occasional visits home both they and the missionaries were instrumental in bringing about a more genuine understanding of China in New Zealand.

Political relations, meanwhile, remained little developed. China through the first half of the twentieth century suffered under a series of unstable governments, more preoccupied with survival than with developing relations with minor powers, while New Zealand was for the most part content to consign questions of foreign policy to the British Government.

The Second World War (for China the Anti-Japanese War) brought about far-reaching changes in the nascent relationship. The position of Chinese resident in New Zealand came gradually to be regularised, through agreement first of all that wives and dependant children could join their husbands in New Zealand for the duration of hostilities, and later that they could stay for good. At a governmental level, New Zealand supported China against Japan in international meetings, and at the individual level, New Zealanders became involved in humanitarian relief, through organisations such as the Friends Ambulance Unit, and through participation in the major reconstruction programme spearheaded by UNRRA (the United Nations Relief and Rehabilitation Administration). At the end of the war, Rewi Alley's efforts to promote development in the far west of China caught New Zealanders' imagination, and became a focus for the efforts of CORSO, an umbrella organisation formed to channel the efforts of voluntary agencies in New Zealand.

Popular opinion regarding China was by this time generally positive, shaped by the experience of those who spent time there, and the reports they sent back. Bolstering this was sympathy for China's privations through its long struggle against Japan, and some realisation that one effect of that struggle had been to tie up Japanese military resources that might otherwise have pushed further south. The Government went so far as to enter into negotiations to conclude a Sino-New Zealand Treaty of Amity, although that eventually foundered on the sensitive issue of entry to New Zealand.

There was no inherent reason why this generally positive atmosphere should not have carried over into a successful relationship with the new government that came to power in China in 1949. The New Zealand Government, however, opted for a cautious approach, one that by steering a path between 'undue haste' and 'perverse procrastination' ended up stuck in the middle. It had still not settled upon a firm course of action by the time of the Korean War. China's entry into that war on the side of North Korea, coupled with New Zealand's interest in reaching agreement on a security pact with the United States, saw the possibility of recognition shelved for a period—a period that ended up lasting more than twenty years.

Following the advent of the People's Republic the level of personal contact between the two countries became less. The long-standing missionary effort came to an end, and there was little scope for continuing cooperation on humanitarian projects. As New Zealand technical experts left China, they were not replaced. New Zealanders who chose to travel to China, individually or as members of delegations such as the one led by Ormond Wilson, were regarded with suspicion and sometimes hostility at home.

The break was never absolute. In New Zealand a group of those who wished to keep the relationship alive formed the New Zealand China Friendship Society, then seen as a dangerously subversive organisation, today one eminently respectable, although neither its objectives nor its methods have changed in the intervening years. In China, Rewi Alley wrote prolifically, documenting in prose and in verse the achievements of the New China. The New Zealand Government never placed barriers in the way of travel to China (so that photographer Tom Hutchins, for instance, was able to take up opportunities denied to his American colleagues). Individual traders took advantage of the government's 'hands-off' attitude to begin business in a small way.

Remarkably, the closest thing to a formal link was the party-to-party relationship enjoyed by the New Zealand Communist Party. Insignificant in New Zealand, the NZCP was accorded a high profile in China because it was one of the few communist parties world-wide to side with China at the time of the Sino-Soviet split. Its leader, Vic Wilcox, was feted in Beijing, and at least once took his place beside Mao on the reviewing rostrum for the May Day parade. The New Zealand Communist Party newspaper, the *People's Voice*, was offered for sale at Chinese news outlets, and in later years it was not uncommon to meet cadres for whom it had been a daily resource material in their English language classes.

Given the paper's somewhat idiosyncratic view of New Zealand's ripeness for revolutionary change, it is not surprising that this avenue of contact gave rise to some misapprehensions that subsequently required to be corrected.

The normalisation of relations, when it came, in fact paved the way for a more realistic view on both sides. Early reporting from the New Zealand Embassy in Beijing reflects a dawning realisation that China was more concerned with bettering the lot of its people than fomenting world revolution. And China came to accept New Zealand as a small, stable Western democracy, unlikely soon to be diverted from that path into the orbit of its giant communist neighbour. Mr Wilcox's visits to China continued for a time, but they were no longer accorded the same high profile. When China organised a study tour for New Zealand journalists in in 1975, the *People's Voice* was absent from a group that included such mainstream publications as the *Nelson Mail*, the *Christchurch Star*, and the *New Zealand Listener*.

From the time of Associate Foreign Minister Joe Walding's first meetings in Beijing in 1973, it was accepted on both sides that a successful relationship had to be based on robust political understandings, but that it needed to extend much more widely than that. The people to people links that had sustained contact through the period of non-recognition were acknowledged, and to them were added the possibility of enhanced trade, cultural, sporting and educational ties. (Mr Walding invited Vice Foreign Minister Qiao Guanhua to consider training English language students in New Zealand; Qiao suggested sending 1,000 in the first batch. Nowadays the suggestion seems less remarkable than it did then.)

In the years immediately after the establishment of relations, governments were closely involved in the exchanges set under way. China sent an acrobatic troupe; New Zealand reciprocated with the National Youth Orchestra. New Zealand provided scholarships for students from China (initially three rather than 1,000); China accepted three New Zealand students at the Peking Languages Institute. As familiarity and confidence grew, however, individuals and institutions developed links independent of the central authorities, and many relationships became self-sustaining. That has continued through to the present, when activities such as sister-city links, academic cooperation, and cultural interchanges find their own justifications and impetus, without the need (or indeed the desire) for the involvement of central government.

New Zealand had modest hopes for its trade relationship with China in 1972. It was with a sense of real achievement that New Zealand's first Ambassador noted, on relinquishing his post in 1975, that exports to China had risen to $20 million, and imports to $18 million. No one then foresaw the spectacular growth in the Chinese economy, beginning in the last two decades of the twentieth century, that has turned China into New Zealand's most important trading partner bar Australia, with exports in 2011 reaching $5.9 billion, and imports more than $7 billion.

The trade relationship is important in its own right, but it is important also for what it has to contribute to other aspects of the two countries' dealings. If a good political relationship is a necessary prerequisite for a good trading relationship, a good trading relationship in its turn helps to underpin the wide range of other activities that go to make up the totality of the dealings between the two countries and their peoples. It lends such dealings relevance, it multiplies the points of contact, and it even at times provides the financial backing to carry worthwhile activities forward. He Pakiaka, the distinctive expression of Maori identity at the New Zealand Embassy in Beijing, is a gift of the Maori people, but it is a gift facilitated by the contributions of companies involved in the China trade.

As China's economy has opened up, so has its population become more outwardly mobile. For New Zealand, this has meant in effect a second wave of Chinese migration. The long-established Cantonese-speaking community that traces its roots back to the gold seekers has been joined by a new generation of immigrants from China. Many studied in New Zealand before establishing a right to residency. Taken as a whole, the Chinese community now forms a substantial and fast-growing sub-group within New Zealand society. A growing sense of cultural identity has been reinforced by the work researchers such as Professor Manying Ip and Dr James Ng have done in charting the past. What it means to be at once Chinese and a New Zealander is increasingly finding imaginative expression through the work of a younger group of writers and artists—Alison Wong, Tze Ming Mok, Chris Tse, Kerry Ann Lee and others.

The present collection does not set out to chronicle the growth of contacts between New Zealand and China in any structured way. Rather it aims to provide glimpses of the people and the events that have helped shape the relationship, for better and sometimes for worse. Readability and interest have been the main criteria. If this has at times led to the trivial being elevated above matters of real significance, that is arguably a fair reflection of the way relationships do develop, between nations and between people.

Readers who seek consistency of approach in the romanisation of Chinese propers names will find themselves disappointed. In general the commentary adopts the romanisation used in the text, with the standard (pinyin) equivalent included in parentheses where it seems this would be helpful.

Many people have provided suggestions about what might be included, and helped track down sources and shape the material for publication. My thanks go first to my wife Sharron and son Barnaby for their forbearance during the process of assembly, then to Victoria Boyack, Anne-Marie Brady, Duncan Campbell, Matthew Dalzell, Pam Dunn, Karen Evans, Alexandra Grace, Shirley Inwood, Steven Lulich, Pip McLachlan, James Ng, Wen Powles, Rhys Richards, Neil Robertson, Jill Trevelyan, John Turner, Margaret Watson, Wu Ming, Jamie Xia, the members of MFAT's North Asia Division, Fergus Barrowman and all at the Victoria University Press, and the many others who have helped put together a selection that aims to be, like the relationship itself, always eclectic and occasionally surprising.

Vice-Minister Qiao Guanhua greets Hon Joe Walding at the outset of talks in the Great Hall of the People on 28 March 1973.

A NEW BEGINNING

New Zealand formally established diplomatic relations with the People's Republic of China through a communiqué signed in New York on 22 December 1972. The Associate Minister of Foreign Affairs, Hon Joe Walding, led a small delegation to China in March 1973 to make the first contact at Ministerial level. In Peking the Minister met Premier Zhou Enlai, and had formal talks with Qiao Guanhua, the Vice-Minister of Foreign Affairs.

OPENING REMARKS BY THE ASSOCIATE MINISTER OF FOREIGN AFFAIRS, HON JOE WALDING, PEKING, WEDNESDAY 28 MARCH 1973

Mr Minister,

Thank you for your welcome. My colleagues and I are very pleased to be in China and to have the opportunity of meeting you and other members of the Chinese Government.

The Government to which I belong came into office only three months ago, after the Labour Party had won a majority in our general elections.

We are determined that New Zealand shall take a more independent stand in international affairs: we do not intend to take orders from any other country. We are also determined to work more closely with our neighbours in the Pacific and in Asia. We belong to the Pacific world and we want to play our part in it.

For many years New Zealand has been cut off from China. The Cold War pushed our two countries apart and there was little contact between us. My Government set out to rectify this situation. One of the first things we did on coming into office was to open negotiations with you for the establishment of diplomatic relations between New Zealand and the People's Republic of China. We were delighted that it was possible to announce agreement within two weeks of our taking office.

New Zealand is a small country, and we have limited resources. We are particularly short of trained diplomatic staff. The joint communiqué announcing the establishment of relations between us said that ambassadors would be exchanged as soon as practicable. We explained in the course of the negotiations that we would not be able to do so immediately but we would aim to open our embassy here by the end of 1973. That is still our intention.

We did not, however, want to wait until our embassy was set up before establishing contact with your Government. We recognised that in working out our own policies we needed to talk to you so that we could take full account of China's position and China's views. The best way to do this seemed to be to send a Cabinet Minister to China to establish contact with your Government at the ministerial level. it is my privilege to have been chosen for this mission.

I should make it clear at the outset that we have no specific proposals or requests to put to you. We are here primarily to get a better understanding of your outlook and to explain our own. This we believe is essential if our two countries are to work together in the future.

We would naturally like to explore with you the possibilities for developing relations between China and New Zealand. As a country that depends heavily on international trade, we are particularly interested in the expansion of trade, and this is one of the things I should like to talk about. But it is by no means the only one. I should also like to discuss the possibilities for technical and scientific exchanges between our two countries, and for further exchanges in the fields of sport and culture.

Another aspect of our bilateral relations that I would like to discuss is the establishment of a New Zealand Embassy in Peking. On my way here I met the group of Chinese diplomats who have gone to Wellington to open your Embassy there. I can assure you that my Government will do all it can to help them. We ourselves want to set up our embassy here in Peking within the next few months: we are hoping that you will be able to help us with the practical problems involved. I have brought with me an official from the Administration Division of Our Ministry of Foreign Affairs who would like to talk to the appropriate people in your Government about this question.

Finally, I would like to discuss with you international questions that are of interest both to China and to New Zealand. Although our countries are a long way apart, they are both in the Pacific region. We at least are anxious to do what we can to maintain peace and promote economic and social progress in that region. We believe there is scope for closer cooperation between the countries of the area to advance these goals, and not least between China and New Zealand. We look forward to hearing your views.

Unused to working through an interpreter, Mr Walding delivered his entire statement without once pausing to allow for translation. The interpreter, Nancy Tang (Tang Wen-sheng, later a member of Mao's 'kitchen cabinet'), who had up to that point taken no obvious interest in proceedings, then provided an exact translation, paragraph by paragraph, sentence by sentence. It was an impressive introduction to Chinese diplomacy.

COMMISSIONER BIGGE'S REPORT

John Thomas Bigge, in the course of his appointment as a royal commissioner in the colony of New South Wales, provided this report to the British Secretary of State, Lord Bathurst, in 1823. Much of his information is based on a visit to the Bay of Islands on board HMS Dromedary. *His reference to English vessels' access to China relates to the obstructive behaviour of the East India Company, at that time still concerned to assert its monopoly rights to the China market.*

MY LORD,—   27 February 1823

. . . From the limited information even that had been obtained of the character and resources of the Northern Island of New Zealand, it appears to possess a great superiority over the settled districts of the Colony of New South Wales. In rivers, harbors, climate, soil, and natural productions, the superiority of New Zealand is manifest, and the only impediment that presents itself to the colonisation of the island arises from the savage and revengeful disposition of the inhabitants. It does not appear that they are averse to the settlement of Europeans—on the contrary, their natural shrewdness has already pointed out to them the advantages they derive from the presence and intercourse with strangers. The missionaries have hitherto confined their settlements to the Bay of Islands, but they were in treaty, when the Dromedary left the island, for a large and fertile tract of land, in which it was intended to make a settlement that was to receive the name of Gloucester. It is the opinion of Mr McCroe that although the natives would not hostilely oppose the settlement of a body of Europeans, or of English in New Zealand, landing with pacific and friendly objects, yet that their indiscriminate revenge and sensibility to injury would expose individuals to a great degree of personal danger. During the period in which the crew and guard of the Dromedary were engaged in cutting wood, and in making a road for carrying it to the harbor, they were encamped on shore; they were frequently visited by the natives, but were never molested by them, and several of the men, as well as women, remained on board the Dromedary when the crew was greatly diminished in number without any symptom or disposition to violence. Quarrels took place between the natives and the sailors, but by the prudence and discretion of Captain Skinner, the commander of the Dromedary, indemnity or satisfaction in some shape or other was rendered to the injured parties, and all feeling of national insult was appeased. Among a body of English settlers not subject to any control the same discretion is not to be expected, and it is on this account, and for the purpose of affording protection against the sudden movements of revengeful passion in the natives, that Mr McCroe considered that a small military force would be necessary, in case it should be deemed expedient to give encouragement to the colonisation of New Zealand. Whenever the China market shall become accessible to English vessels, the value of New Zealand, as a place of deposit for the produce of the whale and seal fisheries, cannot fail to attract them to its harbours. The Americans, who

15

are freely admitted to the China market, are already sensible of the advantages to be derived from an intercourse with the New Zealanders, and will succeed in establishing it, notwithstanding the partiality and preference that the natives entertain for the subjects of Great Britain, and the knowledge they have acquired of the distinction between these and the Americans. . . . All of which is very humbly submitted to Your Lordship.

JOHN THOMAS BIGGE
To the Right Honourable the Earl Bathurst, K.G.

CAPTAIN WILLIAM ANGLEM

Basil Howard

William Anglem was one of the earliest European settlers in Southern New Zealand. In 1835 he took up residence at the Neck on Stewart Island with his Maori wife, Te Anau, and their children. After the events of 1843, described here, he took no further interest in the possibilities of the China market, finding employment as a ship's pilot.

Anglem was an Irishman of an intellectual calibre unusual among whaling captains of the day. According to his son-in-law, Gilroy, he had been destined for the Catholic priesthood; but before his theological studies were completed, his restless nature overcame his intentions, and he went to sea in search of adventure. Whether he found in this new life realisation or disillusionment cannot be suggested even in conjecture, and nothing can be written in record of his career until he arrived in New Zealand in 1829 in the employ of Bunn and Co., at the Preservation Inlet whaling station. As one of their sailing captains he cruised the southern grounds and voyaged across the Tasman Sea to Sydney, carrying the season's cargo of oil and bone. . . .

In 1842 he appears in a new industry—the export of greenstone to the Philippine and Chinese market. The origins of this undertaking are to be found, it is said, in 1830, when a Captain Dacre obtained possession of an excellent *mere*. Years later he exhibited it at Manila, and merchants there enthusiastically offered to buy all he could bring of such stone. It is impossible to discover when or how Anglem became involved, although the solution may be found in the fact that he and Dacre were both sailing out of Sydney to New Zealand in the early 'thirties. Dacre is said to have been responsible for the fitting out of the schooner *Royal Mail* at Sydney for the venture. She left Wellington ostensibly on a sealing voyage, and after calling at Stewart Island and Bluff for a crew for that purpose, made for Milford Sound. At this time the *Anita* was there, presumably in search of greenstone also, for the bay in which the stone is found is named 'Anita', and a point nearby, 'Fox Point', after her captain. Leaving some of her complement at the Sound, sealing or quarrying, the *Royal Mail* left for Sydney to obtain provisions. She returned in November, 1842, under command of Anglem, via Nelson, bringing also ironwork for a small vessel to be built in the south.

In January, 1843, the *Royal Mail* returned to Nelson with the captain and some of the crew in urgent need of surgical assistance. Anglem had lost an eye, and had had both arms fractured; three of the crew were said to be more or less blind. The *Nelson Examiner* found the victims reticent, but gathered that a boat's crew had ascended a large river for greenstone, and that in the course of blasting operations a premature explosion had inflicted these terrible injuries and lacerations. Ten days passed before the unfortunate men reached port. The report continued: 'Captain Anglem reports that there is a fine white marble in the neighbourhood of the spot where the accident occurred, but for some reason is unwilling to give precise information whereabouts it was.' The schooner sailed again for the southward about mid-February, and no further trace of her is found in New Zealand shipping news. It is said that the venture was a failure; it had been undertaken with enthusiasm and secrecy under the irresistible spur of a promise of £1,500 per ton. The schooner's ten-ton cargo, however, found an apathetic market; the stone contained small black flecks which displeased the eastern lapidaries.

THE SOUTHERN CROSS:

EXTRACTS.

VALUABLE GREEN STONE.—We have been put in possession of a curious fact connected with the development of the mineral wealth of the southern island, namely, that the green-stone, or *poonamor* of the natives, a species of talk slate, is in such demand in the Chinese market for the manufacture of their idols, ornaments, &c., that as much as £1,500 per ton can be had for it. We refer to the fact that a vessel had actually been fitted out from this port in May last, by Mr. Elger, of Sydney, for the purpose of speculating in a cargo of it; that vessel, the *Royal Mail*, proceeded down to Milford Haven, on the west coast, where she is now trading, and is to be joined by the *Anita* in about a month hence, to proceed to China and dispose of her valuable cargo. Mr. Deans, one of the most intelligent and persevering of our colonists, has returned from an extended trip down the east coast of Middle Island. We hear he brings highly favourable information of that locality, and some curious account of the *Royal Mail* being at anchor in Milford Haven, engaged in collecting green stone for the China market, where it is said to be worth £1,500 per ton. The account further states that the *Royal Mail* has already secured ten tons of green stone, to the value of £15,000. We wish Mr. Deans would favour the public with a report of his trip, as we feel confident the public would, with justice, place every confidence in any statement coming from his pen.—*Spectator.* (New Zealand.)

The above we copy from the *Bombay Times*, and we insert it to show what very exaggerated and erroneous opinions obtain currency. A consignment of the green stone above referred to has arrived here, and it proved to be utterly valueless. It is undeniable that New Zealand abounds in minerals of great value, but for many years, we much doubt whether it will find a more valuable export than its native flax, and for which there will eventually be a large *debouche* in China.—*Hongkong Gazette.*

ILLUSTRIOUS ENERGY

"...one of those magical, dream-like films that quietly and slowly draws you into another place and holds you there, mesmerized..." - Helen Martin, NZ Listener

Mirage Entertainment in association with the New Zealand Film Commission presents a Leon Narbey film Illustrious Energy
SHAUN BAO . HARRY IP . PETER CHIN . GEELING . DESMOND KELLY . HEATHER BOLTON . PETER HAYDEN . DAVID TELFORD
Designer JANELLE ASTON Cinematographer ALAN LOCKE Music JAN PRESTON Editor DAVID COULSON
Screenplay MARTIN EDMOND and LEON NARBEY
Producer DON REYNOLDS Assoc Producer CHRIS HAMPSON Director LEON NARBEY
Digitally re-mastered by Park Road Post Productions with funding from the New Zealand Film Commission
Approximate running time: 102 minutes. Aspect Ratio 1.85:1 / Soundtrack 5.1

In 1866, the first Chinese goldminers entered New Zealand in response to an invitation issued by the Dunedin Chamber of Commerce. The film Illustrious Energy *is based on the miners' experiences in the inhospitable landscape of Central Otago. Released in 1987, it had the misfortune to be seized by the receivers when its production company failed, and never achieved very wide distribution. In 2011 it was remastered and shown at film festivals in New Zealand. The text provided here is from the fifth revision, and differs in some respects from the shooting script.*

ILLUSTRIOUS ENERGY

Screenplay by Leon Narbey and Martin Edmond

SCENE 7. EXT. LANDSCAPE NEAR HUT MORNING   7.

As the rising sun touches the tops of the hills, WONG is seen walking through the landscape. He wears a jacket and carries the casket of bones and a flourbag on a carry-pole.

At the summit of the slope, he pauses for a breather, looking back down the hill.

A view of the hut below shows the tiny figures of CHAN and KIM out front. They are dwarfed by the landscape.

They shoulder tools, ready to set off to the diggings for the day's work.

WONG cups his hands round his mouth and calls down to them. The SOUND echoes round the valley. They look up.

From below, the tiny figure of WONG, waving. He turns and disappears over the ridge.

SCENE 8. EXT. THE CLAIM DAY   8.

The claim is situated at a bend in a small river, just before it enters a rocky gorge.

They are working the base of a cliff made up of alluvial deposits. There is a wide sandy beach between the stream and the cliff. Water has been diverted from further up river, so it runs, via a race, parallel to the face of the cliff.

Piles of large and small stones mark the limits of the work area. A cradle stands by the race. There are sluice forks and gold pans on the ground.

CHAN is working the cradle.

KIM, with pick and shovel, is at the base of the cliff. A couple more shovel loads and the wheelbarrow is full. He picks up the handles and trundles it along a plank to the race.

KIM tips the load up just as CHAN takes a shovel load of dirt for the cradle. The barrow load of dirt crashes onto his shovel, nearly wrenching it from his hands.

                              KIM
          Watch out!

                              CHAN
          My fault!

                              KIM
          Too slow!

KIM picks up a sluice fork and starts lifting larger stones from the race into the barrow.

CHAN returns to the cradle, rocking it by means of the vertical handle attached and sticking up from its top, while pouring water from the race over the dirt with a ladle. He dips and rocks, dips and rocks.

KIM wheels the barrow load of stones off to the tailings. A SHOUT from CHAN.

                              CHAN
          Cradle full! Time to pan out!

KIM wheels the empty barrow back. Together, they lift the top off the heavy cradle, to reveal deposits of fine sand on the hessian base. The sand glints with mica. It is removed into the gold pans.

Crouching together by the race, CHAN and KIM swirl the sand in the pans, every now and then tilting them into the race to get more water. Their eyes eagerly search the bottom of the pans for flakes of colour.

A few tiny fragments of gold are extracted from the pans with tweezers and placed in an old tobacco tin.

Beginning the sequence in wide shot, we now move closer and closer, until all we see is the pan, the hands, the tweezers, the minute flecks of gold.

Voices come over the latter part of the action.

                              KIM
          Not much . . .

>   CHAN
>   Such hard work, so little reward.

>   KIM
>   We must work harder.

CHAN stands and stretches, rubbing his back. He SIGHS, then looks up at the sun.

>   CHAN
>   Lunch time.

SCENE 9. EXT. NEAR THE CLAIM DAY   9.

In a cool overhang of rock a little distance from the river, CHAN and KIM eat their midday meal — cold rice and vegetables left over from the night before. There is the SOUND of running water nearby.

The billy of tea is hung over a small fire. They drink from enamel mugs.

CHAN is stretched out on his back, his hands clasped behind his head. KIM squats on his haunches near the fire, finishing his rice. He gulps a mouthful of tea, swirls it round his mouth, swallows, then reaches over to refill his cup. He looks sideways at CHAN.

>   KIM
>   More tea?

CHAN doesn't answer.

>   KIM
>   Won't answer when spoken to,
>   talks when should be quiet.

CLOSE UP of CHAN. He opens one eye.

>   KIM
>   Rude to elders and betters,
>   discourteous to guests.

KIM stands up and empties the dregs from his mug. CHAN tilts his head up to watch.

>   KIM
>   I can't read or write,
>   but I know how to behave.

He stalks off down the path back to the claim.

CHAN sits up and watches him go, a quizzical look on his face.

                              KIM (shouting)
                    BACK TO WORK!

CHAN gets to his feet, shrugs and follows.

SCENE 10. EXT. A CLIFFTOP LATE AFTERNOON   10.
_____

CHAN is seen in profile before a landscape that recedes into the
distance. Rocky outcrops, scrubby vegetation. The sun has set, the
sky is purple behind him.

Squatting on his haunches, he has been re-reading the letter. A
CRACKLE of paper as he folds it away.

Beginnning almost under his breath, he repeats the following poem by
TU FU, in ENGLISH, as if recalling the words to himself.

                              CHAN
                    A hawk hovers in air.
                    Two white' gulls float on the stream.
                    Soaring with the wind, it is easy
                    to drop and seize
                    Birds who foolishly drift with the current.
                    Where dew sparkles in the grass
                    The spider's web waits for its prey.
                    The processes of nature resemble the business of men.
                    I stand alone with ten thousand sorrows.

At the end of the poem, he repeats the last line softly in CHINESE,
then stands and CHANTS it loudly over the landscape, so his voice
echoes down the gorge.

Then he bends to pick up his load of firewood. It is made of skinny
sticks, pieces of bracken, twists of tussock — anything that will
burn. The pieces are lashed together with rope, the bundle is carried
via two loops of rope, one for each arm, so it lies across the
shoulders at a slight angle from the vertical.

CHAN turns and disappears down the hill, the bundle of sticks
jumping up and down behind him.

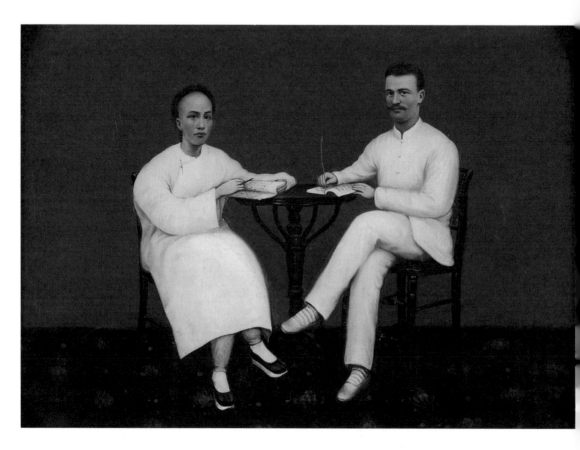

Artist unknown. Teacher Chau Yip-fung and Alexander Don, Shameen, September 1880.

STONE-HORSE VILLAGE

Rev Alexander Don

The Presbyterian Church of Otago and Southland sent Alexander Don to Canton (Guangzhou) in 1879 to study the Cantonese dialect. This was the first step towards establishing a mission to the Chinese gold miners in New Zealand. Soon after his return in 1881, Don began the series of inland tours around the diggings in Otago, Southland, and the West Coast that continued for the next 20 years. In that time he undertook 18 tours and covered 30,000 miles, more than half of the travel on foot. A return visit to China in 1898, described here, led to the establishment of the Canton Villages Mission at Kong Chuen, intended to build on contacts with miners returned from New Zealand.

We took the first night boat to Canton, and at 5 a.m. on January 12th heard the three characteristic Canton sounds—a gong clanging on a passing junk, a watchman's drum ending the fifth watch, and a volley of firecrackers. During the night I had tried vainly to recall this journey seventeen years ago: these three sounds brought back Canton so vividly that it seemed only yesterday that I had left. . . .

TO SHEK-MA

This is the 'Stone-horse' village, which I reached next morning, thus realising the desire of many years; for hundreds of Chinese in Otago come thence. Here live five clans, each in its own 'side' of the village, numbering in all some 7,500; —'3700' the villagers tell you, but only males are counted. It faces east, with Clear Hill a mile to N.E., Star-Scraping Range some fifteen miles in front, and to the S.E. the White Cloud Hills hiding from view the pagodas of Canton city. A small stream touches the village plantation (every village here has a wood to rear and sides, and an artificial pond in front) at the corner where stands the lately renovated temple; and behind is a low hill, over whose shoulder the path runs to the nearest market town 'River Village', where we anchored. There by the path-side is a large flat rock, on which one of the Immortals stood awhile: Is not the impression of his foot clearly visible to this day? Each clan has its Ancestral Hall, with tablets of ancestors back to the founders of the village. The Hall of the Chans (= Smith, because the commonest Chinese surname) is finest: the money to build it came almost wholly from *Chans* in Otago and Westland.

RECEPTION

Walking to Shek-ma I greeted every man met, and was delighted at the friendliness of the responses. At once I felt that I was not in a strange land; for scenes hitherto visited only in dreams were now realised. A group of men and women, on their way to the Bridge-head market, chatted freely as I walked with them part way.

At parting. they directed me across a flat of rice fields, with its thin forest of well-sweeps, and pointed out 'the tops of the tallest trees in Shek-ma wood, peeping over the shoulder of yonder hill'.

At the village, I asked for 'Cloud'—the addressee of a letter I bore from a nephew, mining at Waikaka—to be told that 'Cloud' is dead, but his widow would be called. As I waited, a crowd collected—mainly boys and old men near at hand (the young men are mostly away at Bridge-head, where the market is held two days in five), the girls and young women at some distance. But the elderly women too crowded round, and rather surprised me by their freedom of speech with the first foreigner seen by most of them.

NEWS FROM AFAR

Confucius said: 'Is not it pleasant to have a friend come from a far land?' It would take pages to tell of the wonderfully familiar way in which these villagers met me. I am not a pessimist, but my rosiest hopes were much under-coloured. I shall merely outline some of the incidents during a stay of two hours. What happened here happened too everywhere in this district.

A pleasant-faced, wrinkled old dame asked if I know 'Shining Face,' her only son. When I answered affirmatively, she said, 'What is he doing?' And when told, continued: 'I am 70 years old, he has sent me no money for years, and I am very poor.' The bystanders pointed out Shining Face's nephew 'All,' popularly known as 'Fatty,' whose looks match his nickname.

One 'Glorious Peace' proclaimed himself the elder brother and uncle respectively of two men I know. I am to tell the former that he must come home when he can pay his passage: the latter, that 'his mother has no rice to eat.'

A man came to say, '"Coral" wishes to see you.' Soon Coral (an old Round Hill man) came and welcomed me warmly. He is on his way to Bridge-head mart, but his brother (also from Round Hill) is waiting at the family quarters to see me.

Cloud's widow now appeared. —I am to tell her nephew that his home has gone to ruin since his mother died, three years ago, and there is no shelter for his father's soul-tablet. She led the way, that I might see with my own eyes half a house, and a tree growing among the tiles and clay of the other half.

The father and brother of 'Perfect Dog'—a Hokitika man—gave me a letter to take to him.

A youngish woman announced herself as sister-in-law of 'Faithful', now of Alexandra.

A still younger woman, sister-in-law of 'True View,' asked for his whereabouts and circumstances. She was not surprised to hear that he is a vagrant.

Coral's brother 'Hill Lake' appeared, and led me away from the crowd straight to his house. But on the very threshold he suddenly thought that it might not be the proper thing for me to be introduced to his wife and mother, or he may have been ashamed of the poverty of his surroundings; for he stopped—abruptly and led me back again to the public hall, into which he ushered me. Then he returned to his house, and brought thence tea and cakes. The crowd increased, but was very respectful. I did not once hear the common epithet, 'Foreign devil.'

The mothers of 'Green Wave', 'Nourishing', and 'Myriad Perfections' gave me letters to their sons, with verbal messages.

Then a messenger came for me to visit a family that has members in New Zealand. My guide took me to a handsomely-furnished guest-room, where two men welcomed me—the son and brother of a Greymouth storekeeper.

After photographing the village temple and stream, I returned to the public hall, where Hill-Lake had hot lunch ready for me.

QUITE AT HOME

This phrase expresses my feelings as I went from village to village—Stone Horse to Basket Weavers, Bridge-head, Great Embankment, Dragon Lake, Lower Rushes, Clear Lake Hill, and View Hill.

Many greeted me as *'Seen-Shang'* (Teacher), some who had returned from Otago insisting on treating me if a tea-house was anyway near. At Bridge-head one caught sight of me in the crowd, and made a rush to me that nearly carried me off my feet. The news spread rapidly among the 8000 or more gathered there, and as I sat at rice in a restaurant one after another from all parts of New Zealand came forward and claimed acquaintanceship. It began then to dawn upon me that here was some result for the years of toil in Otago; but I was not assured till an old missionary said: 'The freedom with which you go about among those people is wonderful. If you had done nothing more in New Zealand than make it possible for you to do so, your work is not in vain.'

Buffalo rest by a pond at Shek Ma ('Stone-Horse') Village, 1988.

TWO POEMS

Alison Wong

Chinese settlement, Arrowtown

Christmas Eve, 2002

Walk from the township through the police camp
not far from the river where the purple and pink
lupins and yellow broom flower. See the poplars
shed sticky white seeds through the air,
on branches and leaves, over the dry ground
like fresh wool caught on fences
like dreams of a foreign (white) Christmas.
Here, Ah Gee was found hanging,
Old Tom pitched forward
burned black in his fireplace,
Kong Kai, excellent cook and blind of one eye,
found up Eight Mile Creek, his clothes
spread over his bones, £70 in his pocket.
Now only relics of chimneys, a huge depression
where Su Sing's store once stood, a few huts
and rock shelters, restored/reconstructed
or not. A sign points the way to the cemetery.
At each of the doorways, a woman
has left white roses.

One hundred pounds

for Wong Wei Jung, Wellington 1914

There is no photograph of the father
of the father of my father
only one taken
from the ancestral home by a man
not related. I imagine him
(inside a cardboard
box, lost in the tenements
of modern Canton)
shot
in pure black
and white, and perhaps aged
the colour of old blood,
and wonder
did he have hair
that swung across his back
in the style of Manchurian
subjection, or was it cut
short and covered by
a trilby? Ah, there
is nothing to see, only brazen black
letters on aged white paper:
a notice of Murder
from the Minister of Justice
the reward as great
as the poll tax.

Author's note: My paternal great-grandfather Wong Wei Jung (Wong Way Ching), who arrived from China in 1896, had a fruit and vegetable shop in Newtown. In 1914 he was violently murdered in his shop. After pressure from the Chinese Community and Consulate, the Minister of Justice offered £100 reward for information leading to the arrest and conviction of his murderer. The case was never solved.

TENTS AND HUTS

Alexander Don

European 'rushers' hither and thither preferred to 'dwell in tents', to be struck at a moment's notice when news came of a better field. But Chinese love not the tent. They come here merely to sojourn: their word for 'to dwell' is chue, but for living in these lands tsaap 'to settle'. He is only a settler, yet he likes a home of firmer stuff than calico. He builds a hut then—of turf on the grassy flats, of slabs in the bush, of cobblestones on the shingle, of adobe where stones are scarce, of whatever stuff came handiest. And for roofing, what better than the bags that held his rice; or a thatch of the great tussock of those days—now dwarfed by rabbit, fire, and sheep? There are gullies and flats where hundreds of Europeans came and went, and after them scores of Chinese. The only relics of the tent-pitchers were sardine and jam tins, gin and brandy bottles; but the walls of many hut-builders still stand after thirty years.

CHIN. 3

TYPICAL OTAGO CHINESE DWELLINGS.
CAVE.   SOD HUT.
SLAB HUT.   SACK HUT.

30

National Characteristics

On the corduroy met a fairly educated man with a bunch of roses in his hand. I smelt one, and said, 'Very sweet scent.' When he turned a scentless one to me, and I said, 'No scent', he appeared very much surprised, and said, 'Can foreigners too smell the scent of flowers?'

Alexander Don at Round Hill, 1884.

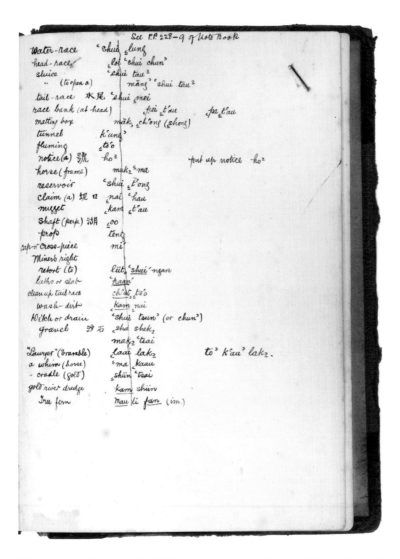

Handwritten glossary of goldmining terms on endpaper of Rev Alexander Don's Cantonese and English Dictionary.

CHINEE JOHNEE

Thomas Bracken

Paper men too muchy say,
        Chinee Johnny,
Too much yabber 'Keep away
        Chinee Johnny,'
Welley good no sabby me,
China make him plen tea.
Emmigration welly flea,
        Chinee Johnny.

Workey hard, too lilly pay,
        Chinee Johnny;
Hump him bamboo all le day,
        Chinee Johnny;
Grow him cabbage welly good,
Dig him garden, chop him wood,
Get him gole-ly, cook him spud,
        Chinee Johnny.

Me no sabby not come here,
        Chinee Johnny;
No get drunky link him beer,
        Chinee Johnny;
Welly good me make him fan,
Cook him puppy in him pan,
Plen loom for Chinaman,
        Chinee Johnny.

Steal him fowley nighty come,
        Chinee Johnny;
Diggy wash-dirt shakey some,
        Chinee Johnny.
Smalley wages me no blame,
Inglisman work ally same,
Eat him Chow-chow Cantong came,
        Chinee Johnny.

Inglies, Ileies, Cotchman, Jew—
        Chinee Johnny;
Plen gammon, talkey too—
        Chinee Johnny.
Chinaman no wifey bling,
No good women, all same ting,
Play on tom-tom, ching, ching, ching!
        Chinee Johnny.

Play him fan-tan all night long—
        Chinee Johnny?
Moke him opey, beat him gong—
        Chinee Johnny.
Ingliesman say 'Tax him Poll',
Me go liggin, make him hole,
Me get lichey plenny gole—
        Chinee Johnny.

What for you no sabby me—
        Chinee Johnny?
Me much lighty you come hee—
        Chinee Johnny.
Get him money, no stay long,
Me go backy to Hong Kong,
Paper talkey welly wrong—
        Chinee Johnny.

ASIATICS RESTRICTION BILL

[PROCEEDINGS OF THE HOUSE OF REPRESENTATIVES, JUNE 23 1896]

Mr SEDDON.—Sir, I rise to propose the second reading of this Bill, and I would ask honourable members if they would to-night agree to pass this Bill through all its stages. I ask it simply as a matter of urgency, and I will give you reasons for it. Every steamer that is now coming down from Australia is bringing a large number of Chinese, and the number of Chinese in the City of Wellington has doubled during the last five years.

An Hon Member.—Not in New Zealand.

Mr SEDDON.—I question very much the accuracy of the census regarding the Chinese. The Chinese are very cunning, and they know just as well as we do, and much better, I think, what the census means. I should like to put the facts before the House, and one is that they are coming in numbers from the other colonies. Very well. As the other colonies have a tax of £100 placed upon them, it is for us to consider whether or not we shall leave ours at £10. Then, the other colonies have a limit regarding the tonnage of ships that is a precaution: we have none. Under these circumstances I ask that the House should pass the same provision as is in the law in Australia. Then, again, there is another thing that wants to be dealt with. We have in the Customs Department a large number of certificates of naturalisation, and there is undoubted proof that there are numbers of Chinese presenting these naturalisation papers, and asking to come in free. The Bill now before us would not touch that phase of the question, but there is this phase of the question I think we might deal with, and that is as to the issuing of these naturalisation papers. As the law now stands in Victoria, I believe each Chinaman has to be photographed, and is photographed.

An Hon Member.—They are all alike.

Mr SEDDON.—Well, at all events, probably it is a precautionary measure. There is some way they have of telling them. I admit they are very similar to each other. However, the position is that we must deal with this question, There are other reasons, I think, why we should deal with it at once. So far as I can gather, we are perfectly justified in passing the law when there is no difficulty as regards treaty, or, that we are dealing with the Chinese in an exceptional manner. From my experience on the goldfields, from what I know personally, and from what has been brought prominently under my notice, I say they are not a desirable class of colonists. You see by the numbers in the City of Wellington that we have something like 270 Chinamen, and we have only two Chinese women. From the police reports that are to hand, and from what is brought under my notice in other ways, it appears that we are getting in the City of Wellington a small

Bourke Street. If any one knows what a small Bourke Street means, we will say that it is not desirable that any part of New Zealand should be put in the same position as that unfortunate locality. . . .

I feel satisfied in my own mind that if we make this a matter of urgency, seeing the Chinese are coming here in such large numbers, and seeing that they are interfering with trade, as they are doing in the cities, we shall be doing only what is right. When they were on the goldfields, and when they were fossicking and working ground which it was ofttimes said Europeans would never work, that was used as an argument in favour of the Chinese being allowed to come here in numbers; but, if we are to believe our census, it means that they are leaving the goldfields and drifting to the cities, and they are coming into trade. In connection with the carrying-out of that trade, there are other things going on which are far from desirable. A state of things has been disclosed which, I believe, the local authorities ought to take cognisance of. I believe, in respect to the Chinese coming into the large cities as traders, they ought to be stopped from keeping sleeping-accommodation for large numbers of their countrymen. Then there are other things of a most insanitary character, most undesirable in a large city, and more particularly when Europeans have to go to these shops and purchase their goods.

Sir R. STOUT—I am in favour—and I have always been in favour—of passing stringent laws against the Chinese, and I only regret that some such measure as this has not been carried out before. The reason I object to them coming here is entirely on two grounds. First, the racial ground—that, I think, is the main point; and, secondly, they have really a lower civilisation, which, if introduced into this colony, is bound to affect our civilisation, and lower it wherever they are situated. I wish, however, to point out to honourable members that I think this interpretation clause will really not work well. It would be far better for the honourable gentleman, whether we pass it in this House or not, to get that clause altered in another place, so as to except the natives of Asia and to put in the races that are to be excluded. . . . That would work far better than to put it in this form. There is another thing which I think we ought also to have—namely, a law against negroes and Kaffirs, just as much as against the Chinese. At the present time there are not many of those races in this colony, but you do not know what might happen in a short time in these days. . . .

Dr NEWMAN.—I think there would be another advantage in the course suggested by the senior member for Wellington City (Sir Robert Stout). The preamble of the Bill says that it is desirable to preserve the purity of the race. Now, not all Asiatics would degrade our race: for instance, the Circassians are one of the finest races on earth, and Circassian women are world-famed for their beauty; whereas this Bill would keep them out like the worst of the Asiatics. I would draw the attention of the honourable member in charge of the Bill to this: that the so-called Assyrian hawkers are really Hindoos. And then there are those men who wander about wearing long turbans, Afghans, &c. They are really British subjects; and I fancy this Bill will need remodelling for the purpose of dealing with them. . . .

Mr DUTHIE.—The necessity for this Bill depends on the statement of the Premier that Chinese are coming here in large numbers; but he has not given us information on the point. Statistics do not bear that out. There is a recent trivial increase in the number of Chinese, but not of any serious moment. The increase, so far as the City of Wellington is concerned, is a transfer from the goldfields— not an influx from abroad. Now, while it is for the moment very popular to run down these people, really I do not know what we should do if there were any exodus. In Wellington we are almost solely dependent upon them for vegetables; and but for these industrious Chinamen the people would generally go short. It is all very well for certain growers to want the Chinamen sent away; but the price of vegetables is even now very high in town. The Chinese do not undersell. I am told the price is higher here than in Auckland—in fact, it is the highest in the colony. It is very desirable for the health of the population that people should be able to get a full supply of vegetables. We should be very much worse off if it were not for the Chinamen. If the agitators would first cease talk and set to work, and produce vegetables, and show that we could do without Chinamen, it might be a different thing. One of the complaints is that Chinamen make money, and, having made it, go back to their own country. If they are able to do that, it cannot be said their earnings are uncommonly low. Customs statistics also prove that this community uses more fruit than at any other centre. It is due to the care with which these people handle fruit that our citizens enjoy this cheap and plentiful supply. It is all very well to abuse these people, and run them down. To do so may catch a little popularity. While, on the whole, agreeing that there is danger from an inferior race and civilisation coming into the country in great numbers, there are no grounds for the urgency sought for this Bill, which is merely a move for popularity in view of the coming elections. . . .

Mr COLLINS—I think the Government are to be congratulated on having brought the Bill down in its present form. As a matter of fact, those clauses which gave rise to the dissatisfaction of last session are just the ones which have been eliminated. And I think that the Bill, as it stands, should receive the general assent of this House. I should like to point out, Sir, what I think to be the weakness off the objections urged against the Bill. The honourable member for Wellington City (Mr Duthie) has told us that we are dependent on Chinamen here—that is to say, Wellington is dependent on Chinamen for its supply of vegetables; but the Bill does not profess to send away the Chinamen already here, or to prevent those who are now working and gaining a livelihood by growing vegetables from doing so. It simply proposes to prevent them from indefinitely increasing, and I think people will admit that it is a very wise provision. The honourable member also says that this Bill is brought in simply in deference to public clamour; but, Sir, if there has been public clamour for this particular Bill, if there were a public demand that the Chinese should be restricted, surely that is sufficient reason why the Government should take action in the matter. There would not be popular clamour for Chinese restriction unless there were a necessity for such restriction. . . .

Mr SEDDON—I am surprised to-night to find the honourable member for Wellington City (Mr Duthie) stand forward as a champion of the Chinese, and his grounds are very weak indeed, because he simply said it was on the ground of expediency, and so that the people should be supplied with cheap vegetables. How did we do for our vegetables when there were no Chinese at all? How do they do for vegetables where there are no Chinese to grow vegetables? The fact is that, when the Chinese go into the vegetable business they drive out the Europeans and if they were not here we should have Europeans doing it, and I say they would do it just as well. The honourable gentleman asked me to give proof that the Chinese are increasing in Wellington. Well, I have got here the returns. . . . There are a dozen boroughs in the colony in which, in 1891, there was not a single Chinaman, and which contain Chinamen now. In the City of Wellington there are 152 storekeepers, eighteen market-gardeners, one cabinetmaker, seven lodging-house keepers, one merchant, five employees of merchants, and there are twenty unemployed, actually swelling the ranks of our unemployed. Well, then, we come to what occurs. I am told that by the *Gazette* notice there is only a slight increase shown; but we cannot deny this fact—and members on those benches must know it as well as I do: that, by several steamers that have arrived recently, twenty-three came in one case, thirty-six in another, and nineteen, I think, in another. Well, nothing like that number have left the colony. Why are they coming here? I know on good authority that they know we are going to restrict, and they are coming, therefore, in anticipation of the legislation which they know we are about to pass. I say the sooner we pass that legislation the better.

The 1881 Chinese Immigrants Restriction Act established a £10 poll-tax, and limited the number of Chinese to be brought in to one for every 10 tons of ship's burden (increased in 1888 to 100 tons). The legislation debated above failed to gain the royal assent, but the measures proposed were set in place with the passing in the same year of a replacement bill, the Chinese Immigrants Act Amendment Act 1896. That act raised the poll tax to £100, and limited Chinese entry to one for every 200 tons of ship's burden.

THAT HEATHEN CHINEE

A NEW VERSION

Which I wish to remark,
    And I do so with pain,
That for ways that are dark,
    And for speech that is vain,
Politicians are often peculiar—
    Which the same I am free to maintain.

When domestic affairs
    Grow unpleasantly warm,
And constituents airs
    Of disgust cause alarm.
A 'Mongolian Invasion', well dished up,
    Disaffection may tend to disarm.

Though statistics appear
    To disclose that of late
We've no reason to fear
    Such a terrible fate—
For the Chinese departures outnumber
    The arrivals of recent year's date.

Still, a good, healthy scare
    Is an excellent thing,
And when treated with care
    Some fresh *kudos* may bring
To political aspirants shady,
    Who of public reproach feel the sting.

So a meeting is called,
    With the mayor in the chair,
And with arguments bald,
    And long since worn threadbare,
The poor Heathen Chinee is well slated ;
    While the welcome applause fills the air.

First the great Mr Reeves
    Takes the floor, and observes
How it frequently grieves
    His olfactory nerves
To inhale the peculiar aroma
    Which a Chinese location preserves.

Mr Collins orates
    On their moral defects,
And he feelingly states
    That he strongly objects
To their habit of toiling and saving ;
    On our own unemployed it reflects.

Mr Russell then tells
    How that once he began
An inspection of hells
    Where they played at fan-tan,
And the opium vice also practised ;
    'Twas a scene to disgust a white man.

Now I venture to think
    Though this picture is sad,
Some intelligent 'Chink'
    Might draw one quite as bad
Of his boasted superior, the white man;
    Many such, you'll admit, may be had.

Though we don't opium use,
    Many praise the creator
Of whisky, and lose
    On the totalisator.
More than all that, we grudge the Chinee;
    Though of gold he's a deft excavator.

Let 'Our Own Unemployed'
    Take the moral from me,
And his vices avoid
    While the virtue they see,
Of the patient and frugal example
    Which is shown by 'That Heathen Chinee'.

'Bohemian', in *The Press*.

THE FUNGUS KING

In the late 1800s a substantial part of Taranaki farmers' income came from the export to China of edible fungus—'Taranaki wool'. Chew Chong was the pioneer of this trade, and subsequently played an influential part in the development of the dairy industry. He was the first Chinese-New Zealander to be inducted into the New Zealand Business Hall of Fame.

COMPLIMENT TO A CHINESE

One of the most remarkable incidents in the history of New Zealand took place in New Plymouth the other day, when Chew Chong was entertained by citizens and farmers and presented with an illuminated address signed by 85 representative settlers of North Taranaki. Of course, everyone who knows anything at all about the history of the dairying industry in Taranaki knows who Chew Chong is and what he did for the industry in the days when it needed all the encouragement it could get. And it is an outstanding fact that it is a Chinaman who must for all time stand as the father of this great industry in our foremost butter province. Chew Chong helped it along in the long ago when it was the means of laying the foundation of the modest and more than modest fortunes of many a man in Taranaki. One of the incidents of those early days he tells himself in speaking of the preparation for the first butter factory (at Eltham) erected in Taranaki—

He had decided to have the factory's machinery driven by water power, and to obtain the necessary power a tunnel had to be driven. This was let to contractors, who, however, encountered so many big rocks that they gave up the job. Mr Chong, however, nothing daunted, undertook the work himself, and his quaint description very much amused those present. He said he ordered about 40lb of dynamite and went into the tunnel himself. As he had been informed that dynamite was better if kept warm, he always carried his supply in his trouser pocket! Many were horrified, and told him he would be blown up—but he was not. Moreover, he succeeded in putting the tunnel through, although it was a tremendously difficult job.

Chew Chong is an unusually interesting Chinaman, and not a few people who know him well have forgotten long ago that he is a Celestial, so different has he shown himself from the Cantonese who shopkeep all over our fair land. Chew Chong—who is now well on in years, for he has been in New Zealand nearly half a century—spent his first three years knocking about the South Island. Then he worked his way up to Wellington, and there he was struck by the possibilities in the despised fungus trade. He went into it for all he was worth—and it proved of so much worth to Chew Chong that he became the Fungus King of New Zealand, although he showed the way for many of his countrymen in this, as he showed the way to Westerners in the dairying industry. It was a Maori who told him that Taranaki was plenteous in the delectable fungi. In his third week up there he paid out £65 one day for this stuff (at the rate of 5s per bag), and soon he had stores going at New Plymouth, Inglewood, and Eltham. His enterprise in this direction helped along many a struggling settler during a bad time. Then came his first butter factory in 1887 ('Jubilee' brand), and he got 95s for his first shipment to London when farmers' butter was bringing 70s; and two years later he won the first and second prizes with his butter at the Dunedin Exhibition. But from now on his pathway was not strewn with roses. . . .

The Fielding Star
Monday, January 30, 1911

A CHINESE VEGETABLE HAWKER.—No work which deals with the characteristics of colonial life would be complete without some representation of this type. Every Australasian legislature has dealt from time to time, and has still to deal further with the influx of alien races, whose presence is extremely obnoxious to the native born. The Chinese, who are content to work for a low wage, and can thrive where the ordinary workman, with his much more expensive wants and habits, would starve, have come in for especial objection. They have, however, proved themselves from time to time exceedingly useful to the community. In quarters where such a thing as a vegetable was once never grown, the Chinese gardeners established themselves, and did well in supplying the whites with vegetables, which they grow with great skill; and around the cities they leased waste spaces of land, and turned them into gardens of wonderful fertility. The vegetable supply of many towns is practically in their hands. They are also in demand as cooks on stations and in hotels, and have a large number of laundries established throughout the country.

THE MISSIONARY EXPLORER

James Huston Edgar

James Huston Edgar grew up on a farm near Tapanui in West Otago. In 1898 he travelled to China to work with the China Inland Mission. For more than 30 years he based himself in Tatsienlu (now Kangding), a market town midway between Szechuan and the Tibetan plateau. From there he carried out and carefully documented many journeys of exploration in the Sino-Tibetan borderlands. His acute observations and scholarly writings earned him Fellowships of both the Royal Geographical Society and the Royal Anthropological Institute. He died, still in Tatsienlu, in 1936.

The account below is drawn from a lecture Edgar delivered in Australia and New Zealand during one of his home leaves.

We are, generally, rather afraid of speaking of the missionary as an explorer. Still, is not such hesitancy the outcome of unsanctioned prejudice rather than Christian common sense? Even if Livingstone and Chalmers are ruled out, it still remains true that someone must explore the uttermost parts; and as long as the missionary keeps away from the Poles and the uninhabited deserts, the claim that he is an explorer should, as a rule, carry with it a compliment. For is not the pioneer missionary to the Mission Boards what the scouts are to the armies? And because both organisations are not as a rule prepared to take unwarranted risks, they endeavor to have at their disposal a mass of facts relating to climatic and geographical conditions, as well as the density and distribution of populations, and the customs and temperaments of the different tribes and races. So I can say without exaggerating that there is a need to-day for men who will be able, with incontrovertible facts, to emphasise the needs of heathendom.

Still, even now it is with some hesitation that I present for your consideration an investigation of a part of unknown Asia. The journey was in one respect frankly negative in results. On the maps of China about a generation old we find a town called Lakiang, which might have influenced missionaries interested in an unknown region north of Chongtien, in Yunnan. But in 1907 Mr Muir and I found it was not in the position claimed for it on the best maps, nor had it ever existed in any other part of China or Tibet. But Lakiang was put off the map to make room for something more important. In July of 1907 Mr Cecil Polhill, the China Inland pioneer in Tibetan lands, and one of the Cambridge seven, sent me to report on conditions along the eastern frontiers of Tibet proper, and then proceed south-west and explore some blank spaces, probably Tibetan country, south of Litang. This programme, although Hsiang Cheng was not on the maps, was intelligible enough to me, but must have been very much like Double Dutch to the authorities in Shanghai. As a rule, such regions have been traversed by non-missionary expeditions. But Hsiang Cheng was terra incognita. The Chinese, however, told of a mountainous region with a cruel, turbulent population, which openly defied China. Indeed, in 1902 one of the agents of the Suzerain had been inhumanly flayed alive, and his skin exhibited in the Lamasery Museum of curios and wild animals.

The Hsiang Cheng people were an unknown migration—mentioned by DuHalde—who had accepted Lamaism and had become thoroughly Tibetanised. The plague spot of the region was an enormous monastery inhabited by 2000 warrior monks, who, by years of unremitting labour, had made it a veritable castle of misanthropic giants. Under Litang in theory, this fortress took its orders from Lhasa, and remained a thorn in the side of China. Impudent slavers preying on Chinese victims passed through its territory to the Salwin, and neither the wisdom of Confucius nor the logic of Mencius could modify their barbarian instincts. Hsiang Cheng was anathema to the rulers and people of the frontiers, and certainly not without reason.

The continued atrocities of the Hsiang Cheng outlaws at last aroused China to vigorous action, and during 1907 the region was being 'pacified,' that is, experiencing the fury of an unsympathetic enemy. But the foresight of the lamas had provided against such a contingency. They had early retired to their great monastery. The walls were thick and well built; they had food in abundance, and underground pipes conveyed water from secret springs. Moreover, innumerable instruments of worship made their religious exercises a series of rollicking concerts. So they remained safe from the Chinese fury, and their joyful worship and ironical remarks ate into the souls of their starving and depressed enemies. As time went on, incipient mutiny was at work, and it seemed as if China's most successful general was to retire from the field baffled by the men he most wished to ruin. But just in time a traitor, under torture or for gain, divulged the secret of the water supply, and, that being cut off, Hsiang Cheng was doomed. And one morning not long afterwards the head abbots concluded act one by hanging themselves and their wives in full view of their astonished enemies. Act two soon followed and it has little to record of a humane or merciful nature.

It was about this time that Mr Muir and I made an effort to visit Hsiang Cheng. And, later, one afternoon, from a low larch-clad pass, we viewed not Lakiang, but the most interesting and most infamous monastery in the land of the lamas. Ours were the first European eyes to behold this stronghold of iniquity, and mine might easily have been the first Anglo-Saxon grave to have usurped a position on the thorn-clad slopes of its environs. We found the Chinese army in possession of the town, and an unfriendly official occupying the quarters of the high priest. We were distinctly unwelcome to the conquerors, and the Tibetans saw no reason to court persecution by taking sides with the aliens. Indeed, to annoy us might be considered as good service. Moreover, in such places there are always sycophants who are in readiness to take hints of this kind. And the opportunity to act came in due time.

We were making excursions in the adjacent valleys, and using the Government animals. Naturally, the Tibetans do not bring out the best, and the continual changing is not the surest guarantee of safety. So far, however, we had escaped unpleasant incidents. But my last mount had a restless eye, and was giving disquieting exhibitions of his kicking propensities. It was emphatically condemned, but someone in a rollicking mood offering to lead it, I jumped into the saddle. Then, with an hilarious shout, the mad, unbridled brute was turned loose. There was no means of controlling it, and to keep my seat was impossible, so, unsaddled, and with my foot firmly caught in the stirrup, I was soon a plaything of fate, an actor in one of the wildest performances ever staged.

It may have been light opera to the Tibetans, but was tragedy to Muir, and I was certain that my last hour had come, for the maddened brute not only jolted me over bushes and boulders, but ever and anon would stop and give classic exhibitions of footwork—dancing on me, and jabbing savagely. Fortunately, owing to an unusual amount of clothing donned for climatic reasons, the force of the vicious attacks was considerable softened, although the dragging and bumping were not a bad imitation of Hsiang Cheng's speciality of flaying alive. At one time I nonplussed the animal, and curtailed his activities by holding up a foreleg, but the real climax was only averted by the stirrup leather breaking just before my senses fled.

With badly skinned back, many bruises over the loins, and fractured ribs, I was escorted to the lamasery, where I remained for some days. And then, far from well, I set out through a region absolutely unknown, for Litang, 200 miles distant. On the way pleurisy attacked me, which, with bruises and fractured ribs, made my work on passes 15,000 feet, in autumn hail and snow, little less than slow torture. And finally, a circuitous entry into Litang about 11 p.m. one cold night was anything but triumphant. But all the same we had been through the heart of an unknown No-man's land, and were loaded with information that no one else could give. That, to the pioneer, compensates amply for any inconvenience in the valleys of the shadow of death.

THE NORTH GATE OF TATSIENLU, WITH A TEA CARAVAN ENCAMPED OUTSIDE

OPEN TENDER

G. L. Meredith

I also heard a good story about Dunedin in its early days. It is claimed that then all the inhabitants of Dunedin were Scotch with the exception of one Chinaman. History does not report what induced the solitary Chinaman to take up his abode amongst the hardy Scots at Dunedin, Possibly this 'Chow' wanted to study economy in its higher branches, as the following incident would indicate. The municipality called for tenders for a smallish contract—clearing scrub from the side of a road or something of that nature. When the tenders were opened, one Alexander McPherson was the lowest tenderer. He received notification of the acceptance of his tender, coupled with a request to attend at the council chamber, on a given date, to sign the contract. At the hour specified the only person in sight was Ah Chow, who was politely asked his business. Ah Chow said he had come to sign his contract. He was told that Alexander McPherson was the successful tenderer.

'All-li,' said the Chow, 'Me Mackee Pherson. No Scotchmanee here, no gettee workee.'

THE GOVERNMENT AND THE YELLOW PERIL

André Siegfried

It fell to a Frenchman, André Siegfried, to have the last word on the Yellow Peril. Democracy
in New Zealand *was published in French in 1904; it was another ten years before an English
translation appeared. When, many years later, a New Zealand diplomat met the then aged
Siegfried, he had no recollection of ever having written the book. Perhaps it is just as well.*

European immigration is looked on with disfavour in New Zealand; but Chinese
immigration raises absolute disgust, and public opinion has demanded and
obtained the most Draconian measures against it. In fact, in New Zealand, and
for that matter in the whole of Australasia, there is a real Asiatic question. China,
that vast human reservoir, pours forth an unceasing stream of emigrants upon
all the shores of the Pacific. California, Mexico, South America, the Hawaian
Islands, the Philippines, the Sunda Islands, not to speak of Indo-China, which
is actually colonised by them, have made the acquaintance of the Chinese. No
climate daunts them, no work is too hard for them. Australasia has not escaped
them; they have appeared there, as everywhere else.

The Chinaman is no ordinary competitor. Too often the Westerners are led
to look on him as a being of an inferior race, less dangerous than the Japanese
in the economic struggle. In point of fact, the white man has no more powerful
opponent. His qualities of labour and endurance make him almost invulnerable.
His calm energy, never worn out, makes him capable of working without halt
or rest. His extraordinary economy allows him to live on next to nothing, and
to be satisfied with the most absurd wages. His indifference to comfort keeps
him from many a temptation to spend. At the same time he unites in his person
many gifts which as a rule are wanting in the cleverest trader. He is a tradesman
of the first rank, with a wonderful grasp of detail, who, so to speak, never handles
a farthing without making some profit out of it. He is also a born merchant,
full of initiative and confidence, and his 'go' reminds one of the most brilliant
American business men. His enterprising but prudent spirit, his suspicion ever
on the alert, his prodigious cunning, together with his genuine honesty in the
fulfilment of promises, make him a wonderful business man and as a competitor
often invincible.

In tropical countries like Indo-China, where the European is hardly able to
work by himself, and the native races are weak and apathetic, the presence of
the Chinaman is a necessity. It is he who really makes the country productive,
not perhaps actually with his own hands, but by the life and development which
his commercial genius can bestow on trade. He becomes the right hand of the
white man, his natural intermediary in business; but later, and this is the danger,
he becomes the white man's almost always victorious rival. His settlement in the

spot which he colonises is not, as a rule, permanent, for often he has in China his home and his family. That does not, however, prevent him from setting up a new home in his adopted land and giving birth to half-breeds who gradually form a new race. This is going on all over the Far East, and, looking at the results of this immigration, one cannot regard it as an evil. The English, who are acknowledged masters in the art of colonisation, had no hesitation in allowing Singapore to become a town of Chinese.

In Australasia the question of the immigration of the yellow races is in a different setting. Instead of tropical regions, with the exception of the north of Queensland, there are only temperate climatic conditions. Instead of an already over-populated country there are only immense territories as yet thinly peopled. Instead of lower races to be directed and exploited, in Australia there are only a few thousand savages, and in New Zealand only a few thousand Maoris, who, from an economic point of view, do not even count. The difference is radical. Australasia is not an exotic country, a colony for purposes of trade; it is a colony to be settled, a country for Western civilisation, where the Asiatic is as much out of place as in Europe.

The Chinaman, however, does not allow himself to be put off by new and unfavourable conditions. His marvellous adaptability makes him fit for any climate, any trade, any circumstances whatever. After passing many weeks in some ship's between-decks, he lands at Sydney, Auckland or Wellington, generally penniless; his whole capital is contained in some tiny parcel which he carries in his hand. He comes to earn his living, and is ready for the hardest work and the greatest privations. But he will not live on charity, especially not on white men's charity. During the first few days after his arrival his fellow-countrymen support him; they are organised into mutual-aid associations; they have societies for helping each other, and it is a rare thing for them to abandon one of their race. Thanks to this aid, which he hardly ever fails to receive, the newcomer has time to look about him; he finds a lodging, looks for work, and, as a rule, is very soon in a situation.

The work he chooses is most varied. In mining countries the adventurous and gambling spirit of the Chinaman often leads him to become a prospector. Those who want safer and more regular employment become servants, cooks, or day-labourers. They are excellent servants, sober, attentive, sometimes even faithful; they are neither unruly nor pretentious; they take the most cutting reprimand with a smile, and are content with absurdly low wages, on which, however, they are still able to save. Part of these savings generally finds its way back to China, to the man's family; with the rest, the Chinaman amasses a small capital which sometimes allows him to start work on his own account.

It is then that he shows his true qualities. He begins, for example, market-gardening. On this ground no one can compete with him; he gets up at dawn and works without a stop; if his business increases, he gets in one of his fellow-countrymen to help—as a rule his nearest relative, whom he hardly pays anything, but who, according to Chinese custom, becomes a sharer in the profits. The white gardener can do nothing but give way. How could he, with the expensive wants of a civilised man, with his smaller powers of endurance, compete with a being like the Chinaman? Anyone who has any close acquaintance with the Celestials knows that it is impossible. The New Zealanders have actually given up the struggle, and near large towns market-gardening has for the most part fallen into the hands of Asiatics.

Other Chinamen take up trading in a small way; they open third-rate hotels or restaurants, groceries and shops of every sort, where their activity, grasp of detail, and economy seldom leave them without profits. Their zeal for their clients is boundless, and they will undertake to carry out the most extraordinary orders and commissions. They are, besides, born exporters and importers. The distinction between wholesale and retail trading, which with us is so marked, hardly exists for them. As their business increases they keep pace with their conditions and often become thorough capitalists.

Indeed, it must not be supposed that they are indefinitely confined to the lower trades. Many, beyond doubt, are skilful capitalists, who are able to make use of Western economic machinery with extraordinary success. Their judgement in making investments is remarkable; and more than one New Zealander does not despise the advice which they freely offer—and which nevertheless it is just as well to be on one's guard against, as the following anecdote, which was told me at Dunedin, will show. It was about a mining company, whose shares had gone up enormously. The question was whether to go on buying or not. An English capitalist thought that it would be prudent, before doing anything, to ask advice from a rich Chinaman of his acquaintance. 'Very good: you should buy,' was the reply he got. Next day the capitalist bought some ten shares which just happened to be in the market. A few days later the decline began; and he discovered that the man who had sold the ten shares had been no other than his adviser, who had found in him an excellent opportunity for getting rid of uncertain securities at the top of the market.

It is, then, certain that the Chinese do very well in New Zealand. But it cannot be said that their presence is a benefit to the land. They only settle there for a time, spend very little, and when they have made enough money, once more take ship and return to China, leaving their relatives or their friends to inherit their work. Any hope of assimilating them is vain; they are and will remain strangers.

It was not long before the Australasians became alarmed at this invasion; not, however, because it was numerically disturbing. In 1881 there were only 5000 Celestials in New Zealand, and since then their number has considerably diminished. But their presence constituted a danger at once moral and economic.

The moral danger is what the New Zealanders, like the Australians, are most inclined to place in the foreground; and this is no mere pretext used to hide the ill-feeling with which a disturbing and dangerous competition fills them.

The Chinaman is the object of a genuine and undoubted race-hatred. When Mr Reeves says that his fellow-citizens think Chinese competition to be 'foul, contrary to nature, and unjust,' he only gives a faithful expression of their attitude, which is an attitude of contempt and disgust. In point of fact, these temporary immigrants, who never dream of settling down for good, can lead nothing but an immoral and degrading life. They do not bring their families with them, and, as they cannot start fresh ones, they find themselves in a situation which is contrary to nature, and which has the effect of developing among them the most deplorable vices. It is true that they trouble no one and are always mild and good-natured in their manner, in the hope that they will be unnoticed, and that they will be able easily to amass their money without attracting anyone's attention. They are not unruly and unbearable like the negroes. But nevertheless it is understandable that the New Zealanders should fear the presence in their cities of these members of a race which cannot be assimilated, and that they should honestly believe that they only lose by coming in contact with them.

It has been argued,' Mr Reeves writes, 'that the Chinese are not a degrading element; that they are an industrious, peaceful and frugal people, with a civilisation, a learning, and an education of their own. It has been said by many Englishmen, Mr R. W. Dale amongst others, that the Chinese have been hated in Australia for their virtues, not their vices. The reply to this is that, to begin with, the Chinese are admitted by all observers to be utterly unfit to use political rights in a democracy. They have no conception of government and public duty, as these are understood in Europe. Their *literati* may be entitled to be called civilised, but the classes from which their emigrants are drawn are not *literati*. Industrious they are, but industry without certain social qualities is a doubtful virtue. A man may be industrious, and yet be dirty, miserly, ignorant, a shirker of social duty, and a danger to public health. All these most of the Chinese immigrants are. It is said that they commit few crimes. A man may be a very undesirable citizen without infringing the criminal law.'

Such, expressed coolly and with moderation, is the average New Zealander's opinion on the moral and political dangers which the Chinaman's presence may cause his country. If we care to remember that these race hatreds are the most violent and the most irreducible of any, just because they are the most instinctive, we shall not find it difficult to understand how it is that in this concert of reproaches no discordant voice is heard—the more so because to their feeling of repulsion and contempt there is added that of threatened interests.

By the side of the moral danger that we have just set forth there is an economic danger, which causes much greater alarm to the Australasians. The Englishman, quoted by Mr Reeves, who said that the Chinaman was hated as much because of his virtues as of his vices, was not entirely wrong. Had he said his *commercial* virtues he would have been entirely right. The Chinaman is too successful; and that is the principal grievance against him. There are even some naïve or cynical people who say this without any circumlocution, as, for example, the Wellington baker who, before a commission of inquiry, expressed himself thus: 'We all know that the Chinese are a very industrious race, and that is just why we are against them.'

It is true that the yellow race has a dangerous advantage in the economic struggle. With wants fewer than those of the white man, the Chinaman works longer and sometimes better; he is always willing to let the scale of wages be reduced, and he accepts work at any figure. How could a civilised man, living a civilised life, possibly be able to compete with him in such circumstances? Remembering the terms which Mr Reeves used in qualifying this kind of competition, we shall find that we too, in our turn, cannot but regard it as unjust and contrary to nature. Following Mr Reeves, we must observe that the New Zealand workman is seriously handicapped as compared with the Asiatic.

'The white workman in the Colonies,' the ex-Minister for Labour wrote, 'is expected to be clean and comfortably dressed; to marry and rear children; to have a home, decent, bright, and which looks a credit to the neighbourhood. His children have to be healthy, well fed, and properly clothed; and he has to support them until their thirteenth or fourteenth year. The father and mother are expected to read books and newspapers and give a certain amount of time and intelligent attention to public affairs. The Chinaman, when allowed, will live in a hovel and scorn sanitation. Without family responsibilities, without social interests, without political knowledge, he comes to a Colony to extract what he can from it, and to take his savings back to China.'

This contrast is a true one, and the conditions of the competition are not the same for both sides. There is no fair play, as the Anglo-Saxons understand it. Is it reasonable to expect the Australasian workman to give up his civilised life in order to be able to compete with the Chinaman? Can he be expected to be content with smaller wages, on the ground that the Chinaman is quite satisfied with them? Certainly not, unless the attempt to make New Zealand into a settled Colony be given up, and unless it is destined to be changed into a colony for exploitation in which the white man is nothing more than a chief and director over inferior races who labour for him. There are the two policies, and a choice must be made.

If the Chinaman were a necessity, as he is in IndoChina, his presence might have been borne—perhaps it might even have been desired. Such is the case in the north of Queensland, for the reason that the white man can hardly take the Chinaman's place. But in a temperate country like New Zealand, which means to remain a land of Western civilisation, there can be no two opinions. Chinese competition is immoral and bad, and must be eliminated at any cost. Set forth in this way the problem seems much clearer; and this is how it was stated by Sir Charles Dilke in his work, *Problems of Greater Britain*:

'To the colonies the Chinese question appears to present itself in a very different aspect from that in which it is viewed by us at home, and it is difficult to induce the men of the colonial lower middle or working classes, dependent upon labour or trade for maintenance, to take what we should call a broad international view of Chinese immigration. That the Chinamen shall be excluded from white colonies means only in the minds of the working colonists that they intend to protect their own position. 'Canada for the Canadian,' 'Australia for the Australian,' are the prevailing cries and colonial labour, knit together in its powerful federations, desires to limit competition, and above all wholly to shut out the competition of the cheapest of competitors—the Chinese.'

Now that we realise the feelings of fear and hatred with which Chinese immigration inspires the Australasian, the rigorous legislation which has resulted from these feelings need cause us no surprise. Supported and even coerced by public opinion, the politicians of the different colonies would have nothing but immediate action. Queensland began, in 1876, by imposing a tax on Chinese immigration. Other colonies followed suit, and in 1881 New Zealand set up a Chinese immigration tax of £10 per head. Such legislation, in this form, gave rise to international difficulties, and for a long time the Colonial Office refused to recognise it. For there are treaties between China and England in virtue of which the Chinese are placed on the same footing as other foreigners, and hence they cannot be detained in any port of a British Colony merely because they are Chinese. Besides this, England owns in the Far East Hong-Kong and Singapore, and there are consequently many British subjects who are of Chinese race. These, as well as the Chinese proper, were excluded by the Australasian legislation.

The mother-country, however, inquired whether they seriously thought of prohibiting a British subject from entering a British colony. This legal point could hardly be met; but all the same the Australasians remained firm in the attitude they had adopted. They are far from Europe, and strange to the subtleties of law, and no doubt they thought of international treaties as vain formula which it is just as well to disregard if they are in the way, especially when they deal with China and the Chinese. Moreover, when they want something, Australasians are in the habit of going straight towards their goal, with a simple spirit that makes Europeans smile, but which always ends by attaining their desire. 'Neither His Majesty's ships of war,' Sir Henry Parkes said bluntly, 'nor his governors, nor his colonial secretary will make us abandon our scheme.' In short, England had to give in. The Australasian legislation was not formally confirmed, but it was tacitly accepted.

At present Chinese immigration into New Zealand is subject to the restrictions laid down in the Chinese Immigrants Act Amendment Act of 1896, and also in the more general law on immigration, which we mentioned in the preceding chapter, and which is called 'An Act to place certain restrictions on immigration into New Zealand, 1899.' The immigration tax was raised in 1896 to £100 per head. Moreover, the more effective measure was taken of limiting the number of Chinese immigrants allowed under the Act to one for every two hundred tons of each ship coming to one of the ports of the Colony. Captains and shipowners caught in the act of violating the law were liable to very severe penalties; the

New Zealand legislator showed no tenderness for them, because they had always encouraged an immigration which, of course, increased their business. In this case, New Zealand interests, or, if you will, Australasian interests, are in conflict with English interests. Much annoyance arose because of this, and we find traces of it in these severe words of the Agent-General for New Zealand: 'When the Australians are criticised in England for their egoistic exclusive policy, they bitterly think how their national life and their future are threatened by this very spirit of English business, which, while poisoning China with opium in the interest of India, is ready to take up the cause of the Chinese, if only there is money to be made in flooding Australasia with yellow barbarians.'

It is a severe judgment. But England has had to accustom herself for some time past to the remonstrances, often harshly expressed, of her colonies. In the case in point, as almost always, the colonials had the last word. The law was rigorously applied. The Act of 1899 even furnished new weapons, to be used in the most improbable event of the former Act not being sufficient. Every immigrant has on landing to sign a form on which he states his name, his place of birth, and a great deal of other information. But what Chinaman can make out in English, as the law requires, such a document? So that if the Government wants to pick a quarrel with him it always has some pretext for sending him back to his own country. This method of procedure is most effective, and it has the advantage of being more correct, from the international point of view, than the other. For the immigrant is detained at a port in the Colony, not because he is Chinese, but merely because he cannot write. The Chinese Government could raise no objection to such a measure. Mr Chamberlain, in the conference of Colonial premiers held in 1897, recommended this expedient as unimpeachable from the treaty standpoint.

It is long since this Draconian legislation began to be effective. In 1886 there were 4542 Chinese in New Zealand; their number fell to 4444 in 1891, 3711 in 1896; and, finally, there were only 2846 in 1901. We may suppose that, if this policy of exclusion is maintained, the number of Asiatics established in the Colony will still further diminish. At the present time it can be said that the New Zealanders, by their brutal action and their inflexible prejudices, have succeeded in removing from themselves the yellow peril.

Poster against Chinese immigration, early 20th century.

JADE TANIWHA

Jenny Bol Jun Lee

Being Maori–Chinese is:
eating pork bones and puha with chopsticks,
washing your hands after taking food to the cemetery to worship your ancestors,
calling my grandparents popo, gungung, kuia and koro,
celebrating Chinese New Year and attending poukai and the koroneihana,
being told that your work ethic comes from the Chinese side
and your rhythm from the Maori side,
feeling like the odd one out at the marae,
or at the Chinese social,
dumbfounding Pakeha,
being made to feel different,
being told that different is 'cool',
avoiding the issue of ethnicity with strangers,
developing a sense of who it is safe to speak with,
negotiating three worlds,
being rejected because you're not:
a 'real' Maori,
a 'real' Chinese
and will never be Pakeha,
forever being on the boundaries,
getting blamed for Maori land occupations and the 'Asian Invasion',
challenging notions that you can only be one or the other,
embraced by my Maori whanau and supported by my Chinese family,
knowing that I see double,
jade and pounamu
taniwha and dragon.

PRIMARY CARE

Dr H. B. Turbott

Dr H. B. Turbott was best known to an earlier generation of New Zealanders as 'the Radio Doctor'. His weekly radio talks on issues of public health attracted a nation-wide audience. They were informed by his long experience in the field, culminating in a term as New Zealand's Director-General of Health. Here he recounts the early experience at the Presbyterian Mission Hospital at Kong Chuen that sparked his interest in finding ways to improve public health in New Zealand.

I just volunteered to serve in the hospital at Kong Chuen and was accepted, and that was after a year's house surgeoncy in the Waikato Hospital in New Zealand . . . I really wanted to be a surgeon and the proper thing to do in those days [1923] was to go home and sit the exam in England. We didn't have one in those days and everybody went home to sit the exam. I was going to do the same thing but I happened to top the group in the final exam in Dunedin, and the Professor invited me home and said what are you going to do with yourself now you've passed. I said, well, I've got a house surgeoncy in Waikato Hospital and I'm going there now. Oh, he said, what do you want to be? And I said I want to be a surgeon. Well, he said, if you want to be a surgeon the best thing to do is to go to either India or China. I said, why? And he said, well, because you get there the experience in a few months you wouldn't get for years in New Zealand, and a very varied one too. So that's how I originated the idea of going to China. I don't know why it was China instead of the other but that's how it happened. Well, when I arrived there I was put into language school for six months.

Then I was shifted up country to start the real work. And that was as staff in a hospital with a hundred beds, with two Chinese house surgeons and two Britishers—Scotch—the Kirk brothers. And now myself as an extra. The Kirk brothers had got involved in many other things besides working in the mission. The senior one, John, was tied up with the Medical Association throughout China and he was away a lot travelling and so on. The other, the younger brother, was a good surgeon and he got himself involved in the School of Medicine of Hong Kong and he used to teach down there periodically and come back and go back and come back. The result was the work of the hospital was really left to the two Chinese and myself as a beginner.

It was purely hospital work with priority calls from the villagers for urgent help. For example, I was called out one night at 10 o'clock to a woman who couldn't deliver a baby, which was very rare in China. And I sent a message down, to say, I'm coming down—don't shoot. Because they had a wall around all the villages, they were all walled in, with night guards walking around with muzzleloaders, that's really what they were, against robbers. Anyhow, when I got within, I suppose, 200 yards they started popping at me. Didn't make any difference if you sent a message. Anyhow, they were no good at shooting so I got past in the end. When I got to the hut, through the spirit door—it was just a simple little hut of sun-burned bricks, with a trestle bed on one side and a trestle bed on the other side. The woman was in trouble on one, and underneath were two or three pigs and half a dozen fowls and so on, underneath the other and around about. And she was completely helpless. I said no, I'll have to take you to the hospital. . . .

It was totally new, I had no idea at all. I was very pleasantly surprised. I liked the Chinese and they seemed to like me all right, there was no worry about that. But they were very, very hard working, putting up with things that in New Zealand you wouldn't dream of putting up with, in the family and so on. And also battling against difficulties of all kinds. Smallpox was rife. Sometimes when I crossed the river between where I was at the language school and the town, the bloke rowing me would be an open pocked, smallpox, in the middle of having a case of smallpox. Because there was no action against smallpox at all, except some local doctors gave the vaccine occasionally. That was only because of outside influence, not Chinese influence. It was a purge at the time. And typhoid fever and dysentery and so on. They were wracked with troubles but they didn't have any national build up to overcome them.

There was no really national health service. It was old Chinese medicine, that's all, and Chinese drugs. They were building the elements of it when I was there. There was the Peking Medical School taking a hundred a year with two hundred professors teaching them to be very good doctors. They taught so damn well that most of them got jobs overseas. I'm not kidding, they did. That was a very fine medical school actually, the Peking Medical School in those years. But the money was put up to help China to get proper medical attention instead of its traditional folklore, you know, and so on. But in the end it failed because they were so well-trained they couldn't resist the temptation to earn very big money for surgery and God knows what not in the China ports like Shanghai and so on, or go overseas to jobs . . .

I had three months up there [at the Peking Medical School]. I mean, that came about by accident really. Because when I'd been up there in our Kong Chuen hospital for about three months or so, around came a request from the American research crowd. They were going to run a series to find out just how bad and how widespread hookworm was in South China. And they were very grateful if any one of the doctors in the various hospitals in the region would volunteer to help. Well, I asked my senior, one of the Kirks, and he said oh yeah if I wanted it'd be very good. And so I volunteered and for three months I worked for a fellow called W W Cort who came from Harvard. The only other volunteer was a woman, a Canadian from the Canadian hospital in Canton, and the pair of us worked like slaves for this damn fellow for three months analysing all the field stuff we gathered from various farms and all around the place to find out just which kind of hookworm was there and how much there was etc etc. He enjoyed all our work—he certainly gave the ideas and so on, but he never mentioned or gave us credit in his book which he wrote afterwards. He did send me a copy of the book.

By and by some few months later I got a letter from the American research group saying here's a job in—I can't remember which state it was—but it was a job in tuberculosis and it was offered to me. Obviously it had been at the Cort fellow's prompting, you see. But I wrote back and said no, I wasn't prepared to take that job but what I would like, if they could do it instead, I would like a course of training in x-rays because we hadn't got one and we wanted one. And blow me they came back and said yes—up you go to Peking Medical School and take the three months course there. So I did that, and that was very hard work because it was a professor from, again I think, Harvard, and he was a slave driver. We used to work all morning and all afternoon, and had an exam on Saturday morning and anybody who failed was packed off, goodbye. So we all had to work hard, you see, nobody wanted to go home. A couple failed—there were about thirty, and about twenty-eight passed. So after three months I got my certificate and the day the certificate was presented the anti-British riots in China broke out. So they said here's your certificate for competence in running the x-ray machine. The final exam, by the way, was some written paper in the morning. In the afternoon go to the laboratory, get the gear you required, build your x-ray machine, take a picture of your hand, present it to the examiner. So there were twenty-eight of us doing that. No idea of guarding against the x-rays, there was none, you took the risk. And I did that—I've still got the picture I took of my hand and it was a bloody clear one, a good one. That was three months of very hard work actually.

And then the anti-British riots broke out—instead of reaping the result and being able to build my machine for the hospital which I'd been trained to do, we were packed off out of the country, the whole lot of us, and the place was shut down for a while. And I never got back, several of them didn't ever get back. Because I decided I can't spend months here, in Hong Kong. I was driving a tram car because we were all put to something to stop the strike and so on, and for six weeks I drove a tram car in Hong Kong. I still have my certificate as a licensed motorman of the Hong Kong and Shanghai Corporation.

I sided with the Chinese [at the time of the anti-British riots] I'm afraid. I was very sympathetic with our two Chinese doctors because what was throughout China at the time was extra-territoriality. And that was simply handed down to all the Chinese who were coming along, as a result of the war. But my two—one was fairly young and the other was quite a young man—resented it, very badly. This right of the [British]—as it happened in Canton, and in other places it could have been the Germans or someone else—the right of you people to walk unchallenged into various areas of our cities and so on, whereas we've got to have a passport. And why was it, and I said well, I don't know and I don't like it.

Several times when passing through Shameen, which was the Canton foreign settlement, with foreign extra-territoriality, side by side with a Chinese, sometimes still with a pigtail, being held up for his passport, and examined, and so on. It was wrong—this was their country—and the most beautiful bit of Canton city too, that they took. And of course that went on in Shanghai, Nanking, all over the place. And it was a festering sore among the educated, coming-along young Chinese. Well, I sympathised with them . . .

My time in China was invaluable to me all the rest of my life. Because not only did I get in touch with all the possibilities in tropical medicine, but I got the—what would you call it—confidence and the ability to take on anything that came along. Because I never knew what was going to come along in China—I mean, I was dealing with various quite tropical things including some leprosy and so on, and I took it all in my stride. And learnt not to worry about whatever turned up each day. You had a sort of wider vision of things, you didn't worry about things, you were there to do what you could with whatever turned up.

The Kong Chuen Hospital complex in June 1989.

A CHINESE NEWSPAPER

William Quinn

Mr Quinn was a Southland businessman on a tourist visit to the East. His visit to a newspaper office in Canton (Guangzhou) was part of a programme arranged for him by staff of the Canton Villages Mission, in consideration of his association with the choir of First Church, Invercargill.

I had the opportunity of going through the typesetting room of a Chinese newspaper. It was a large room opening to the street and was in half darkness, owing to the poor light from outside. How the compositors sorted out the fearful and wonderful characters of the Chinese alphabet kept me wondering. The Chinese are a most polite race and the following letter from a Chinese editor will take some beating for 'the soft answer that turneth away wrath'. It is a literal translation of a letter sent back with a rejected manuscript and compares most favourably with the curt, 'Declined with thanks', of European and even New Zealand editors.

> Sir,—We have read thy manuscript with infinite delight, never before have we seen such a masterpiece. If we printed it the authorities would order us to take it for a model and henceforth never print anything inferior to it. As it would be impossible to find its equal within ten thousand years we are compelled, though shaken with sorrow to return your divine manuscript, and for doing so we beg one thousand pardons.
> Yours obediently
> Tung Cheek (editor).

WHERE LIFE IS CHEAP

Family Cult in the East

SACRIFICE OF WOMEN

DOMINION SPECIAL SERVICE

Citing examples of the slight value placed on life by the Chinese upon the life of the individual, Mr J. A. Brailsford, in the course of a lecture to the Masterton branch of the Workers' Educational Association on 'Family Life in the East', stated that during the three years he resided in Hankow, quite a dozen Chinese were accidently killed by European sportsmen.

It was seriously suggested by the sportsmen that the Chinese were deliberately putting themselves in the way of being shot because they received $5 or so if injured in this way and the heirs received $10 if they were killed. It had been alleged also that for a few pounds Chinese condemned to death had been able to find substitutes prepared to be executed in their stead. When disease was sweeping away the labourers employed on the construction of the Panama Canal, no difficulty whatever was found in getting Chinese to carry on the work. At certain seasons of the year the navigation of the Yangtse was very perilous, but it was carried on. A friend of his had seen three of four boats destroyed with their crews in the Yangtse rapids. The men who were lost had thrown away their lives for the sake of a few shillings.

Sacrifice of the individual for the sake of the family was expected in the East. Factory life in Japan for girls was anything but pleasant until recently, but many girls had undertaken factory work—some an even worse life, perhaps—in order to pay for the education of their brothers.

Mr Brailsford mentioned later in his address that side by side with the desire for large families, and particularly for sons, there was in the East a very high level of infant mortality. In some parts of China it was estimated that 70 per cent of the babies died in their first year.

The lecturer said he thought the lack of progress in the East—exemplified by the fact that China had stagnated for 2000 years or more after inventing, among other things, the compass, gunpowder and printing—was due less to large families, though these were a contributory cause, that to the deadening effect of ancestor worship which implied that it was useless to think of trying to improve upon what had been done so wonderfully in the past. Many educated Eastern people declared, however, that Europeans were too much concerned with material things and too little with the things of the spirit.

The Dominion, 5 August 1931

SEEKING A NAME

Alison Wong

An extract from Alison Wong's novel As the Earth Turns Silver, *published in 2009. The novel is set in Wellington in the early part of the twentieth century.*

FIELD

It seemed the strangest question to ask after they'd known each other for so long, perhaps the hardest, because it seemed so intimate. If it had been anyone else, Katherine would have known—she knew the baker next door was George, even though she only ever called him Mr Paterson. Everyone knew. (George's pies were famous in Newtown, in all of Wellington by the way people talked.) But no one knew the names of the Chinese. Occasionally someone might say Mr— Mr Wong or Mr Choy. But usually it was the Chinaman next door to Paterson's or the John on the corner of Tory and Webb. They were all called John, the Chinese. And even if anyone bothered to find out, who could remember? Their names were like birds that never came in to land.

Katherine was afraid to ask. Afraid he would speak his name and it would hover close to her ear, her cheek, her tongue, then fly away from her. How could she ask him? Again and again. As if his name was unimportant. As if he merely provided a service for which she paid and dismissed him.

He was wrapping turnips in a page of the *Evening Post* and she'd expected him to open his full, wide lips. Without realising, she had turned her face a little, still looking intently at his dark eyes, his mouth, straining her ears as if spreading a net. But instead he'd leaned in closer; held out his left hand for her to see. She did not understand, yet she'd looked into his palm, as if to read his life line, his heart line, the lines of the number of his children. And then he lifted his right index finger like a pen, and wrote stroke upon stroke on his hand.

'*Wong,*' he said, and started over, slowly, kindly, as if to a child. 'My name has grass on top,' he said, drawing a short horizontal line on his skin and then two small ones down through it. Then a longer horizontal line underneath.

A name, she thought, has a sound which disappears, and now also a physical presence, a shape on skin, an apparition.

'The belly of my name is a field,' he said, drawing a grid like a window dissected into four small panes. How strange, she thought, the way the Chinese draw windows, how they draw three sides of the frame, then the two bars within and only last the bottom sill, as if there is no need for closure unless there is something of importance to close. No, a field, she thought again, not a window on the future, but something more earthy. Now two strokes underneath, like two short legs dancing, holding his name up to the world.

61

She watched him write his Christian name (but what does that mean, the word Christian?). *'Chung,'* he was saying, and she was lost, somewhere after the symbol for China, the centre of all things, and three strokes of a heart beating. 'Faithful,' he was saying, 'loyal,' and she thought about faith, about loyalty and what might be true. *'Yung,'* he was saying, 'courageous,' and she thought about courage, about what she had always been afraid to do, what she'd always been afraid to be.

She thought about how his surname came first, how his family had the ultimate priority. Katherine came first for her. Not McKechnie, which was only her husband's name; not even Lachlan, her father's name. Only Katherine. Whatever she could count on for herself.

She watched his finger move across the skin—this strange intimacy of language—and asked him without thinking for a Chinese name, an opening into his language, a window into his world.

GHOSTS, DREAMS

It was 4.30 when she came in on her way home from work. She said he looked tired. He remembered smiling weakly. He'd been up at six to go to the market, spent all day unloading the cart, washing and trimming vegetables. Another six hours to go, bringing in the cauliflowers, cabbages, onions, shutting the shop, tidying up.

She was surprised. Did he always have to work such long hours? What about his brother? Of course they took turns: he finished early on Mondays, Thursdays and Saturdays, at about seven when they had dinner and his brother took over. And what did he do then? He might have said that he went down *Tongyangai* and met up with friends like Fong-man, occasionally played a game of dominoes or cards, mostly drank tea and argued about politics, but then he looked at her again and remembered Haining Street was a swear word in English, something like bastard or whore, a place that *gweilo* used at night to frighten their children. He remembered she knew nothing of China, or Sun Yat-sen and the Revolution, and maybe—probably—she didn't care. He felt a nervous laugh rising in his throat.

'Do you like knitting?' she asked. 'I hear that sea captains enjoy knitting. It's supposed to be good when there's nothing else to do.'

'Nitting?'

She mimed some kind of action with her hands, but he didn't understand.

'Don't worry, just kidding.' She saw his bewilderment. 'Joking. I was only joking.'

He saw the twinkle in her eyes. He was still curious—what was this *nitting* she joked about, and what was the other word, did she say *kidding?*—but he did not ask again. Sometimes he'd sidetrack her with his questions and they'd forget what they'd been talking about. Sometimes he was too plain tired.

'So what do you do when you're not working?' she asked again.

'I walk,' he said. Already he'd forgotten the new words. Instead he was swallowed by night, the rocking of one foot in front of the other, everything full of shadow and half-light—moon, star, lamplight—the streets emptied of people and filled with ghosts, dreams, strange possibilities.

'I like walking too,' she said, and he was surprised, and didn't know what he'd told her and what he'd only thought, because there was always a gap between thought and its expression, especially in another language. 'It's a good time to think,' he heard her say, and he looked up from the cauliflower he'd chosen because it was the biggest and freshest and whitest, and he asked her where she liked to walk.

'Sometimes we walk to Oriental Parade or even down to the beach at Island Bay. If it's fine, that is. The children like to play in the water.

'Robbie kicks a ball or if there are other boys down there he'll join them for cricket . . . Edie makes elaborate—big—sandcastles . . . Sometimes we just go to the Basin. It's so much closer . . .'

She sighed. 'Sometimes I think I need time to myself. Away from Mrs Newman telling me what to do. Away from the children . . .' She smiled.

He nodded. He needed time away from the shop too. Away from his brother. But perhaps he had too much time. Alone.

There was silence, just the crinkling and rustling of newspaper. As he handed the wrapped cauliflower to her, the small bag of Brussels sprouts, he told her about the place at the Basin, under the cabbage trees, where he liked to lie down and think and look at the night sky.

The next evening, Thursday, he did not go down Haining Street or Frederick or Taranaki. He walked to the Basin. There was no one under the pine or cabbage trees. He walked a circuit, then another; and another. Then he lay down under a tree and looked up at the moonless sky, at the stars shining out of darkness.

It was different here. The stars made unrecognisable pictures; they told other stories.

He could feel the damp coming through his clothes from the grass underneath, even from the air. His mother would scold. *Cold-to-death,* she'd call. *Rice bucket, is that all you can do? Eat rice and nothing else? Your brother can't read but is he so stupid?*

Yung laughed and gazed at the stars, which glowed larger and more wondrously fuzzy because of myopia.

He thought about how far away they were. He thought about the cowherd and spinning-maid, of whom the heavens disapproved because passion interfered with their work—two lovers whom the Jade Emperor turned into stars, whose paths crossed only once every year, on the seventh day of the seventh month.

He sighed. Who could understand women and their complicated thinking—especially a foreign woman. He could feel the damp moving through his clothes, through his skin, even through his flesh to the marrow at the heart of his bones, when he heard her voice.

'Hello,' she called from a distance.

He lifted his head and saw her silhouette. 'Hello,' he said, and realising that she might not be sure whether it was him, he stood up and tipped his hat in the manner of a *gweilo* to a lady. 'Mrs McKechnie,' he said.

STROKE UPON STROKE

He'd looked into her eyes as he told her about moonlight, starlight, the place under the cabbage trees at the Basin. Katherine blushed and left the shop quickly.

But she couldn't stop thinking. As she cooked dinner; as she sent the children to bed. She couldn't sleep.

The next day she gazed at the black typewriter keys and thought of his hair, his eyes, the gentle, husky sound of his voice. What had Mrs Newman just said? What was she supposed to be doing?

She passed by the shop on the way home, saw his brother stacking pumpkins. Did not go in.

Her stomach felt tight. At dinner, she could not eat.

'Are you all right, Mum?' Edie asked.

'What? Yes, I'm fine. Just got a stomach-ache.' She put down her fork.

'Brussels sprouts give me stomach-ache too,' Robbie said, pushing his plate away.

Katherine could see him looking at her, waiting for her to argue with him, waiting for her to make him eat, but for once she said nothing.

The children went to bed and the house fell silent.

Katherine opened a book and closed it. She picked up her knitting and put it down again. She looked in at the children. Came back downstairs and paced from room to room. Not a sound from upstairs. Not a sound.

She put on her coat and walked out the back door.

It was a new moon; she could barely make out his silhouette under the cabbage trees. 'Mrs McKechnie,' he said, as if he'd been waiting.

How did he know it was her? How *could* he be waiting?

She was suddenly afraid. She'd made a terrible mistake with Donald. And now, what in God's name was she doing?

He stood up and walked towards her, and she didn't know what to say. She had to say something.

'You haven't given me a name,' she blurted out. 'I asked you over a month ago and you still haven't given me a name.' She wanted to cry. What a stupid thing to say. As if she'd come all this way—as if she'd left her children asleep in bed—just because he'd forgotten. What had come over her? It had been a stupid, stupid thing to ask of him, even then. And now . . .

A tram rattled past, turning out of Adelaide Road, into Rugby and along Sussex; another travelled along Kent Terrace. A drunk called out as he stumbled out of the Caledonian, the clip-clop of a horse-cart, the ragged sound of a motorcar.

What was he saying? Was he laughing? Not his usual gravelly laugh but something quieter, more hesitant.

The leaves of a cabbage tree shook above them.

Her face felt hot. She was shaking. She wanted to run, but her legs felt weak, as if her bones had softened, as if she were falling. 'I . . . I have to go . . .' she whispered.

But then he moved closer, took her in his arms as if to still her shaking.

He turned her hand and slowly traced onto her palm with his finger. She could hardly see, only movements of darkness within darkness, but she could smell ginger and aniseed, the smell of a man's fresh sweat, and she could feel the shape of her name, the sensation of skin against skin.

'Lai,' he said. 'This is Chinese family name, not name we give foreigners, not name like English. You put this name with word for bright and this is sun come out of night. You have all these colours.' She could hear his breathing, feel her own short breaths. 'Bik-yuk,' he was saying. 'This is Christian name. It means jade.' And he was writing again, stroking her palm with her name. 'Bik,' he was saying. 'This is word for king and this is white. Under is rock. Yuk. This is three jades,' he was drawing horizontal lines, 'and this string hold them together. Many woman have name like beautiful or flower but you are pure and clear . . .'

She heard a tram swing through her silence into Adelaide Road, felt him touch her hair, her cheek, brush her lips, which parted and left a line of moisture on his fingers.

THE FACTORY INSPECTOR

Rewi Alley

Rewi Alley travelled from New Zealand to China in 1927. He initially worked for the Shanghai Fire Department, and then as a factory inspector in Shanghai. He was a driving force behind the Gung Ho movement, setting up small industrial cooperatives in inland China, out of the reach of the invading Japanese. Later he assumed control of a technical school in Shandan that became a focus for New Zealand developmental support. From 1953 until his death in 1987, Alley lived in Beijing, where as one of the People's Republic's 'foreign friends' he wrote many books and articles in support of New China.

April 10th [1951]: Looking through the bookstalls in Tung An market today, I saw a kids' pictorial called 'Factory Safety'. These simple pictorials fit the pocket easily, and are cheap. Street libraries rent them to readers for a tiny sum, and their circulation is very wide.

This book on 'Factory Safety' was a joy to see. In the old days of factory safety work in Shanghai, we had always wanted to get out something like this, but we were never able to get the cash for it. What the old Shanghai Municipal Council wanted of their factory inspectors was to keep the city tidy, make things easy and pleasant for big business and silence criticism. It lent much 'face' to be able to introduce well-known visitors to the factory inspection system, as an example of the up-to-date methods of the administration.

As I look through this little book, a hundred memories come to mind. A whole series of books could be written about the tragic incidents of each day of some 10 years' work. Many would leave one with a sense of impotence and anger that such things could be permitted. Gunther Stein, the writer, said when I took him around one day, 'I wonder how you can stand it!' In truth, I could not have gone on standing it had I not known that change for the better was generating itself.

Shanghai Power started as a municipal enterprise. It was sold to Electric Bond and Share, a Morgan subsidiary, and renamed Shanghai Power Company. What chicanery was used, what foreigners were bought in order to allow a public utility to pass into the hands of one of the most vicious foreign trusts in the world, is another story. My chief concern was the number of workers who fell down chutes of the self-feeding boiler apparatus and went into the furnaces with the coal.

I would call on the American manager at Riverside. He would chew his cigar meditatively while I explained how we needed a light chain and belt which must be worn by workers who had to work naked on top of the stack of coal-dust. Then when the coal caved in under them they would not go down with it. 'Christ!' shouted this representative of a Christian nation, 'if the silly bastards don't take more care, what can *I* do about it?' A mention of the American court and prosecution brought forth a smile. In those days of extra-territoriality foreigners were tried in their own courts and were thus exempt from Chinese law. The next time a worker died in this fashion the court was informed. They said they would 'speak to the management.'

The Japanese courts in Shanghai administered the same kind of justice. A Japanese who, in a secret part of his home, kept a line of workers making narcotics for sale, had some killed. He was fined one yen by the Japanese Court.

The ease with which raw material could be imported, and the finished goods exported, caused a great consumer goods industry to rise in dwelling houses of back alleyways. A house built for one or two families to live in would be converted into a factory employing several hundred children making flashlight bulbs for the five and ten cent stores abroad.

In the steaming heat of a Shanghai summer, when the foreigners and their compradores lay exhausted in deck chairs on shaded lawns, sipping cool drinks brought by attentive servants, these children toiled from dawn to dark in crowded lofts, their weary faces close to the Bunsen burners, their legs swollen with beriberi, their sweating bodies covered with sores from bed-bugs and lice. In the not too distant future their hearts would stop working, for they were already enlarged.

From the famine and the flood, from the civil war and all the disturbances of the interior, a fresh wave of children would arrive in the city and be bought up by the loafers and gangsters who ran small industry. Of these there were many.

One of the worst dives was a place called Tien Kai Ziang, in an alleyway off what is now Peking Road West, in Shanghai. The management of this concern would subsidise orphanages to give him children. They had a battery of punch presses, making parts for the sockets of electric light bulbs. The children would sleep beside the machines. They worked a 14-hour day. The factory was unlighted except for a blazing naked bulb over each machine. There was an armed guard at the door to prevent the escape of any child. Foremen could beat the children at will.

Of one batch of orphans sent in by the 'Child Welfare Association,' practically all received injuries from the fast-running, unguarded punch presses. Of 29 children, 11 had suffered amputations. Out of some 64 children working at one time it was found that over 30 had fingers or portions of fingers missing. When a child had had more than two amputations, he was kicked into the street to fend for himself and fight with other waifs for scraps from the garbage cans in the alleyways, at the backs of the restaurants.

The manager of the factory smoked opium. The raw material—brass—came from Japan. The produce went to South America to help force down the wages of workers there. All that China got out of it were the import and export duties on the finished goods. The children would be worn out by 30, if they lived so long. The manager would have a pack of useless fat women and spoiled brats. This was small capitalist industry.

One day I went to a place where one of the apprentices had been beaten to death by the manager. 'Very bad boy!' this gentleman shouted. The police arrested him, but when I passed the place a few months later he was back there again.

But there were many other ways of doing away with people. In the hot summer-time, in badly ventilated workrooms, they died of fatigue or stumbled against unguarded machines and were caught by the old-fashioned clothing they wore. The dead body would be pulled away at night and tossed on the rubbish heaps at the back of Yangtsepoo for the dogs to eat, or taken out on the river and dropped in. But it was usually easy to see who would die and, as a rule, he would be 'sent back to the country.' The kids in the battery-making shops, all of whom had lead poisoning, the silicosis cases, the beri-beri cases in the last stages, the TB ones and the badly injured—they could be sent back to the villages for their relatives to bury. More would come in.

Stinking urinals in workrooms, no place to wash down and take away the sweat and grease, black bedding, bleeding gums, trachoma eyes, wretched food, industrial hazards and lack of any creative opportunity—these were the wages of the worker of that day. Now recognized as the very basis of society, then he was regarded as something less than human.

Later: I can only write of the Shanghai I knew. The Shanghai of luxurious clubs, sleek cars, well-trained servants, was the Shanghai in which one slept and ate one's food. But one's working and emotional life was spent up and down the alleyways where the vast majority of the Chinese people lived . . . Where every tiny room held a family, where the rows of nightpots lined the streets . . . Where clothing, hung a certain way on the bamboo poles in which it was dried, would speak a definite language, 'Come and get the message that awaits you,' or 'Don't come, the house is watched.'

The gangster-run factory to which I was called one Christmas morning, to see the floor covered with the dead bodies of workers who had been killed in an explosion of inflammable gas from an annealing furnace, annealing the tops of water bottles for the KMT army . . . The gangster woman manager with a flock of Taoist priests chanting and mumbling prayers to get the devils out of the place . . . The factory where another woman manager, a great fat mountain of a woman who beat her apprentices while they worked, screamed with rage when made to effect a simple improvement; and to emphasise her words, snatched up a live chicken, tore it to bits with her hands and stamped on it . . . The wonderful machine tool men who turned out marvels of machinery with rotten old machine tools . . . The long lines of serious, sweet-faced village girls who stood in the cotton mills.

The dark, brooding, set faces of the Japanese foremen and technicians, driven on by some force they seemed powerless to stand against . . . The irrepressible gaiety of dying apprentices in lead battery factories when I would go to take urine from them for testing for lead content—'What, you're not going to drink all of that in one day, are you?'—as they saw me handing in the boxful of bottles to the driver . . . The chromium-plating workshops in alleyways, the apprentices covered with grinding dust, sleeping with grinding dust, hands and feet bitten deep with chrome holes that bored right down to the bone and suppurated.

A Shanghai where anything could be done if one had money, and where there was only one sacred word, and that was 'PROFIT'.

But the thing that made one most sick was the support given by the ruling powers to the worst elements and their complete indifference to the fate of the mass of the people.

The Shen Shing Cotton Mill, in the western district of Shanghai, built latrines in the exit doors. A fire on straw matting outside caused a panic. Many girls were crushed to death trying to get out of the doors. The manager, who had been warned many times to keep the exits clear, was treated with tender consideration by the court. When some small fines, and various officials, had to be paid, Shanghai society cried, 'Poor fellow!' But the girls were buried, and that was that.

So also when the handrails of the stairway at a silk filature broke and 13 children were stamped to death; so when 400 women were blasted to death in a rubber factory; so when some 90 women and children were burned to death in a celluloid factory explosion—and so on, and on . . .

The Settlement could build fine buildings, make roads, set up schools for the rich, parks, and even a municipal orchestra, but it could not and would not lift the burden from the backs of the poor. Its *taipans* lived the lives of princes, surrounded by many servants, in lovely houses out in the western district. They would belong to exclusive clubs, holiday in Japan, or Tsingtao, or Pei Tai Ho. They would pass their lives without ever going down the main streets of the industrial parts of Hongkew or Yangtsepoo, let alone the alleyways, with their reek of urine and garbage. 'One half of the bloody world,' one Public Works inspector would say impressively to me, 'doesn't know how the other half bloody well lives!' And having said it, he would escape in his car and get out as fast as possible.

Jessfield and Hongkew parks were beautiful. Nursemaids and babies would frolic there, and the fashionable of the town parade, expensively dressed, on Sundays. The tens of thousands of working girls walked down the paths from the villages before daylight in the morning and back after dark at night seven days a week.

Memory rakes up a jumble of pictures and incidents, each rather more fantastic than the last . . . The White Russian detachment of the Settlement armed forces standing to attention under the old Imperial Russian flag when important guests came in state to visit the Shanghai Municipal Council . . . How, when I began to study Chinese, the foreign officers of the Fire Department laughed and said, 'What do you want to learn that monkey language for?' (My teacher, a gentle slip of a lad, in long white gown, would wince and pretend he had not heard. He had to teach foreigners Shanghai dialect all day for a living.)

Bill Tozer, head of the Yangtsepoo Fire Station, who would come home in the early hours of the morning after a drunken spree, driving like a demon in his car . . . 'Knocked down another yellow belly on the way home. One the less now!' he would triumph. (It was a considerable pleasure, when attending another fire amongst some hundreds of straw huts, to see the worthy Bill, drunk again, fall up to his neck in one of the manure ponds where human manure is soaked prior to use on the land. He stank for some time after.)

And the conversation of the messroom, with its dull topics of drunken excess and lechery, its racial insanity, the wretched airs of superiority overlying the basic unhappiness and boredom because these puppets of colonial imperialism, part of a false, superimposed structure, could have no part in the rich and varied life that surrounded them.

Educational though this phase of my life was, I longed to end this lesson and spend my days amongst people who were struggling. Factory inspection was the next stage, and gave one a chance to pass from one place to another, Chinese and foreign, big and small, workroom and dormitory, seeing all kinds of conditions, knowing that better ways must come and that change would cleanse eventually— though that change had to come via all the horrors of the Japanese invasion, with dogs worrying at freshly made corpses, pillage and rape until the whole world seemed to be in the hands of a horde of maniacs.

Shanghai, a world in itself, has been a city of tragedy. It deserves the chance to make of itself the city it can really be—the city where the worker of the future will have some of the comforts and amenities the pampered westerner had in the past.

Sinza Fire Station HQ staff, August 1931, Rewi Alley on the right.

REWI ALLEY

YO BANFA!

THE CITY OF PEKING

A VISITOR'S MEMORIES

(SPECIALLY WRITTEN FOR THE PRESS)

(By Pleasure Seeker)

The Legations

The quiet of the Legation quarter makes an extraordinary contrast to the activities of the Chinese city; it is like passing into an English cathedral town—through dignified gateways, where soldiers in the uniforms of many armies do sentry go, you look into beautiful gardens. The stories of some of the Legations are as picturesque as the building themselves. The French and British were the first to establish Legations in 1858, but the Russians had the right of residence in Peking as early as 1727, and a church they built there, though much repaired, is still in use. I had luncheon with Sir Miles Lampson in the British Legation. He had just returned from Nanking, a pestilential city which the Ministers leave gladly to return to their quarters in Peking. This estate was given by an Emperor to his thirty-third son. It was falling into decay when the British leased it for £500 a year. For 40 years the rent, in silver dollars, was put into a mule cart and paid over, on the Chinese New Year's day, by the Chinese secretary of the Legation. It is now British Crown property, and two stone lions crouch appropriately at the entrance gate.

My friends took me to a reception at the Italian Legation, memorable for the charming courtesy of our hosts, and for the Italian conception of the American short drink, served in a garden with the bridges, fish ponds and miniature trees that I had wrongly associated only with Japanese gardens. Among other interesting people I met Mei Lang-Fang, just returned from a successful season in New York; a little too plump perhaps for the perfect portrayal of those female roles for which he is so famous. A very high-born Chinese lady was gracious and vivacious with a word or two of English. She was pleasant to look upon in a long straight robe of peach coloured brocade and many jewels. When I pointed downward with much force, she understood that I lived right through the earth, in an island called New Zealand, and laughed in the hearty way the Chinese do, and the Japanese do not. With her were her two sons, one just returned from Germany and the other from America, faultlessly dressed, to their white spats, in the Western manner. Rather pathetic these boys looked, standing apart, watching. They appeared grateful for the effort we made to converse with them.

The Press, Saturday March 4, 1933

THE TWELFTH OF DECEMBER

James Bertram

After attending Oxford as a Rhodes Scholar, James Bertram accepted an invitation to study the Chinese language in (then) Peking. In 1936 he was the first foreign correspondent to travel to Sian (Xian) and report on the 'Sian Incident', when Chiang Kai-Shek was held captive by his own troops until he agreed to enter into a united front with the communist forces against Japan. The following year Bertram travelled to Yenan to conduct a series of interviews with Mao Zedong that have found a place in Mao's Collected Works. *Captured fighting for the Volunteers in the defence of Hong Kong, Bertram spent four years in Japanese POW camps. After the war he returned to New Zealand, and in later life became Professor of English at Victoria University of Wellington.*

While dawn broke in Shensi, about the time that Generalissimo Chiang Kai-shek was scrambling up the hills behind Lintung in his night-shirt, stealthy activity of a rather similar kind was going on in the schools and universities of Peking.

Through back gates and over dormitory walls, small groups of students were making their way out into the dim lanes of the city. They wore padded winter gowns and woollen mufflers; many of the girls were in blue slacks and flannel shirts. All this advance guard carried with them rolled-up banners and bundles of printed handbills. They were preparing for a patriotic demonstration, and the police had got wind of it.

Foreigners living in Peking do not as a rule take much notice of student demonstrations. The phenomenon is recurrent, and has had at times important political consequences. But there is a general impression among foreigners that the students only organise at end of term, apparently preferring the known risk of bullets to the unknown hazards of the examination room. That solemn and admirable institution, the British Embassy, still believes that these children are paid twenty cents apiece to face machine-guns and arrest, and the traditional Chinese torture that is reserved nowadays for political prisoners. Some of them have certainly earned it.

But Peking society is a world of its own, upon which living China seldom impinges. Its amusements are graceful and slightly decadent, as becomes life in an ancient capital. This polyglot society that revolves in the vacuum of the Legation Quarter and the East City is an anachronism, a picturesque survival, like the foreign colony in Florence before the War and Mussolini arrived. Only Proust and Musset together could do justice to its charming irrelevance and acrid fatuity. It is a world in which no one grows up, in which serious events are an invitation to a cocktail party, or a moonlight visit to the Temple of Heaven. The charm of Peking, like the charm of Oxford, is fatal. Those who have lived in both places seldom recover.

Peking people are proud of their 'culture' (though only the Americans call it this), which they absorb from palace walls, Sung paintings, and the most intelligent book-store in China. They have a justifiable contempt for the commercially-minded inhabitants of the treaty ports, who shout at their boys in pidgin English, and do not know the difference between Han and Ming. Most Peking people have, indeed, a real feeling for China: and they will defend this feeling as passionately as a lover.

But so often it is for a China of the past. They look for what is old or quaint or beautiful: their fine susceptibilities are bruised by a radio in a temple court, or a latinised text that threatens to supplant the picturesque Chinese character. They go to uncomfortable theatres to hear Mei Lan-fang or Ch'eng Yen-ch'iu, the most accomplished virtuosi of the old Peking drama that flourishes outside Ch'ien Men; but they find attempts at a realistic modern drama grotesque and slightly indecent. The flavour of the past comes to them from the exquisite pages of T'ang poetry, not the bitter futility of the present from some surreptitious news-sheet. All that has happened since the Manchus seems to them a mistake of history.

They are interested in China as pattern, not in China as change.

And Peking—that home of lost imperial causes—is all on their side. It brings them fewer reminders than any other large city of the social ferment at work over all China today. It guards them gravely with its ponderous walls, charms them with its annual fairs, delights with a vista of golden roofs above brooding cedars, and the far, delicate line of its Western Hills. Peking is the last sanctuary of the Soul of China.

And the Soul of China is a dangerous myth. It may draw a new Golden Horde of tourists from luxury liners to this old capital that withstood the Mongols, gladdening the hearts of the curio-dealers and the traffickers in temple-lore. But it has had devastating effects on the foreign population in the one city in China where foreigners are often intelligent and not seldom well-informed. Those Peking people who are most in love with China are often most unaware of China's real problems. Peking Culture mists their gaze.

For things of general interest besides diplomatic scandals and peculiarly gruesome murders do happen sometimes in Peking. When Japanese troops fight miniature battles on the glacis around the Legation Quarter, and the Emperor's sacred tanks advance destructively along the main streets, even the foreigner is apt to feel resentful. The Chinese merchants at the doors of their shops watch in inscrutable calm. In the rear of the crowd, perhaps, a blue-gowned student stands scowling.

In all Peking, only the students are vocal. Only they, in the armed truce that hangs uneasily over North China, dare organise and raise the cry of national resistance in the streets where the Japanese tanks lumber at will. And when this happens, when the banners are raised beneath the *pailous,* and the students march in thousands beside the moat and the great towers of the Forbidden City, it is the

Mausers and big swords of Chinese police that scatter their ranks and turn them back.

On that morning of December 12th, when so many things were happening in distant Shensi, a car-load of newspaper-men went in search of the demonstration. The universities of Peking are in the western part of the city, which is perhaps one reason why so few foreigners ever see them. In recent years, no procession has been allowed within a mile of the Japanese Legation.

The streets were filled with the usual crowds of pedlars and water-carriers and nonchalant pedestrians. But we passed the gates of schools where policemen armed with rifles barred an exit to the excited students inside. As yet, there were no gendarmes in sight—the Special Police, whose leather jackets and motor-cycles are a familiar feature on all such occasions. These are shock troops, specially trained for violence; and very different from the amiable Guardians of Public Safety who lounge peacefully at the entrance to any public building in China.

'Looks like being quite a good show,' said my friend Don, a young American correspondent who had seen many student demonstrations. 'With no gendarmes around, most of the middle-schools must be out.' He sucked hard on a pipe, and caressed his unshaven chin. The morning air was crisp, with a tang of frost.

West of the main street that runs north and south through this part of the city, we came across the first group of students. They were walking fast and purposefully along a narrow *hutung,* continually joined by twos and threes who seemed to emerge from every gate and corner. Couriers on bicycles scouted vigilantly in advance of the ragged column. If police should appear at this stage, it would be easy to break up and reform later on.

We stopped an earnest-looking youth with a peaked cap, who carried a sheaf of flimsy, gaily-coloured handbills. 'Where are you meeting?' Don asked genially. The boy frowned suspiciously, and began to turn away: but a girl student with short hair falling into her eyes ran up, eager to explain.

'These are foreign journalists—they are our friends.' She thrust a handful of manifestoes and cartoons into the back of the car. 'At the Western Arches—as soon as we can get there. The Peita students are coming from the east. Mass meeting behind the Coal Hill at ten.' She left us with a wave of the hand, and the little group, aware of an audience, shouted their slogans: 'China must not perish! Down with Japanese Imperialism!' It was all very youthful and light-hearted. Trouble would come later, when the groups joined together in the main streets.

At the four Western Arches, where the great red *pailous* tower above the cross-road, there was the usual police guard; but still no gendarmes. We waited until the front of the marching column, now three or four thousand strong, emerged on the main street, and began to cross it, moving east. The banners were up by now, and the songs had started. A crowd had gathered at the cross-road. Coolies struggling with loads that would tax the strength of a farm-horse set down their barrows, and straightened to watch, wiping the sweat from their eyes. Undersized apprentices from the market ran shouting beside the banners.

There is something curiously stimulating about a marching column—a fact which is appreciated in the Tempelhof and on the Red Square. But I think I have been more stirred by a student procession in China than by Labour Day in Hitler's Berlin, or by a Comsomol anniversary in Moscow. It is such a gesture of desperation, so forlorn a hope in the face of overwhelming odds. The only question is how far they will get before they are broken; before the big swords flash in the sun, or the guns fire. More than half of the students in any demonstration in Peking are children from middle-schools, between the ages of fourteen and eighteen. Yet volunteers will always be found to march in front of the column to break a police cordon or face a rifle volley.

That day, as it happened, was the day of Tuan Chi-jei's funeral; and the former leader of the notorious Anfu clique, the most corrupt government North China ever saw, was being buried from his old capital, full of years and honour. Marshal Tuan was the man who had given the order to fire on the Peking students on March 18th, 1926, when they had been trapped in a narrow lane outside his official residence. When the crowd broke in panic from the fire of Tuan's guards, nearly a hundred bodies lay piled between the walls, their blood soaking quietly into the dust. That day had been the end of Tuan Chi-jei's political career, but it did not affect the magnificence of his funeral.

Still, it seemed that the funeral, leaving from a temple near the wall for the Western Hills, had drawn most of the police from the city. The procession was now five thousand strong, and marching well. Ahead was the gate where they hoped to join with the contingent led by Peking National University, now advancing west.

A small squad of Special Police had appeared, and was keeping pace with the moving column. They were obviously waiting their chance to attack. It came suddenly outside the temple-gate of a girls' school. Students broke from their ranks and ran to the gate, calling to the girls inside to come out and join the demonstration. There was a gap in the column, and with drawn swords and pistols the police charged into it.

In a moment, all was savage confusion. Many girls, running to escape the sudden attack, tripped in their long gowns and fell. Those who stopped to help them up were beaten with the flat of the swords or kicked with heavy boots. The girls did not escape punishment—many were beaten with swords or with the heavy leather straps that Chinese policemen carry to use on rickshaw-men and beggars.

The charge had been well timed, and the column was temporarily broken. A number of banners were captured, and several arrests made. But this was only a check; there were not enough police to make matters really serious. Leaders rallied the ranks, with the cry 'Join forces!' The other column was only a quarter of a mile away. We could see the banners across the street, and hear the sound of shouting.

'Do you think they can make it?' I asked Don. We were on foot, busily taking photographs. He jerked a thumb towards the gate-tower in front. 'Look at that!'

A group of some thirty gendarmes stood before the gate, holding the road between the two advancing columns. They had rifles and machine-guns. This looked more serious. We hurried to the head of the procession, which had halted for a council of war.

Only a few hundred yards separated the two main groups—together, they would total ten thousand. It was a rare chance for the Peking students. And the police were absurdly few in number, to handle a crowd of this size. But there were the guns, and it seemed likely now that they would use them. The day was young, and too promising to invite disaster. It was decided to withdraw.

The order ran along the ranks; there were murmurs against it, but the discipline was good. To turn in this position was to ask for attack. But the banners were reversed, and the unwieldy column began to move. 'Now they're for it!' someone muttered behind me.

Sure enough, a compact knot of leather jackets was approaching at the run. Their intention was clear—to charge the slow-moving mass from behind, so that it would pile up and jam. Students in the rear of the column looked back apprehensively, but they did not break ranks. The police quickened their pace for the charge. This looked like a massacre.

But just as the sergeant—a heavily built man with a Mauser at full cock—gave the order, there came a strange intervention. Behind the police, a student had appeared on a bicycle. His advance was calm, unhurried, almost stately. Smiling cheerfully, he addressed the police as he passed them:

'Fellow-countrymen! Why do you attack us? We are not against you—we are only against the Japanese ghosts. We love our country, as you do. Chinese don't fight against Chinese!'

It worked like a charm, for it had been done so smoothly and easily. The police stopped in their tracks: the fierce expressions they had assumed were wiped from their faces with comical suddenness. Quick to seize their advantage, the students shouted 'Hurrah for the patriotic Chinese police!' After that, of course, there was nothing more to be done.

Such incidents are not uncommon—the Chinese are one of the most emotional races in the world, and a well-timed appeal will almost always have its effect on them. I have seen an officer of gendarmes release a group of arrested students, and break down and weep with patriotic zeal while the students stood around and cheered. It is perhaps an unfortunate irony that with this emotional generosity can go a peculiarly cold-blooded kind of cruelty. Later in the day, these same police who had been pulled up with a word in public, made savage and unprovoked attacks upon the students who had applauded their good-nature. Turning the procession from the main streets into narrow *hutungs,* they rode into it from behind with motor-cycles. Leaders who had been picked out by plain-clothes men were seized and led down alleys, where they were unmercifully beaten as a prelude to arrest. And all the time Japanese officials from an Embassy car looked on.

There are many people who believe that all demonstrations are futile, a waste of time and energy that only exasperates authorities and achieves nothing. But in China, where there is not even the pretence of freedom of speech or assembly, where a vigilant government is only too ready to detect any unwary statement either critical of itself or calculated to cause annoyance to the good neighbour, Japan, these student demonstrations in the past have been the only open expression of other than official opinion. Some purists would quibble at the assertion that the May Fourth movement in 1919 'overthrew the Anfu Government'; or that the Student Movement in December 1935 'frustrated the plans of Japan for an autonomous North China.' But there can be no doubt that these movements were the first open expression of popular dissatisfaction, and made possible in the event what without them might never have been achieved. In China, the students have to be taken seriously, for they are the only articulate unarmed opposition in the country.

The demonstration of December 12th in Peking was a success, though not altogether in the way that might have been expected. It was a mass protest against the invasion of Japanese-paid Mongols into Suiyuan; against the armed occupation of Tsingtao by Japanese marines; against the arrest of certain prominent leaders of the patriotic movement. It was an appeal for stronger action against aggression, and for at least a measure of political freedom at home. And the Japanese authorities took it seriously enough to follow the whole route of the processions with staff cars. Finally they warned that most uncomfortably situated of Chinese officials, General Sung Cheh-yuan, that unless the Chinese troops turned out to keep the peace, the Japanese guards would take a hand. So the early afternoon saw the processions scattered, and the largest remnant—a crowd of some five thousand students—trapped inside the grounds of the Coal Hill, with several companies of the 29th Route Army on guard outside.

This was a strange enough scene, that only Peking could provide. Inside the massive gates, so impressively guarded by police and soldiery, at the foot of the five-coned hill on which the last of the Ming emperors hanged himself, the imprisoned students improvised a mass meeting. Directly opposite the gates, within the golden-tiled palaces of the Forbidden City, alarmed officials held whispered conference. The students had been told that General Sung himself would come and talk to them; but the hours passed, and finally it was announced that the General was in the Western Hills, at Tuan Chi-jei's funeral. It was growing dusk: the five pavilions on the crest of the hill were silhouetted against the evening sky.

We waited outside the gate; no one was allowed in or out. 'I don't like this,' my Chinese companion remarked. 'They'll wait until dark, and then let the gendarmes loose on them.' This had happened before.

But suddenly there was a stir among the officials at the palace-gate: the Mayor of Peking had arrived. Silk-gowned figures bobbed like marionettes. A little Japanese, very correct in a dark overcoat with fur collar, was talking excitedly. What was the news?

'The Mayor will talk to the students,' announced a fat detective in an astrakhan cap. I looked at my Chinese friend wonderingly. 'Does this often happen?'

'I can't understand it,' he answered. 'But see, he is going in.' In the centre of a solid phalanx of police, the Mayor was swept through the gates, which closed again after him.

The Mayor talked for a long time. What he said, as we learnt afterwards, was not so very much to the point; but he was surprisingly affable. The shouts of approval or dissent that came muffled through the heavy gates were followed with keen interest by the crowd outside.

At last there came a burst of cheering. The gates were opened; Mayor Chin came out hurriedly. He seemed relieved and yet anxious. 'The students will march out again,' we heard the rumour. 'He told them to march back to their schools, carrying their banners, and singing their songs without fear.' Officialdom had melted. But why? Nobody could guess.

Into the darkening streets the students poured exultantly. Police, soldiers had vanished. East and west they marched between the ancient walls, along streets suddenly crowded with onlookers. The shouted slogans echoed back. The white banners passed beneath the street lights.

The familiar songs of 'National Salvation' carried clearly on the night air. Some of them were taken up by the passers-by. But as the last group marched out from the empty park, leaving the uneasy shade of the last Chinese emperor alone with shadows, I heard a new song. It had a strong, rolling rhythm, not unlike the 'Marseillaise,' and alien to the plangent, rather stilted movement of most Chinese music.

'What are they singing?'

My friend turned to me: his eyes were shining behind his thick glasses. 'That is the marching song of the Red Army. It has never been sung in the streets of Peking before.'

CHINESE ART

INCLUDING MANY

EXAMPLES FROM FAMOUS
COLLECTIONS, EXHIBITED
IN
NEW ZEALAND

1937

In 1937 a major exhibition of Chinese art toured the main centres of New Zealand. The pieces on display were drawn both from New Zealand collections (mostly amassed during periods of residence in China) and from collections in England and Europe, including that of the Victoria and Albert Museum. For New Zealand artists such as T. A. McCormack, the exhibition was a revelation. According to his friend John Stackhouse, he visited it daily: 'He spoke of an exhibition of Chinese ceramics at the museum, that he used to go up daily to see and to look, and occasionally you would get a direct influence on his work at that time. Two decades later, some of his pictures were still showing that influence.'

T. A. McCormack, Chinese Pottery.

NEW LIFE FOR CHINA

George Shepherd

On 17 April 1939, Time magazine ran an article about the presence in the United States of Mme Chiang Kai-shek's key advisor, 'a Congregational missionary, Rev George W. Shepherd of Auburndale Mass'. The importance Time ascribed to Shepherd was not misplaced. He was on intimate terms with Generalissimo Chiang Kai-shek and his wife, and together with the Australian journalist W. H. Donald provided their foreign 'kitchen cabinet'. While the Kuomindang regime hired many foreign advisors, Shepherd was the first to be given actual administrative authority in the government.

What Time failed to note is that far from being American, Shepherd hailed from provincial New Zealand. Born and educated in Mataura, he served a 5-year apprenticeship at the Dunedin hardware supplier Patterson & Barr before bible study in the United States and, in 1918, acceptance as a China-based missionary of New Zealand's Brethren Assemblies. It was not until 1925 that Shepherd took up an appointment with the American Board of Commissioners for Foreign Missions.

Within the Nanking Government, Shepherd's special responsibility was for the New Life Movement, an eclectic mix of puritanism, neo-Confucianism and New Testament Christianity that was intended to raise the moral standards of the Chinese people, imbue them with new hopes and ideals, and, incidentally, counter the success of the Communists in garnering popular support.

'Social Work in the Provinces' will give you a glimpse of some of the things that are being done for farmers. We wish we could do more, and do it faster. Under the direction of the New Life Movement it is proposed that we extend this work for the welfare of farmers into all the provinces. During the summer of 1936 students from many universities will give part of their time to this work. We are just making up a simple list of practical things that the students can help the farmers do this summer. . . . You will be interested in some of the chapter headings of this STUDENT'S SUMMER MANUAL:—

I.— What you can do for the local barber shop.
II.— What you can do for the tea-houses.
III.— Some suggestions for the local inn.
IV.— Cooperation in the village community.
V.— Organize recreation and sports for young men and women.
VI.— Conduct discussion groups in the evening.
VII.— What you can teach the farmer about keeping his family healthy.
VIII.— About cooperatives.
IX.— How to improve the farmer's home.
X.— Some things to investigate.
XI.— List of subjects for evening talks in tea-houses.
XII.— Special supplement for work amongst women and girls.

For China

In 1934, China's Generalissimo Chiang Kai-shek "observed a schoolboy behaving in an unbecoming manner in the street." Shortly thereafter the Generalissimo founded a New Life Movement to puritanize and clean up the Chinese, to fight superstition, ignorance and corruption, even to curb such Chinese habits as spitting in public. Chiang turned over the actual running of this movement, obviously Christian in its origin, to his Christian wife. Since then Mme Chiang has been advised, in the New Life Movement and in other matters, by a Congregational missionary, Rev. George W. Shepherd of Auburndale, Mass.

Next to William Henry Donald, onetime Australian newsman · (TIME, Dec. 23, 1936), Missionary Shepherd is today the closest white collaborator of Mme Chiang Kai-shek. Last week he was in the U. S. on a speaking tour. In a precise, controlled voice, Mr. Shepherd spoke part of his piece on the radio last week at a New York Advertising Club luncheon. Its gist: "Left to themselves, the Japanese will never subjugate China. With the assistance of America [*i.e.* with U. S. scrap iron, other war materials], I sometimes fear that Japan will temporarily win this war. I find it difficult to decide whether I am needed more in America than in China."

Although the U. S. is almost 100% in favor of China against Japan, contributions to China relief agencies are relatively as scarce as news of Chinese victories—today scarce indeed. U. S. sympathizers contributed more than $2,000,000 to Spain during its late war, but they have given much less to China; to the Church Committee for China Relief, only $268,709 since its founding last summer. John R. Mott, vice chairman of the Committee, declares that in China is "the greatest area

and volume of relatively unrelieved human suffering of modern times"—30,000,000 people in need of the barest sustenance.

In China such sustenance is among the cheapest in the world: one U. S. dollar will

Associated Press
MISSIONARY SHEPHERD, MME CHIANG
Chiang observed a schoolboy.

keep a man alive for a month. The Church Committee now sends about $10,000 a week to China, to be disbursed by Protestants and Roman Catholics as well.

By special request of the President of the New Life Movement, churches, schools, and all mission institutions, will be invited to take part in this nation wide effort to improve the living conditions of the people. The response to this invitation will depend upon the outlook of church leaders and their ability to adjust their organizations to meet the needs of our day. The New Life Movement is not based upon political expediency, as is sometimes supposed, but holds as its guiding principle, that 'Righteousness exalteth a nation,' and as a method of attaining this end will employ both government pressure and social education, There will be no attempt to dictate fashions to either men or women. Colour, good taste, graceful manners, and all that goes to enrich life, will be encouraged. Ostentation, lavish expenditure, and all forms of wasteful living, will be frowned upon. Simple joyous living will be the standard of excellence.

Injustices, that fall most heavily upon the poor, even though long established in the social order, will come within the scope of this movement. Concubinage, slavery, early marriage, abusive treatment of workers, cruel apprenticeships, extortion, oppression and corruption can all be brought under fire. While I write, an investigation is under way that will eventually lead to better treatment and earnings for ricsha coolies in Nanking. The Salvation Army has offered to erect and supervise hot tea stands for panting ricsha pullers in co-operation with the New Life Movement.

Shepherd, who had been chosen as a result of his success in promoting rural reform, was in many ways Rewi Alley's alter ego. Both came from a rural background in New Zealand, both took a hands-on approach to problems, and both had a vision for China's future. Sadly, the visions appear to have been diametrically opposed. The only record Alley has left of a meeting between the two does not identify Shepherd as a New Zealander, but does single him out as an embodiment of missionary ills:

In Chungking, I was invited to the room of an advisor to Madame Chiang Kai-shek, a Protestant missionary called Shepherd—'Mu Ku-wen', as he was called by the gendarmes of the Gissimo. I had been pleading for the continuation of the United Front against Japan. 'Mu Ku-wen', after a solemn pause, in order to give his words more effect, proclaimed, 'We shall rely on the great middle-class of China. Only they can understand.' And he made it plain that the anti-Japanese war meant little compared with the holy task of crushing the Communists.

MISSIONARY ZEAL

Kathleen Hall

Born in Napier, Kathleen Hall trained as a nurse before travelling to China with the support of the New Zealand Anglican Board of Missions in 1922. Impressed by the need to extend medical care to rural areas, she established a pioneering cottage hospital in the village of Songjiazhuang, in Western Hebei. When the Japanese army occupied the area in 1937, she became involved in smuggling medical supplies to support China's 8th Route Army and the work of the Canadian surgeon, Norman Bethune. Miss Hall was expelled from China at the behest of the Japanese, but travelled only as far as Hong Kong before re-entering China via Haiphong and making her way back to the liberated areas with a unit of the Chinese Red Cross. Ill health finally forced her repatriation to New Zealand in 1941.

During those first months of the [anti-Japanese] war, the courage of the Chinese armies and the able and clever strategy of their leaders, held up the first drive of the Japanese. By 1938 the Eighth Route Army had completed its plans and organized armies and people for the resistance and guerrilla tactics . . . that very clever and successful guerrilla warfare which for so long held up the Japanese advance in North China and prevented them from ever getting a hold on China. The people were mobilized; the partisans worked by day to save the livelihood of the people and to provide for the armies and, with sections of the armies, at night made courageous raids on enemy outposts. They often took with them only a few precious rifles and their hand-grenades made out of scrap-iron, but brought back captured Japanese rifles—sometimes a machine gun and other equipment—and more scrap-metal to be made into hand-grenades and perhaps into some surgical and hospital equipment too! Many a time, in the early hours of the morning, we heard the clatter of the scrap-iron being dragged up the rough, stony tracks into the hills—laboriously carried by the men, or on the backs of mules or donkeys— those sturdy little four-legged friends who did so much for us in those perilous times. How cheering for us too was the cheerful humour of the men and boys— whether hastening down to attack or raid, or wearily returning with their heavy loads; and at other times, on parade ground, or marching at their base in the hills, their stirring and happy songs, looking beyond the hard times and sorrows to the good times to come. But how often, too, would we wait anxiously to see if all our young men (and some not so young), had safely returned. Sometimes it would be to give assistance to the wounded on their way up to the base hospital in the mountains—and sometimes to mourn for those who would never run cheerily down again.

One time, among these was our village schoolmaster—a fine promising young man. He received a fatal head wound one night when with a guerrilla unit raiding a Japanese post down near the railway, where courageous farmers were time after time blowing up the lines to prevent Japanese reinforcements and supplies from coming through. These schoolmasters were doing a very important work under very great difficulties. As the war advanced, food became very scarce. The children might have only one meal a day of a little poor millet, their clothing often insufficient for the bitter cold winter. The schools, and their homes, might be burnt out shells after a Japanese raid, but school books were often hastily buried in the ground before the Japanese arrived and could be recovered later when they retreated, and every endeavour was made to carry on some education of the children, for these children were the people and the possible leaders of the future. When possible, literary classes for working boys and girls and men and women were also carried on. Much could be written too, of the work of the university students who escaped from Japanese occupied cities and travelled tirelessly throughout the guerrilla and free areas, writing and acting plays for the education of the people. All this was a help in keeping up morale.

But as time went on we became distressingly short of medical supplies everywhere. So much suffering could have been relieved, so many lives could have been saved, had we had the necessary medicines and equipment. At that time I was making periodic journeys to our base mission hospital at An Kuo, slipping across the Peking-Hankow railway by routes well-known to us. (Oh, those loyal innkeepers, who stuck to their bombed little inns and so courageously kept us informed of Japanese movements!) But our An Kuo hospital was able to give me only a very limited amount of medical supplies—they had difficulty in getting any for themselves. I was also able to make occasional journeys to Peking for materials. Between 1937 and 1939 the Japanese probably did not want Britain and America in the war. No doubt in arrogance bred of ignorance they expected to have control of China's vast resources in a short time, ready for their next stage of advance into the Pacific—not anticipating the Chinese determined and skillful resistance. Hence, with my British passport, I was able to slip in and out of Peking.

In the summer of 1938, among people and soldiers, I began to hear of a wonderful 'Pai Tai Fu'. The young soldiers seemed to speak about him with some humour, but with admiration and respect and affection too. I never enquired more than necessary about people or events taking place; making journeys as I did into Japanese-occupied territory, it seemed better for me not to know too much in case I was questioned. Hence, it was some time before I realized that 'Pai Tai Fu' was a 'wai kuo' (foreign) comrade—a 'Chia Na Ta jen' (a Canadian).

Then one day he came down the valley to our village to visit me. If I remember rightly that day he was wearing a faded 8th Route Army uniform. His name—Bethune—told me of his Scottish ancestry, and I might soon have guessed it from his appearance and certain characteristics, familiar to me perhaps because of my own Scottish background through my mother's family. It was a great pleasure for me to meet him, for it was a long time since I had been able to talk with my own people. He seemed a little amused at my missionary zeal—I remember his twinkling eyes—but he showed considerable understanding of it too. . . .

But then Dr Bethune came to see me again with a serious problem. He arrived with our magistrate—not the old magistrate of the corrupt regime in the county city—but a very fine man of the new government for whom we had a great respect and affection. They came not only on a friendly courtesy visit but to speak about the growing anxiety because of the continued shortage of medical supplies . . .

I had on one occasion already brought out from Peking a few supplies for the army with our mission supplies—including some of the sulfa drugs—but only a very small quantity. Although resourcefulness and ingenuity could do much, in many cases the proper equipment and up-to-date drugs were essential. I knew how quickly rubber gloves perished in that climate unless there were suitable facilities for storing them. I always tried to keep some for our midwifery work, and there was danger in operating without them. There was great demand for the antiseptic drugs and there would be a growing one for drugs to combat epidemics. Anaesthetics were needed and other things too. I knew that I must make another journey to Peking. . . .

I look back to those journeys to Peking with much gratitude to all those who helped me. I owe so much to so many brave people: in our mission, the steady, loyal old head of the domestic staff whom I knew I could trust; a leading Chinese surgeon, and an evangelist in a large hospital; a loyal medicine merchant; a university professor and students. Dangerous for them—possible torture and death—but they would never give away secrets. There were also the courageous drivers of the mule carts who brought me safely through; and the men and boys with the pack animals in the hill country. When bringing medicines from the An Kuo Hsien hospital I could carry a fair amount on my bicycle—on the handle-bars, on the carrier behind, and in a bag on my back. But it was heavy work pushing the bicycle up into the hills. There were times of danger but always I was brought through safely.

On this occasion, with the list for Dr Bethune as well as for our mission hospital, I managed to procure quite a large amount in Peking—labelled it all for our Mission—and got it loaded on two mule carts. Some supplies were for the Mission hospital at An Kuo, some for our Cottage Hospital and Health Centre in the hill country in Ch'u Yang Hsien, and some for Dr Bethune and the army. On our route we usually passed round the outskirts of the city of Paoting, but this time our drivers on enquiring cautiously found that Japanese outposts blocked our way. I was horrified to learn that all traffic was compelled to pass through the city! My heart was hammering as our laden carts approached the northern gate and were stopped by the sentries. I can never forget the little Chinese policewoman (just a girl really), standing beside the Japanese officer and looking up to him with a smiling face, as she told him what a 'good woman' I was and that my carts contained only medical supplies for my Mission hospital. No examination was made and the Japanese officer signalled for us to pass on into the city. But the more dangerous place was when we wanted to pass out the other gate to the southwest. Here the Japanese officer had a Chinese 'puppet' policeman with him. The Japanese officer ordered the sentries to examine our packages and they began to unload them from the first cart. Again my heart thumped. Usually I was careful to bring only medical and educational items but this time I had also carefully packed among the medical supplies some radio equipment for our Chin-Cha-Chi Government! But again the Chinese policeman was evidently able to convince the Japanese officer that I was an innocent, good missionary, and after a few large hamper baskets had been taken off and just unfastened, the men were told to put them back and we were allowed to pass. I felt sure that those two Chinese 'puppet' police were really with us in the 'underground' and I was very grateful to them for their courage. . . .

On reaching our mission health station at Sung Chia Chung I sent on the supplies for the government and Dr Bethune and had the satisfaction of knowing that they received them safely. But oh, such a small amount when so much was needed!

医疗队进了孙家庄，遇上了从前线下来的伤员。白求恩下了马，跟随担架进了临时搭起的手术室。

THE WAY TO YENAN

James Bertram

Blue is the smoke of war, white are the bones of men.
—Tu Fu (8th century)

At Nanyuan, under air and artillery attack, lightly armed soldiers of the Twenty-ninth Route Army together with many of the student cadets died where they stood, or were ambushed and shot by Japanese machine guns as they piled into trucks and drove blindly to the West. With Edgar Snow and a number of military attaches I went out to inspect the battlefield on the morning after: it was my first close look at the face of war, and it wasn't pretty.

On 7 August [1937] the Imperial Japanese Army made its triumphal entry into the city of Peking. First tanks and armoured cars, then cavalry (small men in khaki sitting high on big Australian Walers), then infantry in American-built trucks, with the Asahi beer-wagon bringing up the rear. Only one man in history, the Great Khan of China and Korea, had ever led an invasion into the islands of Japan. Now the island people were marching as conquerors into Kublai Khan's old northern capital. It was time for Snow and me to leave.

We had to wait for the trains to start running again to Tientsin and the coast. It was a strange, unreal interlude, in which foreigners were bombarded with gifts from Chinese friends for 'safe keeping'. Ed soon had a handsome limousine which he enjoyed decking out with an American flag and driving past Japanese sentries. He had also, under the bed at home, a small treasure chest of gold and jewels, loot from a Manchu tomb in the countryside he had been asked to turn into hard currency for the benefit of the Chinese resistance. It was a nice moral problem; but we supposed there wasn't much point in leaving loose treasure of any sort for the Japanese. I was offered some fine scroll paintings, which I parked with Ida at Hsiao Yang Yi-pin hutung. And when, in the first cooler days of autumn, we fought our way onto the overcrowded Tientsin train, we had with us a couple of extra attendants.

One was a Communist cadre passing himself off—as Miao had once done—as my secretary. Ed, more seriously, had acquired an unobtrusive household amah in white tunic, black trousers, and blue cloth shoes; she carried his parcels for the journey, keeping always a little to the rear. This was Teng Ying-ch'ao, wife of Chou En-lai—perhaps, in all China, the woman the Japanese *kempeitai* would most have wished to lay their hands on.

Mme Chou had come to Peking's Western Hills for hospital treatment for tuberculosis; it was possible for her, under an assumed name, to pass for an ordinary private citizen. A Japanese security check was another matter. For her to slip out overland to the west would have meant a long and arduous journey through mountain terrain. Now she planned, like Snow and myself, to make her way out by sea from Tientsin, go ashore at Tsingtao and travel by rail through Tsinan to Hsuchow, where she could pick up with the Lunghai railway for Sian and points north.

In another year, Teng Ying-ch'ao's features were to be so well known that she could never have attempted so simple a disguise. And indeed, she has denied that she ever tried to pass herself off as a foreigner's servant. That claim was understandable, in one of the most able and distinguished figures of People's China. The fact was that she did travel with us, on the assumption that Ed or I would claim her as our personal amah if she ran into any trouble either on the railway platform at Tientsin or on the wharf at Tangku, where we were to board a British steamer. In the event, she got by on both occasions.

On our way down the coast, Ed and I stopped briefly at Chefoo (where Ida had been both pupil and teacher at the foreign school). I remember some excellent ice cream, American style, in the Navy 'Y'. We came ashore at German-built Tsingtao, admiring the marine promenades and the twin-steepled Marienkirche. Shantung was sleepy and unalarmed: we had no trouble in getting the train connexions we wanted.

Sian was familiar ground to both Ed and me; the Guesthouse was the first point we made for. Mr Peter Chou, the benign Christian manager who had been so friendly with all foreigners during the Tungpei rising, hailed me with special enthusiasm. 'Ah, Mr Bo, so nice to see you again! You have come to meet Miss Smedley?'

'What, is she here? And Mrs Snow?' We found we had missed Peg by an hour or so, but a telegram to her train soon called her back, and before long we could all forgather in a true Sian reunion. Ed, as a regular agency correspondent, was overdue in Shanghai, where the main battlefront was now joined. Peg would go with him, nursing her heavy swag of notes on leading Communist women—one more of whom, Teng Ying-ch'ao, had just reached Sian: we celebrated her safe arrival at the new Eighth Route Army transport centre. For now, under the United Front the Sian rising had made possible, the old Red Army had become the new Eighth Route Army. Its three divisions, duly recognized by Nanking as part of the National Forces, were already disposed through Shansi and the north. In that month of September 1937 we had the news of their first major victory—the defeat of General Itagaki's Fifth Division at Pinghsingkwan, at the hands of the 115th Division under its brilliant commander, Lin Piao.

That called for an impromptu concert at the Transport Office, with songs and music. Agnes, in grey cotton army uniform, sang cowboy ballads; I fell back on Maori hakas. We heard a spirited account by a one-armed veteran of the Red Army's crossing of the Tatu bridge—one of the epic feats of the Long March from the south. I felt like celebrating on my own account, for I had just received a radio message from Mao Tse-Tung, inviting me to become the first official British visitor to Yenan.

I left Sian crouched beneath a pile of rice sacks in the back of an Eighth Route Army truck. North Shensi is pretty barren hill country; the prevailing soil is the packed yellow earth known as loess, eroded dust blown from Siberia by the great winds sweeping over the Gobi desert. Travel is always difficult, especially in the rainy season, through the deep cuttings and over the precarious natural viaducts linking the bare uplands. We sampled all these hazards of the road, until after several days we had to abandon our vehicles and fall back on hardy North China ponies.

That was more like it, I felt, as our little troop pounded into a narrow valley, running straight to a pass crowned by a watch-tower and a sentinel pagoda. We swept down the slope, galloped through shallow fords in true Mongol style, and arrived breathless beneath the crumbling walls of Yenan.

From my lodging in a bare guest-room at the lath-and-plaster 'Foreign Office' of the Border Region Government, I was invited on my first morning to attend graduation at the 'Anti-Japanese Military Academy'. A thousand cadets were squatting on the ground in front of a temple-style building decorated with

James Bertram as war correspondent with 8th Route Army, 120th Division near Shansi 1937–1938.

Mao Zedong lecturing at the Anti-Japanese Military and Political College, Yenan.

the crossed flags of the Kuomintang and the hammer and sickle. An English inscription on a white banner read:

'WELCOME TO THE FOREIGN FRIENDS OF CHINA!'

Room was made for me on a wooden bench; someone passed an enamel mug of tea. A tall, slightly stooping figure rose and extended a hand: I looked into shrewdly puckered eyes, under the brim of a faded blue cloth cap.

'Chairman Mao,' said Wu Liang-ping, the youthful commissar for Foreign Affairs. 'Have a cigarette?' said Mao, offering a crumpled packet of Pirates, his favourite brand—he had a special allowance from the Border Government to keep him in tobacco.

Mao Tse-tung in that autumn of 1937, though no longer gaunt, still showed signs of the privations of the Long March. With his long hair parted in the centre and hanging down over his ears, his gentle quizzical manner, and his unbuttoned tunic, he looked more like an absentminded scholar than a military or political commander.

When he stood up to address the cadets he didn't bark slogans or tick off his points with a Firstly, Secondly, Thirdly, in that painstaking Chinese style of political exposition that was so like old-fashioned Presbyterian preaching. Mao talked easily in his thick Hunan accent, with a lively play of peasant humour and bawdry—often his audience was swept with gales of laughter as he made an unexpected crack. 'Our task,' he told the cadets, 'is to find out in practice the weaknesses of the Japanese Army. Then if we are resourceful and determined, we shall be able to destroy it piece by piece . . .

'Remember that you must not take even one sweet potato from the peasants, for if you take one you will want to take more! This has been the weakness of old-style Chinese armies in the past. We must make the Eighth Route Army into a model army: both by our fighting, and by our work among the common people. Remember the Last Will of Dr Sun Yatsen—that the Chinese revolution has not yet been completed, because all the people have not yet been roused. Our task is to rouse them, because we are a People's Revolutionary Army!'

Simple points in homely language; a few jokes to clear the air, then the main points over again: that was Mao's public style, and it certainly worked. His humour was impish, almost schoolboyish. At the outdoor meal that followed the graduation ceremony, he had to initial the chit from the restaurant cooperative. He used the same ink-brush to scrawl another bill for me in English, prompted in the correct form for an IOU by Wu Liang-ping:

'Promise to pay—$10 in Chinese Yuan—after 100 years . . . ' I added my initials, and Mao carefully folded the paper and stowed it away in his tunic pocket.

'If anyone ever claims this bill,' he told me solemnly, 'there won't be enough money in the English Treasury to pay it—at Chinese rates of interest!'

八路军的政治工作的基本原则有三个，即：第一、官兵一致的原则，这就是在军队中肃清封建主义，废除打骂制度，建立自觉纪律，实行同甘共苦的生活，因此全军是团结一致的。第二、军民一致的原则，这就是秋毫无犯的民众纪律，宣传、组织和武装民众，减轻民众的经济负担，打击危害军民的汉奸卖国贼，因此军民团结一致，到处得到人民的欢迎。第三、瓦解敌军和宽待俘虏的原则。我们的胜利不但是依靠我军的作战，而且依靠敌军的瓦解。

《和英国记者贝特兰的谈话》（一九三七年十月二十五日），《毛泽东选集》第二卷第三六九页

The political work of the Eighth Route Army is guided by three basic principles. First, the principle of unity between officers and men, which means eradicating feudal practices in the army, prohibiting beating and abuse, building up a conscious discipline, and sharing weal and woe — as a result of which the entire army is closely united. Second, the principle of unity between the army and the people, which means maintaining a discipline that forbids the slightest violation of the people's interests, conducting propaganda among the masses, organizing and arming them, lightening their economic burdens and suppressing the traitors and collaborators who do harm to the army and the people — as a result of which the army is closely united with the people and welcomed everywhere. Third, the principle of disintegrating the enemy troops and giving lenient treatment to prisoners of war. Our victory depends not only upon our military operations but also upon the disintegration of the enemy troops.

"Interview with the British Journalist James Bertram" (October 25, 1937), *Selected Works*, Vol. II, p. 53.*

大力支援农业

Shanghai, The Bund, 1930s.

A LETTER FROM SHANGHAI

Robin Hyde

The New Zealand journalist, novelist and poet Robin Hyde (Iris Wilkinson) travelled to China in 1938 to observe and report on the Anti-Japanese War.

(March 7th, 1938
Rue de la Tour,
French town, Shanghai)

I can only write this in a hurry and it's not really an article only an elongated sausage of a letter which mayn't even reach 'Woman To-day' for the Japanese censorship, applying to foreign correspondence has been officially acknowledged (guessed at for some time!) and today the first batches of censors, about 22 Japanese, moved into postal rooms prepared for them. This is one finger of a closing fist around Shanghai—put Customs control as another, barbed wire fences and entanglements where foreigners may squeeze through on a pass, but Chinese coolies and peasants are frequently shot on the most trivial pretexts as a third, terrorism of the more outspoken Shanghai newspapers, both Chinese and foreign, as a fourth—and maybe the genius behind all this is just sucking his thumb, so I can't say what shape it is.

NEWSPAPER TERRORISM

The newspaper terrorism takes two forms, bombs through your window (the Shanghai 'Post' has been twice bombed), or decapitated bodies of ex-newspapermen left outside on the pavements. This week, by way of variety, a coolie carrying two human arms done up in newspaper was intercepted: another man got human fingers through the post. The heads, so far, have been exclusively Chinese, the point about decapitation being that the Chinese believe your spirit will have a very bad time if your body doesn't reach the underworld in one piece. I was in Hong-Kong, about three weeks ago, when the widow of a Shanghai publisher whose headless trunk had been picked up, buried him with a head of straw, hoping the spirits might make allowances—as I should think they would, if existent.

That was one reason I had for stopping off at Hong-Kong (where thousands of fugitives, in bitterly cold weather, were sleeping out in their rags on the streaming pavement, with an epidemic of small-pox helping to account for the scores of dead men, women and children picked up by the police every morning), and coming up to Shanghai for a brief while. I felt a city where newspapermen are systematically decapitated by terrorists behind whom is, unquestionably, foreign Fascist organisation, would be interesting to a writer and occasional free-lance.

So it is—and at present I am installed in a little Chinese house, whose hostess is a very plucky young German woman—Nordic blonde in appearance but not Aryan in beliefs. She tells how two months ago this alley, a stone lane with half a dozen high-spiked green gates on each side, was always full of wounded soldiers, now at nights there are beggars, some professionals—tiny babies, girls especially, taught to run in their ragged clothing and bare feet after any foreigner, while their masters and mistresses lounge about in some sheltered place, but a good many others, peasant refugees, who have lost all they had and won't go into the refugee camps.

THE REFUGEE CAMPS

If you saw some of these camps, you wouldn't blame the peasants for wanting to die outside! A few are excellent, like the enormous one in the Chiao Tung University building, taken over by the French, the Salvation Army and the Red Cross. Thousands are living there, in healthy if hard-up conditions. But now the Japanese say they are taking this University as compensation for a Japanese college here, burnt during the hostilities. It's plain grab, for they themselves have bombed, burned and looted every university and school building they could lay hands (or bombs) on, reducing the whole educational systems of Shanghai, Nanking and other occupied districts to a shattered mess. This, of course, was by no means accidental, or plain spite. The first step in the Japanese mission to 'culturise' China is to make sure China shan't continue in any misguided culture of her own—shall be blind, deaf, helpless, with a broken back from which nerve centres can't function or brain cells be fed.

So in this 'backyard of war,' which is my pet name for Shanghai, in camps alone are 80,000 refugees. Hundreds of thousands have passed through the city, but many have moved on towards the south, Hong-Kong and thereabouts, many more have died, some have gone truck-loaded to slave-labour in 'Japanese' cotton mills—some really Japanese, others Chinese ones, taken over by the invaders—and there's a drift towards the provinces which would be stronger, if so many thousands of harmless villages hadn't been smashed to pieces. But getting these peasants back into the interior and helping them to restore not only their old way of living, but a far more self-contained means of carrying on, seems to be the only healthy hope on the programme, and very strong efforts will be made in that direction, I think.

HUMAN LANDSLIDE

Otherwise the human landslide, once started, may be so appalling that it'll outweigh anything else in this time's history. In China things can't happen by the hundred or even the thousand, but by the hundred thousand or the million. Imagine those masses, once the process of disintegration really set in—leaderless, illiterate up to 90 per cent in a good many districts, cut off from their newly-smashed industrial possibilities and hopes, from the spearhead of literacy which the Chinese Government was certainly trying to drive into them, from even the very small wages and very rudimentary protection they had! It isn't that the Chinese worker, coolie or boy or even slave, hasn't a mind and possibilities of his own—the Chinese types at their best are reflected again, in the courage and humour and natural friendliness of these people. But they have so much against them that if their present poor but improving means of State-help and self-help are taken away, one can't see them able to maintain the level they had reached, and that was a pretty bare level of existence. That the Chinese problem is almost completely a problem of, and for, the working masses can't be doubted—and, after the first killing blows at the educational institutions, which naturally helped to draw the sting of the rebellious student movements, Japan's greatest activities in occupied or part-occupied territories have been aimed at these very masses. Workers' night school centres, like the big Yangtze Poo once here, are all gone—the rickshaw pullers, among the poorest and most exploited people in China, had achieved a mutual aid and protection society, and that's knocked on the head—in the great Wing On cotton mills, where girls work 12 hour shifts for tiny wages, but were lately provided with factory classes where they learned to read and write and had their formal 'graduation certificates'. I was told that 'classes have been suspended owing to the hostilities' and that is true everywhere. If the old junk fishing-fleets attempt to go back to their fishing grounds, they are burned in such numbers that salt fish is substituting for fresh in the markets here. Peasants who used to have shipping and road facilities for their produce now come dragging along their rice (on which they are taxed), in great sacks, pushing it in wheelbarrows. Women slump down, vegetables and firewood too heavy for them—some of them walking on bound feet, which in the country are anything but uncommon. Even the little children carry their loads of twigs, bundles of rubbish which may fetch a copper. This unending stream, which I've watched for hours, is NOT bringing in really substantial crops, for the reason that no replanting has yet been allowed. When the men reach the Japanese barbed wire, the Japanese amuse themselves by beating them up. A coolie was shot the other day, for coming in with five men in a row instead of four. In the heart of the city, one sees the very worst—people selling rubbish and living on an indescribable rubbish heap. A man tries to sell rotting oranges, probably out of rubbish-bins: another tinkers with a tuppenny watch beyond repair: children have the most aimless things 'on sale'—a handful of sticks, twigs, just any rubbish. Behind them, water and mud on the broken bricks, whole mountains of rags and rubbish, and such tenement buildings—their bricks have slithered, more are obviously about to fall, they are in a rotting 'house of the dead,' but it's the living who are crammed into them—people to-day, rubbish tomorrow, but still people. Behind them a refugee camp—I meant to tell you about these camps—four styles, the best housed in now disused educational buildings, next best the reed shelter type, IF there is a bit of space, third the tenement camps, which are like a black pit into which you descend by ladders black and rickety, and the faces of the huddled women nursing children or new born babies are the colours of fungus. Why can't I draw? It would be better than words for a place like this: three or four dead children placed outside the wall any morning was ordinary here. I've seen the corpse-waggon, open at the back, go through the streets, with the body of a child in his pink little padded suit tipped on top of the canvas covering the rest. The Temple courtyard provides the other type of camp. I've seen one very good one, in the beautiful Temple of the Jade Buddha, and another very bad one. But I should emphasise that bad camp conditions don't reflect on the camp workers, who give their services voluntarily, sharing the same conditions, and who seem decent young people, of the medical student and nurse type. The nurses at the Chinese National Child Welfare Home, which is full of refugees and camping in still another disused college, sleep in rooms poorer than those of the children. In some camps there's good vocational work, but I'll never forget the Cantonese one, with families sitting on three-layered bunk-like bamboo structures, cages in everything but bars. Yes, it was like seeing animals in a dark, crowded Ark, with narrow passages between these rows of cages, and a family to each partition. Yet they smiled and were pleasant—a huge majority of the Chinese people are, whatever their circumstances.

But I'm tired and have probably written all the wrong things, certainly given a pessimistic picture. Remember Shanghai is the backyard of war; not the war or the great unoccupied territories like the North-West. The Chinese armies have a marching song called 'Challei!' ('Arise!') which they took over as a legacy from the Manchukuo struggle. I was trying to scribble some four-line verses in imitation of the old Chinese ones translated by Arthur Waley, and here's one— brief, if of no other virtue.

In the heart of the reed is a secret
In the heart of the green bamboo, a spear:
In the heart of a boy is 'Challei! challei!'
They will take a long time, ere they stamp out these.

Woman To-day, 1 June 1938

TWO POEMS

Robin Hyde

Ku Li

Two words from China—'ku li'—bitter strength!
'This coolies' war'! tinkle the sweet-belled idle:
His face and Hundred Names sweep on below,
Child-like, he plays at horse without the bridle
And carts a world along, and carts a war.
Winning perhaps to mountain heights at length:
The new vernacular chronicles exhort him,
And waste their breath.

                    His grinning face can't know
Half the fixed reasons of the flags he saw:
He had a happy childhood; then time caught him,
Broadened his forehead, but forbore his head.
Eight years his life between the shafts: eight hours
(With luck), between Changsha and Hsuchowfu,
Picks swinging like pendulums through a noon of flowers:
Shining their freedom, bombers spot his blue,
But cease to count. Too poor for marriage-bed,
He takes his dreaming in the big dim shed
Wrapped in the quilt where other warmth has dossed.

Turns to Yunnan, hacks the next strategy through;
Cheerful; and mostly killed; and always bossed.
And not on Tiger Head or Purple Mountain
His grave-mound rises: worlds live on, to slake
Their ashy gullets at his bitter fountain
Of blood and vigour. Enemy armies break
Somehow on these, as somehow cracks the stone
Beneath his pick: but now he rots alone
(Not claiming to have died for something's sake),
None but the earth makes ready for his bone,
The green wheat sees him with unflattering eyes:

Too cheap a partisan for man to prize,
Men seldom see him as their broadest river
And burnt in the immortal tiles for ever.

What Is It Makes The Stranger?

What is it makes the stranger? Say, oh eyes!
Because I was journeying far, sailing alone,
Changing one belt of stars for the northern belt,
Men in my country told me, 'You will be strange—
Their ways are not our ways; not like ourselves
They think, suffer and dream.'
So sat I silent, and watched the stranger, why he was strange.
But now, having come so far, shed the eight cloaks of wind,
Ridden ponies of foam, and the great stone lions of six strange cities.
What is it makes the stranger? Say, oh eyes!
Eyes cannot tell. They view the self-same world—
Outer eyes vacant till thoughts and pictures fill them,
Inner eyes watching secret paths of the brain.
Hands? But the hands of my country knit reeds, bend wood,
Shape the pliable parts of boats and roofs.
Mend pots, paint pictures, write books
Though different books; glean harvests, if different harvests,
Not so green as young rice first shaking its spears from water.
Hands cannot say. Feet then? They say
In shoe, not sandal, or bare if a man be poor,
They thread long ways between daylight and dark,
Longer, from birth to death.
Know flint from grasses, wear soles through, hate sharp pebbles,
Oftentimes long for the lightness of birds.
Yet in my country, children, even the poor
Wear soft warm shoes, and a little foot in the dance
Warms the looks of young men, no less than here.
In my country, on summer evenings, clean as milk poured out
From old blue basins, children under the hawthorne trees
Fly kites, lacing thin strings against the sky.
Not at New Year, but at other festivals
We light up fire-crackers
In memory of old buried danger, now a ghost danger.

On a roof garden, among the red-twigged bowing of winter trees,
The small grave bowls of dwarf pines (our pines grow tall
Yet the needle-sharp hair is the same) one first star swam,
Silver in lily-root dusk. Two lovers looked up.
Hands, body, heart in my breast,
Whispered, 'These are the same. Here we are not so strange—

Here there are friends and peace.
We have known such ways, we in our country!'

Black-tiled roofs, curled like wide horns, and hiding safe
From the eyes of the stranger, all that puts faith in you.
Remember this, of an unknown woman who passed,
But who stood first high on the darkening roof garden looking down.
My way behind me tattered away in wind,
Before me, was spelt with strange letters.
My mind was a gourd heavy with sweet and bitter waters.
Since I could not be that young girl, who heedless of stars
Now watched the face of her lover,
I wished to be, for one day, a man selling mandarins,
A blackened tile in some hearth place; a brazier, a well, a good word,
A blackened corpse along the road to Chapei,
Of a brave man, dead for his country.
Shaking the sweet-bitter waters within my mind,
It seemed to me, all seas fuse and intermarry.
Under the seas, all lands knit fibre, interlock:
On a highway so ancient as China's
What are a few miles more to the ends of the earth?

SHIRTSLEEVES DIPLOMACY

Auckland Star

In the 1930s, the New Zealand Government appointed honourary agents in Tientsin (Tianjin), Shanghai and Hong Kong. When in 1939, the Japanese imposed a blockade on the British Concession in Tientsin, the New Zealand representative there, Mr Cecil Davis, was more than once subjected to humiliating strip searches at the concession boundary. Michael Joseph Savage, then New Zealand Prime Minister, rejected appeals to make an official protest to Japan, 'since the Foreign Office would automatically deal with the situation that had arisen in respect of Mr Davis'. The British Secretary of State, Viscount Halifax, chose to appeal to the Japanese Ambassador's better nature: 'I read to his Excellency the latest telegrams from Mr Jamieson, showing the nature of the indignities to which British subjects had been thus exposed. I told the Ambassador that, whatever justification might exist for the blockade in the mind of the Japanese authorities, behaviour such as that reported in the telegrams was unworthy of any civilised people, and I was certain that he would be just as shocked by it as I was myself.'

CRUEL INDIGNITY TO NEW ZEALAND AGENT

TIENTSIN ASSAULT.

Forced To Strip Before Passing Women.

SHOCKING JAP. OUTRAGES

United Press Association—Copyright
(Received 12 noon)
LONDON, June 23 [1939]

Mr Cecil Davis, hon. Agent for the New Zealand Government, who was subjected to indignities at Tientsin yesterday on entering the concession, today was stripped despite his protestation that he was the agent of the New Zealand Government.

'The Times' Shanghai correspondent says Mr Davis, who escaped undressing yesterday, entered the same examination shed today with the intention of leaving the concession. He was told to take off his shoes and complied, but he refused to undress.

A gendarme then hit him three times on the mouth with his own passport, Mr Davis saying each time, 'Thanks.' He then elected to return to the concession, but gendarmes forced him to strip naked and kept him in this degraded position while at least a dozen foreign women passed.

Mr E. G. Jamieson, British Consul-General, has received no replies to any of his many protests.

BIG CITY LIFE

Joseph Needham

The British scientist Joseph Needham's monument is the magisterial Science and Civilisation in China, *which has continued to be published even after his death in 1995, and now extends to 24 volumes. From 1943 to 1946 Needham served as Director of the Sino-British Science Co-operation Bureau, based in Chungking (Chongqing), and travelled extensively through Free China. This serial letter relates incidents on a journey he made in Rewi Alley's company along Gansu's chain of desert oases. The two clearly hit it off: Needham records of his companion, 'I never met a better friend and a more reliable colleague.'*

Chienfotung, Tunhuang,
North-west Kansu,
18th October, 1943.

We are still marooned in this oasis by the failure of the truck, and there is time to write at leisure about our life here. . . . If we knew for a fact that we should have to be here for three weeks more, say, we could make ourselves more comfortable. Or if we knew definitely that the oilfield had been unable to do the repairs, then I should wire Chungking for authorisation to abandon the bloody truck for good, or till next year, and we could make our way by ox-cart or what have you to Anhsi and catch an oilfield truck to Lanchow from there, after which I'd return to Chungking by plane, and that would be that. Meanwhile there is nothing to do but to endure the cold, take all advantage of the sunshine, and carry on as best we can. . . .

We think a good deal about food here. The diet is getting monotonous. Having come up here, like fools, with no firearms of any description, we see rows and rows of partridges sitting and watching us every evening, and wish we could get them in the pot. Rewi and I hanker very much after proper toast, butter and marmalade for breakfast. He, too, was used to a comfortable life in Shanghai, when he was chief factory inspector there. It is astonishing how much hardship he puts up with uncomplainingly in pursuit of the ideal of democratically-run, decentralized industry in China. Living at Shuangshihpu as he does, the amenities are much less than Chungking. When I get back from this Central Asia, Chungking will seem like civilization itself. About the only thing you miss there is butter—I didn't for many months, but now the lack of it is beginning to wear me down. I must try to buy a lot of yak butter at Lanchow, where it is sold in skins or bladders, and take it down to Chungking, as well as jam and marmalade from Chengtu.

24th October

Mafeking is Relieved! Yesterday about 1/4 to 4, just as I was teaching Fieldtown jigs to the boys in an effort to keep warm, Kuan Wei appeared, on horseback, having ridden from Tunhuang city. The engine was brought there by truck from the oilfield, but the driver, who seems quite crazy, and had been fighting with the mechanics all the way up, went on strike, and refused to come out to such a dangerous place as Chienfotung. So today KW has gone in to arrange for a horse—or ox-cart—to bring the engine out, and the boys have gone in for provisions.

Yumên 31st October

This letter is being continued in the military guest-house at Yumên, 880 km. from Lanchow, and therefore way down the main road from Tunhuang and Anhsi. From this you will see that we are moving again at last, but there is a lot to tell you about the interval.

On the 24th KW and the boys went into town, and Rewi and I checked the river-bed to find the best way out. No getting stuck in the sand this time, if we could help it. Next day, on getting up, the old Tao-Se, Wang Tao-Se's successor, brought us a basket of delicious quinces, which, so far as we could ascertain through his enormous beard, was in gratitude for sulpha drugs applied to his sores. The horse-cart with the engine on it did not arrive till evening, and from the hills Rewi and I watched through field-glasses the boys riding out on donkeys to welcome it jubilantly.

The longer we stayed at Chienfotung, the more our repute as physicians spread, which I gather is everywhere the case if one stays long in one country place and has enough medicines to give away. Later the soldiers (the little tiny garrison of 15 whom we had rather neglected) brought us a case of typhus in a young soldier of perhaps 18—with a temp. of 103°. There wasn't much to be done, but we gave sulpha drugs and Rewi demonstrated once again what a wonderful natural physician he would have made, uniting warm human sympathy with strong intellect and apparently no aversion from the body in its diseased states. I shall always remember the day we left, the sunlight coming through the groves of trees, the Buddhist caves behind, Rewi sitting on the sandy bank consoling the young man with typhus, giving him some of our scanty supplies and telling him he'd probably get over it at that age, and the sergeant wildly insisting on our taking back the $120 we'd paid the soldiers for pushing the truck to make it start, which of course we didn't do.

NB: No army medical service within 500 km! Ch. army has never, it seems, been able to organize one good enough to cover all its vast territory.

After a day of reassembling the engine, the 27th was a nightmare, for we were all packed up ready to start, but *it* wouldn't start, and practically the whole population of the oasis spent practically all day in pushing it round and round the little parade-ground. By evening, however, it did, and supper plus two mechanics sent by the oilfield was comparatively cheerful.

Next day we really did get away, arriving at Tunhuang city after a few frights in the sand, but we had taken the precaution this time to provide ourselves with good boards (old temple doors bought from Yi Lama). (Eggs for dinner for the first time for a month). As we were on our way into the city, bumping up and down along the wildly rutted track, Rewi, who was riding on the running-board of the cab, stuck his head inside and said (American accent) 'Now we're going to taste Big City Life'.

Rewi Alley explains the workings of a Diesel engine to his Technical English class.

Formal family portrait in a Canton studio, 1935, on one of Mr Lam's visits home.

THE REFUGEE'S STORY

Lam-Lau Yuet-Sin

At the time of Japan's attack on Southern China, the New Zealand Government granted permission for the wives and young children of Chinese men resident in New Zealand to join them for the duration of the hostilities. There was a requirement that they should return to China at a time of the Government's choosing, and take with them any children born during their stay in New Zealand.

When we got married, I was nineteen. We were born in the same year, he is just two months older. It was at our home village. I can't remember exactly what year it was. Oh, I know, we were both born in the same year, in 1905. Then it must be . . . 1924, yes, 1924 when we married. He returned to China to marry me. What I do remember very clearly is that I was thirty-three when I finally came to New Zealand. It was during the anti-Japanese War, it must be 1939.

My husband came earlier, he was only fifteen, no, only fourteen-and-a-half. My father-in-law, old Mr Lam, came to New Zealand in his early twenties. He told us that he was only twenty-one or twenty-two. He came for gold. He worked near Greymouth, at a place called Blackball. We are all natives of Poon-yue, Upper Poonyue. He just came by himself. I don't remember which year he came, he must have told us, but I can't remember it now. Actually, Father-in-law never said much to me. It was Mother-in-law who told me those things. My mother-in-law, mothers-in-law, rather, all three of them, never came to New Zealand. You see, I had *three* mothers-in-law, and they all waited in China for him. My husband is an only son. So he was brought out to New Zealand, together with some of his male cousins. By that time, Father-in-law was no longer working at the goldmines, he was working as a market gardener, in Lower Hutt. Was it difficult for him to change job? Probably, but didn't all the Chinese miners change jobs, too?

About six months after my husband's arrival, Father-in-law bought him a fruit shop so that he could work there. Only a small shop. Sold by a fellow-Chinese who was selling up to return to China. My husband could only manage a small shop. He didn't know much English then. Lucky if he could earn 100 pounds in a year, very lucky. He just lived above the shop. I am not exaggerating in saying that hardly any Chinese would care to find a separate place to live. Even by the time I came, they all lived above or at the rear of their shops, or in huts built of kerosene tins in their market gardens. People used to say that we Chinese 'dressed shabbily, lived shabbily' and looked down upon us. I suppose we did live shabbily, we were so used to our conditions back home.

My husband returned to China twice. The first time it was to marry me, and he stayed for three years after our marriage. We had a son. Then he went back to

New Zealand. Most Chinese men went without their wives. I had never dreamt of coming here to spend my time with him. No, it was not the price of the boat ticket, I think it was only twenty-eight pounds, not so bad. The journey was rather arduous, and we women never thought that we could help to make a living here. Much better to stay in China. At that time, things were so cheap in China. New Zealand money was really high, one pound could be changed into over twenty Chinese dollars! It was really nice to have him returning home with New Zealand money. Once, I remember one pound was worth *thirty* Chinese dollars! He always sent us money regularly, he really cared for me and our son. Men could not stay in China for too long—who was to look after the business in New Zealand for them? Sometimes you could trust it to relatives, but if they wanted to leave for over a year, many people just sold up and went. My husband moved several times, first to Wellington; he stayed there for a few years and then moved up here to Cambridge. It was 1929 when he moved up to Cambridge. There was to be another ten years before we came and joined him.

Of course I missed Uncle Lam [her husband] but what could I do? Men should go out to earn a living, anyway. Women's only hope was that their men would return once in eight or ten years' time. He sent money to us regularly, always in the form of bank drafts. He would send money for Chinese New Year, and sometimes twice a year. Chinese men really love their families, I think. Some unfortunate women marry bad men, but such a minority of cases. I could not write to him. Write? I don't know how to read and write. Most women in our village were illiterate. In our village, even girls from well-to-do families were not taught to read and write. My family wasn't rich anyway. Mother just said that no man would want us as wives if we were too clever.

It was inconvenient not knowing how to read and write, though. I had to depend on those street letter-writers to help me correspond with my husband. Since we mentioned bank drafts and money matters so much in the letters, I had to be very careful. I wasn't sure which letter-writer to trust. You never know men's minds. Wouldn't some people be envious if they think you are rich? My husband was so far away, I was a woman with a little son, I had to be careful. Each time I would go to a different letterwriter, and I would try not to say too much. Later on, I would not even tell them where I lived. It pays to be careful.

After Uncle Lam left, I bought some lands and tried to grow paddy rice. It was a really exhausting job. I stayed with his family then. But my real mother-in-law died, and Father-in-law married this 'room-filler'. Of course I called her Mother-in-law, but she was not my husband's natural mother and therefore not so close to me. She was not so demanding either. So I needed to stay for only two years and I was allowed to move away to set up my own household. I decided to move closer to Canton city. In the Canton suburb area I bought an orchard, and grew star fruit. You know star fruit? They really grow well in South China. It was much better and much easier than planting rice in the village, much better returns. My sister helped me at the orchard. We tended the orchard and it was very prosperous—I had no idea that I was to leave China for New Zealand soon. By that time, I had a son and a baby daughter. My son started school, and he loved to play in the orchard. Planting rice was a much harder life, I loved the orchard. . . .

We never dreamt that we could come to New Zealand. The government would not allow women to come, probably neither Chinese men nor Chinese women. We came as refugees, and for just two years, I think. When the Japanese invaded South China, Canton fell. I sneaked away to Hong Kong in a 'snake boat'. Many families with overseas connections were in that boat. Everyone wanted to go to Hong Kong. It was safer, and from there you could go overseas.

We were robbed by some pirates as soon as we left Canton. My guess now is that they somehow found out beforehand that we were 'Gold Mountain women' and hoped to get cash and gold from us. We were such easy targets anyway, just women and children. I was very frightened, my boy was howling and my little daughter clinging to my bosom. I saw those pirates coming towards us. I had hidden our cash in the front part of my baby girl's vest. In desperation, I decided to play-act. I loosened my tunic buttons and assumed a dishevelled look. Holding my girl tightly to me, I said aloud, 'Baby, don't be frightened. We have already been searched and we didn't have much anyway. I am not a Gold Mountain woman, just a poor peasant woman going to relatives in Hong Kong.' Since it was so chaotic they actually thought we had been searched, and passed us by. Although one of them pulled my chignon loose. For a moment I thought, 'This is the end!' I had two gold sovereigns and Uncle Lam's last bank draft hidden in it. Fortunately, I had such thick hair then they did not see my hidden treasures, even though my chignon was undone. Yes, I was lucky. We had to stay in Hong Kong for several months before I got word from Uncle Lam that we could come to New Zealand. Without the gold and cash, what would I have fed the children with?

When we came, our son was twelve, and our daughter only six. This year our son is sixty-one! When my husband sent word that we could come, I was so happy. Going to 'Gold Mountain', you see? I was not worried at all. I just heard that some kind-hearted missionaries petitioned the New Zealand government on our behalf. No, we were not allowed to have permanent residency. We were only given temporary permits. We had to promise to go back to China at the end of the war, and we had to leave with all our children, including those born here. I think the New Zealand government was very careful. I didn't mind, I was just excited that I could come, even for a couple of years. It was good to be with my husband again.

We had to be very careful in Hong Kong. People knew that we were 'Gold Mountain women' waiting to emigrate, and quite often bad characters followed us around, trying to rob us. We had to co-operate and band together, especially when we went to the money-changers. I was always careful, and would never walk about alone. The boat journey was good. The whole ship was full of refugees, I knew many of them because we were from the same village. Others I got to know while in Hong Kong waiting for the boat. It took us eighteen days to reach Sydney. We changed boat there, and then sailed three to four days to Auckland.

At the pier, before disembarking, we were asked to sign some papers. I don't know what papers. I just said that I didn't know how to sign in Chinese, let alone in English! Actually, my husband said that it might have been old Wah Lee who signed for all of us. It was Wah Lee who boarded the boat to meet us. I did not know what to say to the officials, none of us knew any English. It was lucky that the procedures were quite smooth. Only later on did I hear about the two hundred pounds security that my husband had to pay for me.

Mr Wah Lee led the whole group out, and I saw Uncle Lam standing at the pier. I felt very confident and at ease. After all, my husband is the closest one to me. I was already thirty-three that year. I really wanted to be with my husband; it was good even if it was just for two years. I wanted to have a good look around, and see for myself all the places where he worked.

I liked New Zealand. It was clean and tidy, and so peaceful. I need not be scared of bandits and robbers any more. Society was very stable, and the people rather nice. But I remember my first great shock on spotting an old friend at a Chinese provisions store. I knew him in China. Whenever he went back for a visit, he was dressed in such a swank style, and spent his money generously. On that first day of our arrival, however, he just had some old sacks covering his head, some old sacks on his shoulders, and some matting around his feet.

It had been raining, and apparently many Chinese men just improvised their rain gear, using rice sacks and straw mattings which they could so readily find. I remember sighing to my husband, 'This is what the ancients described: 'he can earn his rice, but not his clothing'.' Chinese men could be really frugal here, but they liked to show off a bit when they went back to China. I was really shocked when I saw this old friend. Then I realized why so many children of 'Gold Mountain men' were such spendthrifts—they never knew how hard their old men worked, or how frugal they had to be in order to send some money home. Quite a number of these children even took to opium-smoking and womanizing. They thought that money came easily, that their old men were just picking up gold from the ground here.

After we arrived, we had to find a place to stay. My husband used to live upstairs in his shop, but now there were four of us. At first we lived with some friends who had an orchard. It was very inconvenient. My husband decided to build a house for us. It may sound a bit boastful now, but during the War this house of ours was the very first proper residential home built by a Chinese. Most people waited until well after 1947, when they knew for sure that their families could really stay in New Zealand. But my husband didn't wait. Everyone said that he was too bold and rash. 'What happens after the refugee papers expire?' everyone asked. 'If the government makes them go, then I'll sell the house to some Europeans,' my husband replied.

The New Zealand Government and Chinese Immigrants.

In the early years of Japan's savage attack on South China representations were made by the Chinese Association and the Chinese Consulate in New Zealand asking the Government to allow wives and young children of Chinese men already resident in the Dominion to join them for the duration of the war. This was granted and many came, each husband being under bond for £200 which was lodged with the Customs authorities, as surety that these refugees would return to China when ordered to do so by the Government. The permits were renewed from time to time but only for a short period.

After Japan's surrender the economic and political situation in South China deteriorated still further and Christian friends of the Chinese in New Zealand felt that something should be done to give the refugees assurance of more permanent residence. The matter was brought before the Presbytery of Dunedin in May 1947 and the Public Questions Committee of that body asked the Public Questions Committee of the Presbyterian General Assembly to bring this and other questions regarding the Chinese to the attention of the Government.

On July 1 a deputation representing the Public Questions Committee of the Presbyterian Assembly and the Inter-Church Council on Public Affairs waited on the Prime Minister - Mr Peter Fraser. Revs. Davies and McNeur were asked to bring forward the questions for consideration which were:

1. That Chinese refugee women and children, already here, be allowed to remain in the Dominion, not only because of the unsatisfactory conditions to which they would return in China but also because united Chinese families had proved a much healthier and happier contribution to the social life of the country than had men separated from their homes.

2. For the same reason it was urged that permanent Chinese residents who had not been able earlier to have their wives and children join them should share this privilege.

3. That naturalisation of qualifying Chinese should be granted where it was desired.

4. That the New Zealand Government should negotiate a treaty of friendship with the Government of China and appoint a diplomatic representative.

5. That a chair of Chinese studies should be founded at one of the New Zealand University Colleges and that interchange of professors and students should be encouraged.

The Prime Minister was sympathetic and promised to bring these matters before his colleagues in the Government.

The result of these deliberations was that later in the same year (1947) all Chinese who had entered New Zealand under short term permits and had spent upwards of five years in the Dominion were granted permanent residence. This included the refugee women and children, students, business men and visitors, a total of 1320 Chinese.

Early in 1948 the Government decided to admit to New Zealand as permanent residents the wives and minor children of 50 approved Chinese residents who have been in the country for at least twenty years. (At first this privilege was conditional on application for naturalisation. Owing to difficulties raised by the Chinese Government regarding dual nationality this requirement was withdrawn.) The same concession was repeated for 1949. The proposed Treaty of Friendship is under consideration but is held in abeyance by force of present circumstances.

George Hunter McNeur, whose note this is, travelled to China in 1901 to establish the Presbyterian Church's Canton Villages Mission at Kong Chuen. He carried out missionary work there for almost 40 years before his final return to New Zealand in 1939. Following his return, he became a tireless advocate for the interests of the Chinese in New Zealand.

THREE POEMS

Chris Tse

Dig

after Seamus Heaney

Our first back yard hugged
the prickled slopes
of Kelson.
I watched my father dig and
tear his way through bush and clay
to find that richer soil.
The spicy scent of gorse, the path
        he zigzagged.
And beyond him, decades
and oceans away,
his father stooping to dig
gathering ginger and spring onion;
        dreams of richer days.

       ★

Between my finger and my thumb
the sticks rest.

       ★

Below the surface lies
a history of chopsticks.
In the days
of new sight we clung to comfort
as a sign of success.
Eight treasure soups,
the finest teas
        ivory and bone over
        wood and plastic.

       ★

I'll dig
with them.

The Second Wife

Splintered roots,
new roots and
shadows cast on past lives.

But shadows don't erase
they just conceal and feed
the knot at the back of his head.

Strings across land and sea
tied to the feet of his first wife,
the new bride poised with scissors.

These days

She sits at the edge
of front door and
outside world, her hand resting
on the only photograph
she has of her husband
his name still static
in her throat.
The girl betrothed to her son
is cleaning inside.
She shifts and creaks
through each tombstone room,
stacking dishes in the kitchen,
polishing the table
with determination.
Very soon her son will return
to take his bride
back to New Zealand.
But what of his mother—
will he leave her
to fill this house with sound
alone?
The sun hooks her eye
and in the light
she recollects days of
tender architecture,
when all she hoped for
was a life of family
to spill out at her grateful feet.

WARTIME CHINA

Agnes Moncrieff

Agnes (Nessie) Moncrieff was Head Prefect at Wellington Girls College in 1915 and 1916. She taught in New Zealand before travelling to China under New Zealand YWCA sponsorship in 1930. Miss Moncrieff worked with the YWCA of China first in Beijing and Shanghai, and then in Hankou and Chengdu as the Chinese Government retreated inland in the face of the Japanese invasion. She served as the YWCA's Business Manager for Free China throughout the war years. Ill health as a result of wartime privations led to her return to New Zealand in 1945.

I got caught on a Christmas holiday when the Japanese began their onslaught on Shanghai, and I had to go on up to Hankou. I was seconded to the International Red Cross up there—nothing to do with the International Red Cross in Geneva— but a group organised by a doctor at the English Presbyterian Mission, and he collected up consuls and goodness knows bishops and what have you, into an international committee. Because all the waterways from Shanghai were blocked, and everything had gone up the river, and there was no source of medical or surgical supplies for all those hospitals—mission and civil—up in Central and West China, and he organised a supply. He got this committee together and they contacted people in America and in Britain, and New Zealand and Australia too, and got money and goods sent.

All the goods had to go to Hong Kong, and then come up that railway. And I wish somebody could have written up the story of that railway because the Chinese fought to keep it open and it was being bombed the whole time by the Japanese. They even winched one train that I heard about truck by truck over a bridge that had been damaged. They couldn't get the whole train onto it, of course, so they did it truck by truck. And you know they fought marvellously to keep it open. I went down on that railway to Canton and we went through stations that were still smoking and smelling of water on burning wood and there were wrecks and, you know, we'd get an alarm and the engine would be detached and shunted off into a cutting or something like that where it would be a little bit more protected. And we'd be left sitting in the open and just waiting for it to come. It was very exciting and it took about twice as long to get down to Hong Kong.

I was very fortunate really. I was always just out of the way. I had one absolutely fantastic year in Hankou, the year that the government was there, and everybody in the world who came to China went through Hankou. And they all stayed in the same place that I was staying in because the Lutheran mission had an enormous six-floor boarding house-cum-offices-cum-everything else and everybody who went through Hankou in the way of foreigners—and some Chinese too—stayed in the Lutheran mission place. And you really met the most amazing people. I remember meeting an American dairying expert—now what the dickens he was doing in China, which didn't have a single dairy herd, I don't know. But they all came and Robin Hyde, you know the American [sic] author, she was there. I was one of the people who tried to dissuade her from going up to the Front Lines but she was very stubborn and she was just determined to do it, and of course she got caught.

The water table's very close to the surface near that river, and the only people who had bomb shelters were the government party and they had enormous concrete-lined places that had been built for Chiang Kai-shek and his immediate surroundings. But the rest of us were out and about. I always used to feel a little safer if I had my umbrella up.

I was with an American secretary—we'd been having a holiday together and we had to move on up there. And Madame Chiang Kai-shek had been asked—the YWCA, I think, had asked her—to do a nation-wide address in America. And the poor woman, you know, she wanted to get out of it. So she asked this American secretary I was with to write a speech for her. Well, of course, that was a stupid thing to do, because what the American secretary would say in a situation like that couldn't possibly be put into Madame Chiang's mouth. And she wasn't very happy about it. But at the time she asked us we had lunch with her at her home. And we stepped out afterwards with her for some reason—I've forgotten where we were going—and my brother was in a small cinema show in Pahiatua and all of a sudden he saw me walking down the pathway with Madame Chiang. He got up and shouted there's my sister! They must have thought he was nuts! He was so surprised. But Madame Chiang found she had to write the speech herself.

I didn't [have contact with the Communists]. They were away up in Yenan and we used to send medical supplies up from our go-down in Hankou—bags of them. There was a Canadian doctor who was in touch with them and he used to come down and put in an order and old Dr Maxwell, he didn't like the stuff going up to Communists. He and Dr McLure used to have a real dingdong. But he did get materials through, and after all, they were serving injured men and sick people and they should have been served, whatever their politics. But I didn't meet any of them.

Zhou Enlai was in Hankou when I was there, and of course he was being feted all over the place. There was an American Episcopal bishop there, whose name has gone for the moment, and he invited Zhou Enlai to dinner one day. And Zhou Enlai was a little uneasy about eating the salt of the bishop and he said you know who I am, don't you? And the bishop said yes. And he said you know I killed one of your men. And the bishop said yes. And he said well, I'm very sorry about that—it was a mistake. But this bishop was a particularly fine person and he was a great reconciliation agent, you know. And he made overtures to the Communist group that was in Hankou. We were on the edge of it but I never met any of them.

The last time I went [into Free China, after furlough in New Zealand], I went up the Burma Road and had a fantastic trip up there. It was about 2400 miles on a truck and all sorts of things happening, you know—petrol getting more and more scarce, not a garage the whole way up, and our tyres going to pieces. It really was a fantastic journey. But it was the only way in, because there were aeroplanes going from—there was some sort of a spasmodic service from Hong Kong right up into West China—but planes were being shot down. And I wanted to get there. So I went in from Rangoon and that was quite an experience too.

The Japanese occupation affected it [the work of the YWCA] very much indeed. We had a very flourishing industrial department in Shanghai among the girls in the factories who—well, we could hardly believe the conditions under which they worked and the YWCA went in there and taught them to read. And their textbooks weren't the fat cat that sat on the mat, they were really read. Not only really read, but taught them how they could go about bettering their own conditions. And of course all that went by the board but a lot of the girls surfaced up in West China because they tried to get a lot of the machinery out of Shanghai and up the river and of course the workers had to go too if they could. And so these girls came up and we met some of them again up there.

And then we had to find other ways of working. We had cooperatives going up in the rural districts around Chengdu and things like, well, any family that had its menfolk press-ganged could apply for cheaper rice. They didn't have to pay so much. And there were inspectors out who were supposed to help them. What was happening was the inspectors were getting the cheaper rice and the people were being absolutely fleeced. So our girls just went out and informed the whole township or village or wherever they were, of what their rights were in the situation. And they could have been mugged at any point, you see. Again, they were very courageous really. And it was no good the foreigners going out, our Chinese wasn't good enough, and we didn't have the local Sichuan dialect. So they did things like that that really met some of the problems that they were up against.

One of the most interesting things, I thought, when I came back: I had left a China singing. There was a young YMCA secretary who was very musically inclined, and there were a lot of very nationalistic songs being composed, and the music, and he had people all over China singing. Wherever a group moved from one place to another, the songs went with them. When I went back Chiang Kai-shek had killed the whole movement. There was no singing anywhere.

There was something to the New Life Movement but you see, he was afraid, all the time, that another great section of his government would move out as that Wang man did and joined the Japanese. And he had somehow to keep his government intact if he could. And of course armies are all private armies in China, or were then. Every local governor had his own army. And Chiang Kai-shek had crack troops, of course. And he wouldn't let them fight, because if they fought he'd have no defence. And so he stopped fighting, he never did fight the

Japanese air raid on Chongqing, September 1941.

Japanese. It was the Communists up in the north and the northwest who fought them.

I wrote long letters to the National Office here and they got news about me round the country, especially at the times when they were trying to raise money. When I got back to New Zealand and got on my feet again, I taught on the correspondence school staff for about fifteen years. And one of the English teachers there one day said to me—we were talking about China and evidently she hadn't realised who I was—and she said, 'Do you mean to say you're the person we put our pennies in the tin for?' I thought it didn't sound very appreciative. She had been a member of a YWCA club and all the clubs had World Fellowship tins that they put their pennies into. You know, you can always raise money around a person—more than you can around a cause, I think. They used to give very freely really. It's harder to raise money for just a project, unless there's a person in it.

And I used to talk when I came back on furlough. I addressed six Rotaries in seven weeks once. And I was the first woman speaker that the Dunedin University Club had ever had. And you know I just talked my head off around the country. And when it came to going back and I had to go to the Chinese Embassy to get a visa, they thanked me for all the propaganda work I'd done, the publicity work I'd done for China. And I had talked about them because I was impressed by the way the Chinese people were fighting. And they were.

I used to tell them [audiences in New Zealand] a lot about the Chinese and the way they were fighting. And about the communications difficulty and the way they were getting stuff into the country and the use they were making of it. And I used to tell them what the YWCA was doing in the whole picture. And things of general interest. I'll never forget one meeting I had at Wellington College. All the secondary schools were invited to Wellington College so that I could give one address. And their huge hall up there was absolutely chockablock. The only secondary school that didn't join in was Marsden. It was the most thrilling audience I think I had. They were just—you know, their ears were flapping.

I had a huge map—I always insisted on a map—and I showed them the routes by which the stuff was coming in. There was even one—I've forgotten the name of the junction with the trans-Siberian railway—but some stuff used to be coming in that way, just a trickle. And the way they held the bridges and the way they defended themselves during an air raid when they could, and some of the mistakes the Japanese made. We were in Hankou and the Han River comes into the Yangtze there, and up the Han River is another smaller river which comes in. The Japanese had got their geography mixed and they bombed away mercilessly up at the junction of these two rivers, a couple of miles away from Hankou. We looked out our sixth floor windows and admired all the fireworks.

They used to try and get you off the street during an air raid and I'll never forget the first time. I'd been up to the Methodist Hospital, which was across the Han River at Hanyang, with Dr Maxwell's wife, and we'd been getting some examples of surgical appliances, splints and things that we could have copied.

On our way back to the Hankou Bund the air raid alarm went off and I didn't hear it. But our rickshaw boy suddenly got very excited and everybody began putting their shutters up and people were being ordered off the street. And we were ordered off the street too. But right up at that end of the Bund was the big Customs House, and we knew if we could get there we'd be OK. So every time somebody tried to stop us, we told them where we were going and please to get out of our way because we wanted to get there. And when we got there they had great fire hoses lying out along the corridors and all the refugees who'd gone in there were lying flat on their faces on the floor. It was most exciting. We didn't get bombed that day, but I'll never forget my first introduction to an air raid.

I was very ill when I got back from China. We'd been living under rather impoverished circumstances up in West China and I always remember the doctor saying to me when he finally discharged me 'fit for anything but return to China'. And I never went back.

A NEW ZEALAND GUANGYIN

In Rita Angus: An Artist's Life, *Jill Trevelyan writes that 'In 1944 Rita had written of her wish to paint a European girl-child who could be found "in the Bodhisattas of the Buddhist shrines where the Chinese worshipped . . .", and this work seems to fulfil that desire. The floral pattern of the goddess's skirt recalls the designs of Chinese ceramics, while the title evokes the Buddhist goddess of mercy and compassion, Kuan Yin, a much-revered semi-deity who hears the cries and prayers of all suffering human beings. Usually depicted as a barefoot, gracious woman, her palm exposed in a gesture of benediction, and often associated with a willow branch, Kuan Yin is a virgin goddess who protects women, offers a religious life as an alternative to marriage, and grants children to those who desire them. She would have been an immensely attractive figure to Rita.'*

A note to this passage points out that Rita Angus would have seen a bronze figure of Kuan Yin in the 1937 exhibition of Chinese art that toured the main centres of New Zealand. The catalogue to that exhibition lists a 'Figure of Kuan-non. Bronze, on a bronze pedestal, 35 in. high to the top of the aura. In her left hand is a lotus flower'.

Rita Angus, A Goddess of Mercy.

GEE HONG'S WAR

Imogen Neale

It's a timeless story. A young man is torn between filial responsibilities and patriotic duty. Does he stay at home and look after his aged mother and father? Or does he lace up his boots, pin his country's flag to his breast and march off to war?

The story's setting could be Prussia, 1756, France, 1915 or United States, 2007.

But here's the twist. It's 1945 in New Zealand and the story forms the backbone of a Cantonese play, written by a Canton-born immigrant for two Auckland-based Chinese groups hoping to raise money for the New Zealand Patriotic Fund. The play is performed once, in Cantonese, by local Chinese residents, to a capacity crowd at His Majesty's Theatre, Auckland.

The national Chinese population then hovered around 5000, or 0.3 percent of New Zealand's population. The actors are all male although there are six female parts. The audience, an eclectic mix, includes journalists, locals, prominent businessman Sir Henry Kelleher and Auckland Mayor Sir John Allum.

The next day, two local newspapers run laudatory reviews. In one, the reviewer says that that night they envied Cantonese speakers. Remarkable, really given the level of anti-Chinese prejudice that local Chinese were living with.

The highly decorated (QSM and ONZM) Chinese New Zealander Dan Chan was there that night. He had to be: he was the play's official 'Programme Editor, Script Translator and Chinese Calligrapher'. He was also a member of the two groups that had combined to stage the performance: the Dai Tung Music Society and the Auckland branch of the NZ Chinese Association (NZCA).

After noting that, at his age, his memory isn't as good as it used to be, Dan—who recently turned 100—says that although the play, called *Qizhuang Shanhe* or *Human Integrity* and written by Ng Wai Poi, was assembled over a period of weeks, the decision to give it a public performance was spur of the moment. Indeed, in the play's programme there is a detailed preface that notes 'originally, they [members of Dai Tung Music Society] had no intention of appearing in public performances. We, therefore, hope that the audience will not pass judgement on their dramatic and artistic ability.'

Of course their dramatic and artistic ability was exactly what the reviewers focused on. But the society needn't have worried, with one paper stating that 'especially in the group scenes there was a building up of atmosphere and spontaneity rarely seen in European performances' and another commenting: 'Special word of praise must be given to the five men who played the women's parts. So good were they in their impersonation that it was only after perusing the programme that one realised that women were not in the roles.'

So, Act 1: China, July 1937. The Japanese claim that there has been a violent

Chinese-led confrontation at Beijing's Marco Polo Bridge. They also claim that they're missing a soldier and they're holding the Chinese authorities responsible. The Japanese become impatient with the ensuing negotiations and bomb the bridge. The carnage that follows leads China's Generalissimo Chiang to herald a national call to arms. He also issues a statement to the world: 'China has reached her last limits of tolerance with the Japanese and must resist the Japanese aggressors to the end . . . We are combating Japan not for the negative purpose of putting an end to Japanese aggression, but as a means of contributing to a free world order of the future.'

Act 2: we meet Chan Gee Hong, the young man about to face the 'duty to the state or duty to your parents' dilemma. At his parents' insistence, duty to the state wins: he's off to war. To start with, however, his father's boisterous birthday celebrations take centre stage.

Act 3: Gee Hong is wounded and while he's in hospital he meets Lee E-ha, a friend who has become a Red Cross nurse. Two things happen: they fall in love and Gee Hong's mother becomes gravely ill. Once again he's on the horns of a dilemma: to go or to stay?

One might well ask why it was decided to stage *Human Integrity*. Particularly as, in keeping with Chinese theatrical tradition, women couldn't appear in public displays and thus the female roles had to be played by men. Dan Chan says it was all about raising money for the Patriotic Fund, a government-devised trust of sorts that co-ordinated the public and private sector's contributions towards the war efforts. *Human Integrity*'s programme states a slightly loftier, heartfelt raison d'etre: the musicians had volunteered their services to 'help alleviate the terrible sufferings of humanity in this world conflict'.

As historian James Ng highlights in an essay on early Chinese settlement in New Zealand, it's not as though local Chinese communities weren't already making significant financial contributions to the war effort. Indeed, since 1937, the NZCA had been systematically collecting funds to aid China's war effort against Japan: employers were levied 10 shillings per week and employees two shillings in the pound. Even Chinese children had a levy imposed on their wages. Permitted by the government to send these funds back to China, New Zealand's Chinese population is said to have raised, if not the highest, then the second highest sum per capita for an overseas Chinese community.

Conceivably, however, another motive underpinned the performance of *Human Integrity*. For, according to Ng's research, Chinese immigrants here were intensely patriotic towards China. As he says, they believed in the inner strength of China and the Chinese people. Many felt that if only China could once again shine in the eyes of the world Chinese people everywhere could escape ethnic discrimination. Perhaps, then, the underlying intention of the performance was to demonstrate a universality of life story.

Which, of course, is right there in its title.

New Zealand Listener, 3 November 2007

FAMINE IN HUNAN

George Silk

Born in Levin in 1916, George Silk built his photographic skills during five years working at an Auckland camera store. He spent the war years as a combat photographer, first for the Australian Ministry of Information, then for Life *magazine. It was for* Life *that he travelled to China in 1946, shooting a photo essay on famine conditions in Hunan. Silk took up residence in the United States after the war, working for* Life *as a staff photographer. He died in 2004.*

May 1946: During the famine, powdered milk supplies being carried to villages by rickshaws.

Hunan famine: 'dragging a plow through the parched paddy'.

MANDARIN SUMMER

Fiona Kidman

An extract from Fiona Kidman's 1981 novel, Mandarin Summer, *set in Kerikeri in the 1940s.*

I chose one of the ripest-looking fruit and tore it off the tree. I dug my fingers into the skin expecting it to need force like an ordinary orange, but to my surprise it fell away almost like a shell. I tore it apart and crammed half in my mouth at once. It erupted with juice, delicious, wonderfully sweet. I finished that one and started another and then another, discarding the skins on the crisp brown earth. I was almost whimpering with the relief from hunger.

'I suppose it's too much to expect that a city brat would know how to keep the countryside clean.'

The voice was right beside me. Brigadier Barnsley was wearing a fresh linen suit tailored on slightly military lines. My eyes were about level with the button above his belt. In my abject terror a piece of fruit shot out of the corner of my mouth and splattered the beautiful linen. He sighed and flicked a spot of juice away but the stain spread in an ugly blotch.

'I suppose I will have to find someone to clean it for me, won't I?' he said in a languid voice. 'Who do you think will do it for me, eh?'

I was certain I was going to cry again. It haunts me, this business of weeping. I envy people who do not cry.

He watched me with evident pleasure as I spilled the first tears. Then just at the moment, the exact moment, before they became uncontrollable, he said, 'You enjoy the mandarins then do you?'

I stopped crying. 'Is that what they are? I thought they were oranges.' I wiped my face with the back of my sticky hand.

'Grown by the Chinese. Refined by us out here. A lot of us came from the East you know. Shanghai. Becky was born in Shanghai. We were very rich people there.'

'Aren't you still?' I asked.

He smiled. He had a full fleshy mouth under the heavy moustache. 'Rich enough wouldn't you think?'

'I don't know how rich is rich enough,' I said.

His eyes were sharp though he looked at me sideways. 'You're not stupid are you?'

I was not sure whether that was a rebuke or a compliment. 'No, I'm not,' I said. 'I always come top in English composition and spelling and third in arithmetic.'

'I was afraid of that,' he said. He had a little cane under his arm. He tapped gently at the fruit on the tree nearest to us. Some of it fell to the ground.

'Overdue for picking. I'll have to get Freeman busy today.'

'I thought he'd be showing us our property,' I said.

'Did you?' He still had that faintly languid air, but I could feel him thinking. 'Perhaps he could do that in his lunch hour.'

'Why doesn't Dan Cape pick the fruit?'

I was walking on dangerous ground. I could almost see the minetraps waiting to be sprung. 'Mr Cape,' I said hastily, by way of redress.

I had the feeling that the sky was about to fall on me.

'You were stealing my fruit,' he said.

'Yes.'

'Is that part of being clever?'

It occurred to me that nothing I was doing was very clever. In a new wave of terror I had visions of me and my family being forcibly ejected from Carlyle House with all the pots and pans. That didn't seem a very promising prospect.

'I'm sorry,' I said unhappily. 'I'm very sorry. It's all my fault, not my mother or father's. I—just haven't seen fruit like this before.'

'Nor food at all for quite some time I gather. You were put to bed without any supper last night weren't you?'

'I was a bit rude to your—to Miss Barnsley and—Master Barnsley.'

'Dear me,' he said, playing me along like a kite on a string. 'You'll have to learn the rules of the house.'

'I will, I promise you.'

He seemed to have reached some sort of decision, for he said abruptly, 'Then come along with me then. You'd better get to know us a little better.' He turned to leave the orchard.

'Where are we going?' I asked.

'Oh here and there, and then you'll have breakfast with us. I've decided you should have one meal a day with my family. Might put a little grace on that snotty little face of yours. Mosquitoes give you a bad time last night?' He made to touch my face, but I cowered back, instinctively loathing his plump smooth fingers. If he noticed he pretended not to.

'Thank you—sir.'

He nodded approvingly. 'Good, that's good. And we'll teach you the rules eh?'

'Yes sir.'

'I'm not a cruel man you know.'

It was an odd statement. He didn't seem to expect a reply or for me to comment on it.

And so I followed him out of the orchard. The path we now took, and the one which Dan Cape must have taken, ran parallel with the road we had come by the day before. A horse came clopping down the road towards us.

'Morning Colonel,' said Barnsley, lifting his head.

'Morning Brigadier.'

'Out for your constitutional?'

'Just inspecting the troops.' He raised his voice. 'Come on, hurry along chaps, no messing round, look lively.'

The Brigadier smiled indulgently. 'The family and I will see you on your lawn for elevenses.'

'Quite right, come on now what sort of dressing's that, eh? eh? You'll have to do better than that. Lively. Lively.'

My eyes were mesmerised as I followed the movements of his imaginary line of troops.

'Quite so, quite, look forward to seeing you my dear fellow. And you'll be at Mossington's tonight for cards!'

'Yes, of course.'

'Good, good. By the left—oh how is your good lady, Barnsley?'

'Poor, very poor, she keeps to her room.'

The Colonel's eyes suddenly glittered with a sharp intent look. 'I'll have Amy call on her.'

'Very kind,' said Barnsley easily, or did his hand tighten ever so slightly on the little cane? 'But I'm afraid poor Lilian recognises no one. Her specialist called from Auckland the other day, good of him to make such a long trip, says it's better for her to rest at the moment, the effort of trying to make conversation is too—taxing. It distresses her not to be herself.'

'Ah of course. Your charming guest will accompany you then?' Already his eyes were occupied with other matters. 'Qui–ick march no . . . no . . . not that way . . .'

'She is a great comfort to—all of us,' said the Brigadier.

'Quite, quite,' and the Colonel proceeded with his mad instructions, having already dismissed us.

'Colonel Roache. A charming fellow,' said Barnsley. 'A little eccentric. There is a charm in it though, wouldn't you agree.'

'Yes,' I said dutifully.

We were approaching the house in a circular motion from the orchard. There was a thick leafy hedge, pale yellowish green tipped with red. Looped amongst it was a vine hanging with elongated prickly fruit.

'Pick one,' instructed Brigadier Barnsley.

I pulled at one gingerly; the prickles bent at the touch, feeling no worse than my uncle's face in the early morning.

'Now break it in two,' he ordered.

I did as he said, and the fruit inside was soft and fleshy and very bright green with little black seeds. 'You'll need to squeeze it from the bottom, it really needs to be peeled or for you to use a spoon, but as you seem to have such accomplished little sticky fingers it shouldn't be a problem. Eat it.'

I did as I was told though I had rather lost my appetite for fruit. It was tangy and slightly tart.

'Chinese gooseberries,' he said with satisfaction. 'Something else we brought.'

'You seem to have brought a lot of things,' I said.

'Yes, we do rather, don't we? Interesting that a fruit should be as ripe as that, yet so green. I like green.'

We had come full circle and were now outside the pagoda-shaped house I had seen the day before. The smell of the flowers was heavier than ever, as if something had decayed.

To my great surprise I saw that he was unlocking the little house. He had promised me breakfast but I didn't trust him. Perhaps he was simply going to lock me away for the day. Apparently I had caused enough trouble to warrant it.

'The Jade House,' he said. 'You'll find them in most of the gardens round here—my friends' gardens, that is. Mine is the best though.' He pushed open the door. 'Come in.'

I stepped inside the building. It was all one room. The door was closed behind us, and the Brigadier locked it from the inside, intensifying my apprehension, so that it took a few moments for me to concentrate on what was before me, and, for that matter, for my eyes to accustom themselves to the light.

'It is different at every part of the day,' he was saying. 'At each hour the light changes, and it is like looking at different objects. That is why one never tires of it.' As he spoke he frowned in the direction of the windows. 'I see Freeman hasn't cut those ginger plants back,' he said. I gathered he meant the thick rich flowers with the strange smell. 'They have to be contained, I had to cut down a plum tree because it was interfering with the light . . . an exquisite one I might add, with dark red leaves and excellent blossom . . . a great sadness but it was essential, it had to go. You can understand my point can't you, it had to go.' He emphasised the last four words with great care and it was hardly as if he was speaking to me at all. Then, more naturally, he said, 'You will move with great care while you are in here, d'you understand? No sudden movements, no jumping round like a silly child, you will walk carefully amongst the jade.'

And now I was sorting out the objects around me. The place was crammed with the most lovely ornaments imaginable. He had hardly any need to tell me to move carefully for I found myself stealing amongst them, and his voice as smooth as a cat's fur followed me, murmuring the names of things as I stopped in front of them. I cannot recall what was said, or the order in which I saw them, but in my memory and from what he told me, I know that I saw many ornate carved ornaments in a great variety of colours, not all of them jade, but a superb and costly collection of Chinese hardstones. Some were the true nephrite, pale apple green from the S'ung Dynasty, these seemed to be his favourites; and there was jasper carved in fishes and lapis lazuli made into stunning blue turtles, and pink crystal fashioned into peach blossoms, and agate cups and plates; there were figurines made of amethyst, bowls made of alabaster, glowing like golden glass with the everlasting dragons crawling around their sides; rings made of turquoise, and a great collection of items made from chalcedony, and it was these that made me stop and look and look into them, afraid that I would lose their beauty simply by moving, and then find that with the slightest inflection of my head I would see another facet and the object would become more beautiful still. There were many vases, decorated with birds and flowers, with fish and branches, they were brown and blue, pink and white and yellow, and there was one in particular which I will never forget, a vase so translucent that it glowed with a thousand refracted lights. Around its slim waist a lizard, smoky-blue, hung suspended by the most delicate sculptured threads.

'It is not the most valuable,' he said behind me.

'But it is the most beautiful,' I said.

'You're a surprising child,' he said. 'You see a great deal.'

'Yes,' I said.

'The Chinese used to poke out the eyes of people who saw too much,' he said harshly.

I said nothing. I knew, or perhaps I learned later, but certainly half guessed even then, that I was in the presence of vast wealth, that the collection I was being allowed to view would be sought after by the great art collectors of the world. How had this man acquired so much? I knew from what my mother had told me that the East had become hostile to the British years ago and the military and their retinue had prudently found themselves somewhere else to live before it was too late. That was why they were here in their isolated elite little colony. What had they taken with them and at what cost? I think I knew the answers. The Brigadier was a thief. But not a common thief, a most uncommon one, and one with very expensive tastes.

MORE ABOUT KERI KERI

Reginald T. Waters

The world evoked in Mandarin Summer *existed in reality in Kerikeri in the 1930s and 1940s. An ambitious land development scheme targeted expatriates on the China coast as investors and settlers. Numbers chose to take up the opportunity, despite a lively press controversy in China as to the viability or otherwise of the scheme.*

The following interesting letter comes from Mr R. T. Waters of the Tientsin-Peking Railway:—
The Editor
North China Daily Mail
Tientsin

Dear Sir,

During the last nine months there has been a great deal of correspondence concerning Keri Keri in the Bay of Islands, New Zealand, which was very confusing to would-be settlers and most disturbing to those who had already taken up lots under the North Auckland Land Development Corporation's scheme.

I was in Peitaiho all last summer, where I was waiting for China to come to her senses, but conditions being such that one's business, private property, and even one's life were permitted by the Governments of the various Foreign Powers to be at the mercy of rabble Chinese soldiery, I decided to find out personally whether Keri Keri was all that it was made out to be by those who seemed so enthusiastic about it.

Leaving Tientsin on October 30th, I arrived here via Hong Kong, Sydney and Auckland on the 22nd December. Throughout my trip I was continually being told the same old yarns I heard in China, viz—that there was nothing but poor land, scrub and barren country in the North of the North Island, and that the whole thing was more or less impossible, and only another wild land-shark scheme.

I must say that even up to Otiria, the station on the railway where one transfers to a motor car for Keri Keri, my heart began to sink, for I saw no good land, and every fellow passenger whom I questioned seemed to have either no knowledge of Keri Keri, and, having none, only knew for certain that all the North was hopeless. Needless to say, I felt none too cheerful.

After the first few miles of the motor car ride, however, I began to sit up and take notice, for we were running into lovely country and scenery, which made me feel that we were driving through Old English park lands, fair roads, splendidly tree'd rolling hills and valleys, herds of cattle and sheep grazing in beautiful pastures, and in every respect it reminded me of the Surrey country between Leatherhead, Dorking and Guildford. I thought to myself 'if Keri Keri is like this then there was no exaggeration'.

I did not wish to form a hasty opinion, so having been here now four weeks, I cannot be accused of having obtained only a superficial outlook on this much-debated district.

Having been all over the estate, carefully examined the different lots, met all the Directors, consulted with the Government's Horticultural Inspector who has been sent up here to make a report, and listened to most interesting and enthusiastic conversations with the latter, I am more than satisfied that all the false accusations against 'get-rich-quick' speculators in land are not only pure bunkum but what I should call mischievously libellous.

Apart from the Directors, all of whom I have met up here, a fine body of enthusiastic gentlemen, and government interest in the scheme; I have been put in the happy position of meeting many interested New Zealand tourists who, having at last learnt that there are possibilities in the North, have come up to see for themselves. It has been my privilege to escort several of these searchers for truth around the estate.

Amongst them I met one of the most prominent horticulturalists from Auckland, a man of many years experience in citrus growing, who 50 years ago had trekked through Keri Keri, and he told me that even then he saw what a splendid country this was and especially suited for citrus and orange growing. This gentleman had recently carried off gold medals for his citrus specimens.

He was delighted with the Keri Keri scheme and went into ecstasies over the soil, the growth and condition of the orchards planted to date, and considered, as all others I have met, that there is an enormously profitable future in the Keri Keri scheme. . . .

The country is splendid, climate perfect and soil ideal. I came here skeptical and now intend to remain here, as I am convinced that the Keri Keri scheme is all and more than it was made out to be by enthusiasts from whom I had learned of its possibilities.

Let no one run away with the idea that there is no work to do beyond watching lemons ripen on the trees. There is much to do and hard work at that, and I myself am now working 48 hours a week as an ordinary labourer, gaining experience until I start on my own section which I have purchased, and on which I and my family intend to settle, with Government assistance, far from the beastliness of China as experienced by me during the last few years.

Yours truly
REGINALD T. WATERS
Keri Keri
New Zealand
20th January 1929

NORTH AUCKLAND
For WEALTH &
OPPORTUNITY

E.L. MOORE

A missionary called E.S.Little arrived in China about the turn of the century. I don't know whether he was British or NZ but his wife was certainly NZ. After a few years of gospelling Little switched over to commerce and eventually became top man for Brunner Mond (ICI) in China. He and his wife spent their leaves in NZ and bought a huge parcel of land dirt cheap at Kerikeri. Plots of this land he sold to ex-pats from the China coast and elsewhere who were looking for congenial retirement locales. They were told that they could make an easy living growing citrus fruit, but found when they had built their homes, set up their windbreaks, dug their wells and so forth that all they could grow successfully were lemons - not of much market value in Northland where evrybody grew lemons in their back gardens. These settlers then found that they were unable to sell their plots and when I first made contact with them at the end of 1941 when I started my stint with the NZ Army, they were living in each others pockets and not doing at all well. That was forty odd years ago and they have more or less died out and their plantations have been taken over I understand by people from Rhodesia who now produce first class oranges, grape fruit and the like.

SHEEP CAN FLY

Colin Morrison

In 1947 CORSO (the New Zealand Council of Organisations for Relief Service Overseas) sent Colin Morrison to China 'to see how best CORSO, and through CORSO the public of New Zealand, might aid China in relief and rehabilitation'. During his four-month stay in China Morrison drew up an extensive list of possible projects, and helped implement some already under way. Morrison's report to CORSO describes taking charge of 25 stud Corriedales, donated by Canterbury breeders to Rewi Alley's school at Shandan. The challenge he faced was to find a way of transporting the sheep from Shanghai to their final destination, 2,500 miles inland.

We contacted the CAT airline to secure a quote for flying the sheep. The CNAC and the CATC lines had already turned down the job. . . . The CAT line is headed up in China by General Chenault who was famous during the war years, his men going under the name of 'Flying Tigers'. During those years they had flown some mules over The Hump into China, but this operation was the first time that sheep had been flown in China. The next step in this historic transportation of the sheep was advice from CNRRA that they had arranged for them to be flown, and that a special plane was being fitted. I was offered a passage on the plane but was obliged to remain for the CNRRA/UNRRA Welfare Conference, and go to Sandan after that.

The Sheep Arrive
On 12th March [1947], the 'LINDENWOOD VICTORY' a special UNRRA cattle ship arrived at Jugong Wharf on the Whangpo River, Shanghai, having left Lyttleton on February 20th and Auckland on February 27th, carrying 1,001 New Zealand Government sheep for UNRRA and 407 cattle, as well as the 25 gift sheep. In the unloading of the sheep from the ship I was impressed by the expert way in which Mr Harry Sievwright of New Zealand handled the operation, in spite of the excitability and inexperience of the Chinese coolies. A flying stall was used to convey the sheep from the ship to the wharf. There they were taken by lorry some few miles away to the feeding station. . . .

The Flight
On 22nd March, Max Bickerton, who was to make the flight to Lanchow in the sheep plane, and I went to the aerodrome at 4 a.m. in company with UNRRA and CATC photographers, Mr Harry Sievwright and Mr Huse of New Zealand. The sheep were loaded direct from the truck platform into the C46 plane just as dawn was breaking. The sheep were drafted into the largest space at the rear of the plane and were then lifted over the bamboo strainers across the plane and over the double decks of hay bales which served the double purpose of separators and

136

food for the journey's end. There were three such pens. Before emplaning, the markings of the sheep were checked with the lists brought by Harry Sievwright, he and I doing this by torchlight. One of the rams was obviously sick, but he was loaded on to the plane and would receive attention at the Veterinary Station at Lanchow. Taking off at 7.10 a.m., the flight of 1,200 miles to Lanchow had started. The plane touched down at Hankow for refuelling after three hours' flight, then a direct course was steered to Lanchow which was reached at just under another five hours. The plane flew at a low altitude except over the mountains near Sian, when it climbed to 10,000 ft. The sheep were unaffected, and as Max Bickerton writes: 'Whenever the journey got a little bumpy they just looked at me with patient eyes and chewed at another wisp of hay. I wanted to convey to them the historic nature of their flight, and describe some of the beauty of the rugged country over which we were passing, but I was not successful.'

The Transport Section of the Sandan School was waiting with a truck and the sheep were housed at the Lanchow Bailie School for the night. Next day they set out on the last 279 mile lap of the journey along the old silk road to Sandan. On the second day the sheep arrived at Sandan just as Rewi Alley was reading a letter from New Zealand with a picture of the markings of the sheep enclosed. Great was his excitement when told that they would arrive in four hours. This they did, just 25 days after leaving Auckland, or in terms of actual travelling time, 17 days from 'Down under' to 'Under the eves of the world'. There was a continuous procession at Sandan to see these 22 wonder ewes and three super rams. Thus ended what was headlined in the China papers as 'Operation Bopeep', and 'Airlifting New Zealand Sheep Causes Shanghai Sensation'.

I hear of the Sheep Again
On my way later to Sandan, at Wuwei we were asked for a card of the official who was travelling in the truck. I had apparently been linked with the sheep and was thus considered a person of some importance. Rewi wanted to push on in spite of insistent requests that we remain. We were even told that it was dangerous because of the bandits who were prevalent north of Wuwei. However we left, not before I learned that when the sheep had passed through some few weeks before, they had caused amazement. Asked what was in the truck they were told sheep. They asked from whence they came, and were told Shanghai. 'How did they come?'—answered 'By plane,' their mouths opened wider as they plied the question, 'Did they sit in the seats?' . . .

An interesting sidelight of the transport of these sheep was the fact that some of them, after reaching Lanchow by air, were transported several days down the Yellow River on rafts composed of 13 or so inflated sheepskins. Then they were driven two or three days over mountains to their final breeding ground. Truly much travelled sheep.

DESERT HOSPITAL

Barbara Spencer

A young New Zealand doctor, Bob Spencer, and his wife Barbara, a nurse, were sponsored by CORSO in Shandan from 1947 to 1950. There they built and equipped a cottage hospital to meet the needs of the Shandan Bailie School, the local people, and, it appears, much of the animal population in the district.

'Do you see what they're doing?' I gasped. 'They've soaked all that cotton waste in gasoline and now they are setting the pieces alight and pushing them all round the engine—the whole truck will blow up in a minute.'

I glanced at Bob and Don Sutherland, who were looking quite as horrified as I felt. By now the truck engine was completely enveloped in a mass of dancing flame, and with one accord we hastily retreated to a safe distance—but not so at least a dozen of our Chinese friends, who stood as close as possible all trying to warm their hands at the blaze. Occasionally some of them would glance in our direction with such obvious scorn on their faces I imagine they were thinking:

'Those crazy foreigners, why do they stand and freeze over there when we have a good free fire for all?'

It was eight o'clock on a bitter morning in early December, and we were standing in the large courtyard of the inn outside the East Gate of Sandan city, for as money had just arrived from Shanghai Bob and Don were going to Kanchow, a large oasis city sixty kilometres West from Sandan, to buy supplies for the winter. As no school truck was making the journey to Kanchow just then they had to travel 'yellow fish', a term used to describe passengers who paid a sum of money to the driver of any truck on which there was some space available. It was a most dangerous way to travel as most of the trucks were overloaded, and the excess yellow fish only served to increase the numerous hazards. The night before, Chou, who was also travelling to Kanchow to help buy the hospital's winter vegetables, had approached one of the drivers who said he would be leaving at five in the morning, so we were all up early and I walked out with them to the inn, where the truck-drivers stayed overnight. When travelling yellow fish it was always a good idea to be on the truck in plenty of time even if the driver did not appear for several hours, for they never waited, and any excess passengers who were too late would then have to search for another vehicle and often pay another fare. However, on this occasion it seemed we had reckoned without the winter temperatures.

At that moment someone came out of the inn carrying a large pottery dish of flaming coals which he proceeded to place directly beneath the gasoline tank, and just then Chou came running over to explain the difficulties. It appeared that the fluid in the gasoline tank was frozen, as also were the feed-pipes leading to the engine, and this was the customary way of dealing with a situation of this nature.

'No worry,' said Chou. 'Much water in this gasoline—no danger at all.'

He was quite right, there certainly was always plenty of water in the gasoline, and although on this, our first experience of winter travel in the North-West, we were duly horrified at the methods used, we soon discovered we had to do exactly the same thing to get our trucks started—only we used blow-lamps as well. All the gasoline had to be transported by truck from the Kansu oilwells some 250 kilometres West from Sandan, and was carried in fifty-gallon drums. Constant banging over rough roads soon caused many of the drums to develop small holes, but as the drivers had to deliver full drums there was one easy solution—they simply kept on adding water to raise the contents to the original level. When pushing an empty drum across the yard in winter the clanking of ice against the sides could always be heard: the ice having formed from the water previously added to the gasoline.

With five months of piercing cold when temperatures dropped to more than thirty degrees below freezing-point, there were many hazards in driving across that wild, wind-swept desert. But driving at night was the greatest nightmare, for packs of hungry, menacing wolves came down from the mountains and remained

Barbara Spencer and her son Michael, aged two weeks.

close to the highway over the long winter months; and if the truck broke down while a blizzard was raging the intense cold could well be disastrous. There were road-houses at intervals all along the desert highway, but many drivers, particularly army drivers on their first journey through to Sinkiang, did not know where to find the houses and on one occasion fourteen soldiers died from exposure when their truck broke down during a terrible blizzard.

Bob and Chou returned from Kanchow several days later, so we then set about storing winter vegetables. Storing green vegetables was quite an easy task, for they were simply stacked outside, completely covered with earth, then a bucket of water was thrown over the top. As the whole mass quickly froze the vegetables remained perfectly fresh until the spring thaw, and when we wanted a cabbage it was merely a matter of taking a pick and chipping one out. To store potatoes and other root vegetables which were useless if frozen we had to dig pits at least fifteen feet deep where the cold was not so intense.

'You will find the winter has one consolation anyway,' said Rewi, as he watched us digging the hospital potato pit in the large hill behind the Lei Tai. 'You won't have to eat dry bread, as the Mongol traders bring butter into the city during the winter months.'

'How wonderful to taste some butter again after months of nothing but dry bread smeared with rape seed oil,' I replied.

'You'd better not become too enthusiastic until you've seen the butter,' was his only comment.

The yak butter, which was transported in the stomach lining of a sheep, was brought into the city and sold either by the skin, holding about twenty pounds, or in smaller lots. It was incredibly rancid, full of yak hairs and big lumps of curd, but even after boiling it with raw potato and soda bicarbonate, then straining the whole mixture, I still preferred the dry bread. The Mongols and Tibetans, who used brick tea, which was extremely pungent and bitter, added lumps of rancid butter to their bowls of tea. Unfortunately the Mongol hosts, in their anxiety to please a guest, often placed more rancid butter than tea in the bowl, but out of courtesy the guest had to drink the whole bowl, and quite frankly I found this a most nauseating, unpalatable beverage.

It was an afternoon in late December when Chou, who had been sent on a message to the transport section, came rushing back to hospital his eyes sparkling with excitement. 'Two trucks have just arrived from Chungking,' he gasped. 'They are packed very high and I can see some boxes marked CORSO in big red letters, so I think there must surely be some for the hospital.'

We were almost as wildly excited as the boys at the prospect of seeing some of our eagerly awaited equipment—instruments and supplies we had chosen before leaving New Zealand, which had then been bought and transported by CORSO. With many eager hands to help, the trucks were soon unloaded and the crates of hospital supplies safely deposited in the front courtyard. . . .

Even though some of our equipment had arrived we wondered how much

Arrival of eagerly awaited supplies at Bailie School.

we would be able to use it over the winter, for the bitter cold made working conditions almost impossible. If we touched any metal object it simply stuck to our hands, and although we wore thick cotton-padded suits, knee-high felt boots and fur-lined caps, there were only a few hours of the day when we felt warm enough to work at all. Throughout the school we used a type of pipe heating system with a fireplace outside the room, and a series of short pottery pipes covered with mud and straw which ran along one side of the room to a chimney at the far end. As quickly as possible we installed these pipe heaters in all the rooms at hospital, but not before many of our precious bottles had broken, leaving the various coloured dyes and solutions a solid mass on the dispensary shelves. One of the greatest difficulties was to get enough water to keep the hospital going, as all the streams inside the city were just solid ice, so all the water required by the school had to be carried over a mile from the river outside the city, being transported in large wooden buckets on the backs of small donkeys. . . .

When we were not seeing sick schoolboys, or treating the peasants, there were always plenty of animals to attend, and it soon became quite the usual thing to see the New Zealand sheep being brought along to hospital. Twenty-five pedigree sheep had been given to the Bailie school by the farmers of the South Island of New Zealand, and the small farm boys, who thought nothing was too good for these sheep, always tried to insist that they be brought right into the consulting room. But we had to draw the line somewhere, so just before the peasant clinic each afternoon there was a regular procession of sheep, goats, donkeys, and horses along to hospital to have their ailments treated. The boys realized only too well our affection for animals, and I often felt they put one across us whenever it suited their purpose. A large flock of the local sheep were kept by the school for their wool and meat, and at intervals during the winter each department was given a sheep whose carcase quickly froze. Although the meat was usually consumed fairly rapidly these frozen carcases would keep for three or four months if necessary until the spring thaw.

We generally gave the boys a medical lecture in the evenings, but if they had too much school work to complete one of us always went along at nine o'clock to check the sedatives and look at the patients. At this time we had only three wards completed, and I was busy making sheets and mattresses for the next few wards. One evening I went down and after looking at the patients in the three wards I turned to go home.

'We have someone in the fourth ward, too,' said the nurse on duty, who seemed a bit diffident about volunteering this information.

I was rather puzzled. 'But we haven't any beds ready for that ward yet.'

'Well, it's not actually a patient.' Then rather rapidly he opened the ward door, and said: 'It's a sheep. Do you mind?'

Did I mind! The sheep was placidly chewing at a pile of straw, and curled up on another little bundle of straw with one eye cocked warily on the offending creature was our small protector. The animal had obviously been entrenched for at least two hours, and there didn't seem the remotest possibility that it intended going elsewhere for the night. Anyway, by this time the mess was so appalling there seemed little to do but accept the situation.

'I hope you'll get it out first thing in the morning,' I said somewhat acidly.

The small boy was very co-operative. 'Oh yes, of course we will,' he readily assented.

They got it out all right, but not very far! The following morning when we arrived at hospital there was the sheep, strung up on the verandah beams, being skinned and gutted by the hospital cook, to the great interest of numerous small boys and several walking patients.

NEW ZEALAND REPRESENTATION

Colin Morrison

Although I had not gone with any inflated idea of New Zealand's importance in the world of to-day, I was frankly astounded at the abysmal ignorance about New Zealand in China, and even of its existence at all in the Pacific. This was at various levels of people in China. New Zealand is not represented officially nor has it any particular representative. The Australian Legation and British Embassy and Consulates are presumed to look after any odd New Zealand interests that may call for attention, but there was no clear indication on the part of either for these Corps as to what they were expected to do. Often matters are passed backwards and forwards between the two.

I consider quite categorically that New Zealand interests, viewpoint and standing are not adequately represented in China, and this of course is no reflection on the part of either the British or the Australian representatives. It is simply inherent in the fact the one country cannot represent two countries. Through New Zealand's interests being looked after partly by Australia, there is a fairly widespread belief that New Zealand is either a state of Australia or a small island off the Victorian coast.

Some small examples which I encountered were the New Zealand UNRRA sheep given at considerable sacrifice I heard referred to a week after their arrival in Shanghai as Australian sheep and yet Australia had not given one head of cattle or sheep to China.

The Vice Minister of Foreign Affairs, having had my card clearly showing that I was from New Zealand, opened the conversation 'How are things in Australia?'

At an UNRRA function on Anzac Day, the British and Australian flags decorated the hall, but New Zealand's flag was missing, as indeed seemed to be the 'N.Z.' in the celebrations during part of the evening, as a microphone was taken over by the Australians, Australian songs were sung—no reference at all to New Zealand.

It is not for me to speak on this particular point, but I record it as an observation relevant to this particular matter of lack of representation on which I write. The New Zealanders with the Friends' Service Unit in China—some ten in number—have been excellent ambassadors for New Zealand. They have sung New Zealand's praises and have done it well. Rewi Alley who is one of the most notable foreigners living in China to-day, having been there for twenty years, spoke strongly on the lack of New Zealand representation in China. Alley stated that New Zealand as an independent country of the Pacific should have someone in China. He felt it was unwise, to put it mildly, to leave New Zealand interests to another country or countries. Nothing at all has been done to promote relations between New Zealand and China, and to foster the supporting trade to follow. There are a million and one things, Alley says, that need closer attention. Australian wool will undoubtedly be sold in Shanghai, and it is relevant that New Zealand's future wool market in China is being neglected while the Australians are apparently getting in first in this direction.

I recorded this strong conviction at the time, and in retrospect it still seems right, that New Zealand who is represented in countries like the USSR should be represented in China, a continent which is a Pacific neighbour of ours, and contains more than one quarter of the human race.

SQUARING THE CIRCLE

Alister McIntosh

One senior public servant writes privately to another about a 1951 meeting involving the New Zealand Minister of External Affairs, Frederick Doidge, and Percy Spender, his Australian counterpart.

<u>PERSONAL 1/51</u> 16 March 1951

Dear Carl,

I have forgotten whether or not I have written since I came back.

For some days we have had ready to send to you a mimeographed copy of a report on the talks with Dulles in Australia, but the Minister does not agree with the Record. He says that over much emphasis has been placed on Spender's approach, and that Spender is mentioned as having said and thought things which he, Spender, might not like having ascribed to him.

The difficulty—as I understand it from the boys who made the Record—was that Mr Spender said a number of things which Mr Doidge ought to have said but failed to do so, but, in order to get them into the Record, our people, quite faithfully apparently, put them into Spender's mouth because in fact Spender did make points for us, even though he did not believe in them himself, but they had been put up to him in the officials talks earlier in the week and he had agreed not to dissent from our point of view.

The next objection the Minister had was that the Record omitted what he regarded as one of the most significant and important aspects, namely, a move by Spender to get recognition of Communist China. Mr Doidge says he took this matter up with Spender very sharply and told me at length how he had expostulated with him and, as a result, got him to drop his ill-timed proposal. The boys tell me that this is not really in accordance with their understanding. Spender did refer to the question of recognition in a very curious way, but his main point was, they say, if you de-recognise Chiang Kai-Shek you need not, automatically, recognise Mao Tse Tung, but at some stage you could give de facto recognition and achieve the limited objective you wish to achieve, in somewhat the same way as people try to square circles and to swear black is white. This particular incident was left out of the Record because it did not seem relevant, but the net result has been to hold up the Record which we wanted to send to you. . . .

Yours sincerely
(Sgd. A. McI)

His Excellency
Sir Carl Berendsen, K.C.M.G.

THE VILLAGE OF NAM HU CHU

Margaret Garland

In October 1952 the Chinese government held an international Peace Conference in Beijing. Margaret Garland was a member of the small delegation that, in the face of some domestic criticism, travelled from New Zealand for the conference. As well as attending the Beijing meeting, the delegation undertook a number of visits to see activities illustrative of the New China, including this one to a small village not far from the capital.

After taking an enormous meal, we staggered out to visit a landlord or two. The first lived in his own house with his family. His house was much the same as all the others, except that the furniture was better and the roof was of tiles instead of straw. I noticed a pile of books in his rooms although he told us that he could not read, because he had never cared to learn and his father had not made him. He looked about thirty-five but was probably over forty, very browned by the sun, with a shaven head, wearing a white shirt over black cotton trousers. It was the common dress and appearance of the average peasant. I thought he had a slightly nervous look and did not smile as readily as the other men—in fact he did not smile at all, except when I put out my hand to shake hands with him when I was leaving. Then, instead of saying 'Goodbye', he said 'Thank you'. Perhaps he was pleased at being treated like the others. He had never been a big landlord. He had only owned 80 *mou* of land, but he had never done a stroke of work in his life till three years ago. He said, when he was asked to give us an account of himself, that he now realised that his land which at first he felt was his own and which he had inherited from his ancestors really belonged to the people who had worked on it and whose ancestors had worked on it for generations. At Land Reform, when they told him this, he thought it was wrong, but now after three years labouring on the land himself, he understood that it was true and he felt pleased, he said, to have given the land back to the people who really had a claim to it.

This is actually what he said and I noticed that it made the peasants standing around grin slightly—perhaps at the inference that he had given the land back to them of his own free will.

He now owned the same amount of land as other men. Because he had never ploughed the land before, he had to learn how to do it from the peasants, but in spite of their advice, the first year his crop had not been good and he had only just enough to eat. At this time, he said, his body was not strong enough to work. His limbs ached with fatigue and the sun burnt him, but in the second year he had begun to learn and his body was much stronger. He said he did not get tired now nearly so quickly and he began to understand the pleasure of creative work. He reiterated that all his life till three years ago he lived in complete idleness and discontent, but he was proud at the end of the second year when he found that he had produced 50 catties per *mou* more than in the first and he had a surplus. At the end of the third year he had raised his production by another 50 catties and he now had a yield of 300 catties per *mou,* which was quite good. The Government had looked after him and had rewarded him for his efforts by helping him to buy a mule and he owned a rubber-tyred cart. Some of the money for these he had earned in the off-season by working in the brickyard. With his cart he was making a very good living as a carrier to the city (Peking). He told us he was making more money now than he had ever made in his life before. The peasants were good and they helped him. He certainly looked well and strong. Although he had never cared to go to school, his children and the children of all his family were going now. He ended with a queer little speech of gratitude to Chairman Mao, because of the pleasure he had out of ploughing his land and driving his cart, and because his health was better and he was happier and richer than he had been before. More than this, he said, he was friends with all his neighbours and quite free to go among them because he was politically conscious. In two more years he would join a Mutual Aid Group and be accepted as a peasant citizen.

I felt pretty sure that this man had been prepared for this interview; that he was, so to speak, a specimen landlord primed for this sort of thing. I record this impression, not because I think it is of much significance but simply because it was, on the whole, the chief one I got from him.

We went on to visit a second landlord who was older than the first. He had also owned 8o *mou* of land, which is 13 1/3 acres. He and the seven members of his family had never done any work at all. He had no cart, otherwise his story was very like the first and they lived next door to each other.

In each of these houses, as in the peasant homes, we were given tea and we sat on the *k'ang* while we drank it and talked. This man worked his own 3 *mou* (half an acre) of land now and in the off season he worked making bricks. He said that all this at first had seemed terribly difficult, and terribly hard and miserable for him. The first year had been the worst, but now it was all much easier and he said he was quite happy, although I must say he did not look it. When we first went into the room it was his young daughter who answered our questions in a torrent of words poured out as if she had learned them at school, and I did not like this much. The old man stood silent, looking at the ground, while she ranted on. I asked why he did not answer us himself and there was a slight confusion. The girl, very pretty and rather proud of herself, shut up and retired to the outer edges of the little crowd in the room and I felt sorry for her. The old man raised his eyes and looked at me with a half smile. From then on he spoke for himself. I was told that the girl had spoken for him because she liked talking and spoke easily, whereas he was not used to expressing himself and when he saw that we were going to visit his house he had told her to answer our questions if we asked any. Nevertheless, now that he did talk, he did so well enough. He said he only made bricks when his land did not need attention. He had a number of books in his rooms and he said he had been to school as a boy and could read them. As far as happiness went, he said he thought land reform had been a good thing for him just as it had been a good thing for the peasants. He thought he was as happy as he had ever been. He looked well and strong, but perhaps because he had no cart like his neighbour he was not so enthusiastic. He made no speech about gratitude to Chairman Mao, but he did say he was glad to have land allowed him and he said he was doing well enough with the extra money that he earned at the brickworks in the off season.

We wandered through the village as the sun began to set, very golden and hazy in the west. Labourers were coming in from the fields; children were playing games, dancing and singing as they seemed to dance and sing everywhere we went. Groups of people were leisurely milling grain with the help of their little donkeys. Women stood about with their babies in their arms. Sunflowers lent over mudwalls and in the little gardens old men were busy watering tobacco, cabbage, celery, castor oil and onions. A touch of colour was added by the strings of red peppers hanging on the walls of the houses. There was certainly an idyllic feeling in this remote village.

We visited the Co-op shop during the afternoon and I bought some packets of green tea and a cap and some brightly coloured socks for my son David. We came back to a cup of tea in the school and a final farewell speech or two and the children, who were still dancing and singing outside, induced us to take part in their games. Rewi Alley caused a great deal of amusement by dancing round with a look of extreme concentration on his face as he tried to learn the words and actions of the game the children were trying to teach him, which they could hardly do for laughing. Professor Chou, who is tall and lean, also took part, looking every inch the university don trying to be playful. I can only guess how much my own performance contributed to the merriment but I expect it did quite a bit.

As we left the village in our bus with the China Peace Council group and Rewi leading the way in cars, I felt very satisfied with the day's trip. There was an unmistakable happy and peaceful atmosphere in the village which seemed to be reflected in the evening sky with its few faint stars just appearing as we came up to the massive old walls of Peking.

Often as I came back like this from some such expedition I was rather amused to think that I was forming exactly the opinions or impressions that it was undoubtedly hoped I should form. This did not worry me because I felt quite satisfied that I was not being misled. When the headman in the village told us that their troubles were past and that the people were working towards greater and greater prosperity with great happiness and excitement, I could see no reason whatever to doubt it. If the landlord seemed a bit uneasy and careful to say what was expected of him rather than coming out with some of the thoughts that may possibly have been in his mind I did not feel that land reform could be condemned on that score. Nobody ever denied to us that in the heat of the moment after Liberation some landlords came to a sticky end at the hands of angry peasants who hated them. They did not deny it nor did they approve of it, but in all fairness I must also add, neither did they disapprove of it. Those landlords who were murdered as soon as it was safe to murder them richly deserved death in the eyes of people who had for so long seen them get away with murder themselves. And murder was in some cases not the worst that these men had done; they had caused whole families to live in misery and fear and want and seemed to gloat over it. In killing such a landlord the peasants must have felt they were exterminating their mortal enemies and destroying evil.

On the other hand the very fact that there were still so many landlords about, holding small amounts of land, like everyone else, was proof that being a landlord was not considered a crime in itself. Liquidating landlordism in China did not necessitate liquidating all the landlords.

Journey to new China

MARGARET GARLAND

WITH A FOREWORD BY
ORMOND WILSON

THE CAXTON PRESS
CHRISTCHURCH
1954

THE COMMUNIST SPEAKS

James K. Baxter

Do not imagine I could not have lived
For wine, love or poetry,
Like the rich in their high houses
Walking on terraces above the sea.

But my heart was caught in a net
Woven out of strands of iron
By the bleak one, the thin one, the basket-ribbed
Coolie and rickshaw boy

Who has not learnt the songs that ladies like,
Whose drink is rusty water,
Whose cheek must rest on a dirty stone,
In whose hands lie the cities of the future.

ON THE GOBI DESERT, TEAM OF RAILROAD WORKERS EMPTIES BASKET OF ROCK ON EMBANKMENT NEAR YUMEN AS AN OIL TRAIN STANDS IN THE BACKGROUND

RED CHINA ON THE MARCH

A New Zealander in a land off-limits to U.S. newsmen reports on its desperate but impressive effort to make itself modern

Tom Hutchins

Tom Hutchins grew up in Auckland, and worked as a photographer on the New Zealand Herald *and the* Auckland Star. *In 1956 he gave up his job with the* Star *to travel and photograph in China. Apart from the 10-page spread, 'Red China on the March', featured in* Life *magazine, few of the photographs Hutchins took in four months of travel around China have been seen publicly. After China, Hutchins became* Time/Life's *South Pacific stringer, and later a lecturer in photography at the Elam School of Fine Arts. Tom Hutchins died in 2007.*

Girls training at seamless tube plant, Anshan steel mills, Liaoning, 1956.

Social dancing, Changchun automobile workers club, Changchun, Jilin, 1956.

A PIONEER TRADER

Ron Howell

Aucklander Ron Howell was one of a handful of New Zealanders who sought to initiate trade contacts with China within a few years of the founding of the People's Republic. He was a founder member of the New Zealand/China Friendship Society, and later was instrumental in the establishment of the New Zealand China Trade Association. When Hon Joe Walding led the first trade mission to China in October 1973, Howell was an invited participant and a key source of advice.

I went up there [to China] in 1956. Want to know why I went? I'd been in public practice as an accountant for twenty years and I was psychologically unsuited for that job. I used to worry like hell about my clients' worries or concerns while the clients were fast asleep without really a worry in the world. And that really knocked me about and I was at a stage where I had to pull out or else I'd be in a nut factory, quite literally. So I pulled out, and then I wondered what I was going to do . . .

I was interested in China. Not quite sure how this could be explained, except that as a kid books I'd read about China sort of intrigued me. That was the basic thing. The second thing was I was interested in what was happening at the social, political level—was very interested in that. So when I was looking around what to do, this occurred to me—that perhaps I should try to do something in China. I think the main attraction about that was the thought that at any rate I'll get a trip up there and look around. Now, how was I going to do this because, at both ends, there wasn't much encouragement. . . .

I had during the war years made contact with a number of people who would be described as of the extreme left, Communist Party members and associates. And I was on quite good speaking terms with them. So I talked to some of them and said what's the chance of getting a trip up to China? Because some of them were going up at that stage. Ask me just who, not too sure—George Jackson, Vic Wilcox and a few others . . . So, I talked to some of these people about the possibility of going up there and I told them that I was interested in the possibility of trade. They saw this as a useful link, that trade might help them in their efforts to develop good relations.

So I went up there with the blessing of some of these people. I went up there and I met some of the Party people and told them that I was interested in the development of trade, and they put me in touch with one or two of the corporations and I think that coming from them, that was a useful introduction. Nobody ever asked me whether I was a member of the Communist Party—which I wasn't and never have been. At that stage—1956—the Chinese had very, very little foreign exchange, so their chances of buying things were not good. On the other hand, they had very, very little to offer that would have been acceptable on the New Zealand market as far as I could tell. But I made particular contacts with the textile corporation.

The textile corporation were interested in buying wool—if they had any money, which they didn't—and they were also interested in selling textiles to us, although the quality to a layman like me looked pretty rumpty. But I did make contact, and I met one or two people who over subsequent years became very close friends, particularly the Director. So I came back to New Zealand pretty doubtful whether anything could be done, but started correspondence. And as a result of that correspondence I went up again about two years later and by that time the possibility of buying wool from New Zealand was definitely on, and I started that. I knew very little, or nothing, about wool but I had contacts here that were a help, and also they were starting to send down samples of fabrics which looked as though they could be coming right. So I went up again about two years later and about that time I started selling wool and selling their textiles on the New Zealand market. Very, very small, both ends, but particularly what we sold of their stuff. I remember the first order, I think it was the first order ever, was fifty dozen tea-towels. I can't remember what they were worth, but they were worth very, very little. That's where it started.

Because there was no recognition with China, there was absolutely no possibility of any assistance. Well, at least that's what I was told, there was no possibility of any assistance whatsoever. Although of course within the next few years a few other people got into the act, and a little bit started to trickle down. But right from the beginning textiles was New Zealand's biggest import from China and it has continued to be.

I had the sole agency for all the textiles. And that was a very good thing, not only for me but also for the Chinese, that they had a sole agent. That had been helped by the fact that I was also selling wool to them—same corporation, just a different section of it—and for some years I sold wool to them and was probably one of the biggest sellers of wool . . . But of course before long everybody and his dog was in the wool business, and after some—ten or twelve, fourteen, fifteen—years, I pulled out. Because, well first of all I wasn't geared particularly well for it, and I couldn't compete with the big people.

Right through the Cultural Revolution I was in there at least twice and most years three times. I saw a lot of it—you had to see a lot of it. It was a fantastically turbulent period and a tremendous amount of wasted time and everything like that. We always used to stay in those days at a particular hotel in Shanghai—the Peace Hotel, which is right on the waterfront. And every night—and I mean every night—there used to be massive demonstrations along the waterfront there. When I say massive, I mean more than a million people. And they used to go along there singing and beating their drums and making a hell of a noise, all through the night. I remember one night I couldn't get to sleep, there was such a noise, and I got a bowl of water and I threw it out the window. Not the bowl, the contents—the water—well that was a puerile sort of expression of anger. Nobody tore up to arrest me. But, yes, those times were pretty difficult and, of course, you go to the office corporation the next day, probably most of these people had been out all night on the streets. But despite the difficulties that occurred, the trading went on, growing all the time.

During the Cultural Revolution period it was a bit trying—oh, that's an understatement—it was hellish trying for people going up as visitors because everybody that went up there as a visitor was seen as a potential convert to what they were doing. So you had to be talked at, at very great length. You were taken out and you used to either sit down in chairs in the dining room or actually sometimes sit down at the table, and they'd say—before we have our meal, Mr so and so, we'll tell you about the Cultural Revolution, and you'd have to listen to a discourse of anything from ten to forty minutes.

I've often said that if a thing is good in China, it's not just good it's absolutely perfect. And if a thing is bad, it's not just bad, it's not someone's mistake, it's not someone's shortcoming—it's bad, it's really bad, it's hellish, you know. It's very difficult to get anywhere between absolute and complete perfection, and absolute and complete badness. And that's one of the things about the whole Cultural Revolution experience.

I think we in New Zealand have been extremely fortunate in the personal contacts—of course the prime illustration of that is Rewi Alley—but there've been quite a number of people who've been known up there as New Zealanders and the Chinese had reacted well to our country because of the people who've represented it. The Chinese are very, very impressed by personal contacts and personal reactions. I think we all are. But I've often said this when I talk to business people, that I think it's more true of the Chinese than anywhere—that if they like you, well that counts a tremendous amount, and I found it very easy to like the Chinese. Not universally—I can think of one or two that I've found a bit hard to take—but the vast majority are nice people. And that association of individual people has been a link between our two countries. It's been tremendous value.

Until the last fifteen years China has remained a long, long way away for most New Zealanders. When I was a kid, my parents and all my parents' friends and everything, talked of the UK as Home. We're going Home, or we've been Home, or we've had a letter from Home. New Zealand was essentially a part of Europe, and of course China was the Far East. It's only in pretty recent years that for most people China has become closer than the Far East. I always insist on it being called the Near North. Because that is—according to maps that I've seen —geographically correct.

THE CHINESE EARTH

Keith Buchanan

Keith Buchanan was Professor of Geography at Victoria University of Wellington from 1953 to 1975. He carried out research in China in 1958, 1964 and 1966, and became a strong critic of the New Zealand Government's policy of non-recognition.

First we look at the hill in the picture,
And then at the picture on the hills.
—Li Li-Weng

To me, who spent my last years in Britain by the margins of the silver Welsh sea, amid hills parcelled out by an intricate tracery of stone walls, stippled with the cottages and the diggings of eighteenth-century miners, crowned dramatically with the earthworks or the stone circles of men who died over twenty centuries ago, in a valley where (as legend has it) the most beautiful woman ever to tread this earth was conjured up out of the flowers of the oak and the broom and the meadowsweet, the rawness and recency of the New Zealand landscape came as a traumatic experience. I came to an almost empty land, a land seemingly little loved by those who dwelled therein, a land scarred by the gashes of new roads, disfigured by suburbs strewn like confetti across the swelling slopes of the green and gorse-gold hillsides, a land where the intimacy and tenderness of the association between men and the earth which feeds them—and at the end receives them— was lost in a money-oriented exploitation. And at times it has seemed to me that this rawness and this want of tenderness in man's relationship with his landscape is mirrored in the relationship of man to man and man to woman; transients all, not greatly concerned with permanence but greatly concerned with material gain, we build our relationships as we build our suburbs—as temporary staging posts in life's journey, as investments, as something which will not tie us overmuch and from which we can eventually pull out with more than we put in. The land is to be exploited—why not the emotions of our fellow-men and -women (and let us beware of gentleness and tenderness lest that too be exploited)?

New Zealand also emphasized something I had come to realize at an earlier period of my life in Africa and which I had forgotten—and that is how exceptional the humanized and domesticated landscapes of our earth really are. Growing up in such a landscape, in one of the intensely cultivated fruit and vegetable producing regions of Worcestershire, I came instinctively to accept such a landscape and everything that went with it—the historical richness, the acre by acre transformation extending over untold generations, the soil and trees which were cherished because they were the result of the labours of those who went before and must be handed on as a legacy to those yet to come—as the *normal* type of landscape, and the values which went with it as the *normal* values. In fact, such conditions exist on any scale in only two areas of our globe, at the two extremes of Eurasia, in the Mediterranean-derived culture world of Western Europe and in the Chinese culture world. Only in these two areas do we find landscapes that have been transformed by the labours of untold generations of men, men who were heirs to a distinctive and coherent culture, and who have left the signature of that culture on the earth's surface—in the shape of the hedged fields and medieval town patterns of Western Europe, the hill-top village and the dry-stone terracing of the Mediterranean or the flowing lines and curving mirror-surface of the South Chinese rice-field. In these areas so pervasive and so profound has been the impact of man that the geographer is often at a loss to determine which elements of a landscape are 'natural' and which 'man-made'; how far can we regard the intensively-worked soils of lowland Britain or of the north Chinese lowland, transformed by centuries of manuring and cultivation, as elements in the 'natural' environment? How much of the vegetation of Western Europe or eastern China is a 'natural' vegetation? The countrysides of Europe, the countrysides of China, are like ancient palimpsests, manuscripts on which countless generations have inscribed the poetry—and the misery—of their daily lives and the writing they have left behind them is only partly effaced by the bolder characters inscribed by the latest arrivals in this unending succession of peasants and farmers, of village dwellers and city folk.

Of the two great culture worlds of Eurasia, it is the Chinese that has left the most decisive mark on the landscape. It is true that the civilizations of the Mediterranean can rival the civilization of China in terms of their antiquity, but the Mediterranean civilizations lack the continuity of Chinese civilization; their cultural cohesiveness (with all that this has meant in terms of man's moulding of his environment) has been less; above all, the sheer pressure of human numbers, of countless millions draining and clearing and cultivating the land, has been less in western Eurasia than in the monsoonal lands of the continent's eastern fringe. And, if we except certain periods—such as classical antiquity and the Romantic revival from the eighteenth century onwards—Western man seems to have been much less conscious of his links with the land which gave him his livelihood than was the Chinese. He was, perhaps, less of an observer, too, so that contemporary Western literature had no parallel to the vivid word pictures of the eighth-century poet, Wang Wei; no parallel to the Sung or Ming painters who achieved in their landscapes the reality of the unreal landscapes of Kweilin's karstic mountains; no parallel to the subtlety of unknown architects who captured in the curving line of a roof a reminder of the peaceful curves of the hills, the restless plunge of the wave or the lazy curve of river or stream, whose windows were contrived to open out on a vista of skilfully arranged crags, of dwarf shrubs and bamboo fronds—'the real in the unreal', the countryside in the heart of the city.

A CLOAK FOR MAO

Ramai Haywood

Ramai Hayward was brought up in Martinborough by her Maori grandmother. In 1957 she and her film-maker husband Rudall were invited to film in China. They travelled with the poet R. A. K. Mason (Ron) and his wife, and made three films, 'Children of China', 'Wonders of China', and 'Inside Red China'.

October 1st 1957. It was National Day and a most exciting public holiday with many functions being held. We knew that in the evening we would have an opportunity to present the feather cloak from King Koroki, as a gesture of goodwill from the Maori nation, so I was dressed in a piupiu that Princess Te Puia had given me. At the last moment we learned that we were going to be taken up to the top of the Tian An Men building. As we were leaving our hotel Rudall grabbed his camera which was in a silver case, and he'd had the forethought to have Chinese writing put on it. I said, 'You can't take that, Rudall'—but he wouldn't listen to me.

We got there to find very many soldiers lining the wide steps all the way up, and I was expecting one of them to step forward and grab the camera, but no-one did. We reached the top where there were rows of VIPs including one that Rudall recognised who was looking a little askance at him. It was a British Consul on whom Rudall had called to pay his respects a day or two before. There were important guests from all around the world and I found it quite an adventure. By this time Rudall had the camera out of its case and up on his shoulder. Then someone came over and took Ron and me over to where Chairman Mao was standing with Premier Chou En Lai and indicated that I could present the cloak to Mao. He had an interpreter, and I was standing barefooted with my interpreter right in front of him.

Mao greeted me, and then I put the cloak on his shoulders and tied it. I said it was a gift from our Maori king of Aotearoa–New Zealand, a gift of goodwill to the leaders of China. I said

'We are the smallest nation in the world, giving this gift to the largest nation in the world.' He smiled and said, reassuringly, 'The smallest is as great as the largest.' He turned the cloak over and looked at the weaving and wanted to know how the feathers were woven into it. I was quite pleased because my grandmother and mother were great weavers and I was able to tell him. I was shaking like a leaf, standing there barefooted, because a long time ago Guide Rangi had told me that if I was ever meeting an important world figure and I was in my Maori costume I should throw off my shoes. I'd done that and told Rudall to mind them. Then, Mao turned to Ron, and Ron, of course was most eloquent, and I was so thankful to get off the hook. They had a lovely conversation, two poets together, and they had an empathy straight away.

Rudall was filming it all, and that was the real reason why I was in a state—I was terrified of him suddenly being arrested. He was filming away and the Chinese film unit nearby who had also been filming suddenly turned the lights off. Rudall, quite a towering figure standing there, called out to our interpreter, in an irate voice 'Tell them to put those lights on again!' I was terrified—I thought they would grab him and throw him over the wall or something. But they just turned the lights on again and he got his pictures.

THE MAY DAY CELEBRATION

Nigel Cameron and Brian Brake

Photographer Brian Brake worked with Wellington portrait photographer Spencer Digby and the National Film Unit before being accepted as a member of the photo agency Magnum in 1955. His first journey into China, in 1957, was undertaken in the company of Nigel Cameron, the British journalist and author. The two collaborated on a book, The Chinese Smile, *with Cameron providing the text and Brake the illustrations. Brake returned to photograph in China in 1959, and twice subsequently. He died in New Zealand in 1988.*

'Un peuple en liesse' is the phrase of a French writer describing the scene—a people making merry. Whatever the overtones and the details the Peking people on May Day were assuredly making merry with all the spontaneity of the unsophisticated who have something in common to make merry about.

On the south side of the Emperors' Forbidden City lies its front door, the Tien An Men. The mouldering fabric of this huge gate was restored at the beginning of the present regime and at its feet a wide square cleared and paved. And on the square was erected the Monument to the Peoples' Heroes, a column bearing an inscription in Mao Tse Tung's calligraphy, but otherwise unremarkable save for its height. Between these two symbols of the old and the new an excited crowd gathered early in the fine morning. The warm red of the Tien An Men, with its white marble bridge over the moat and white marble columns in front, was flanked by stands for the guests and diplomatic corps, members of the Government and others. Red lanterns like huge pumpkins hung in the arches of the Gate, their tassels swinging gently in the light wind, and a twenty-foot portrait of Mao Tse Tung smiled out from the façade over the square. Opposite were a military band in white, and a sea of schoolchildren beneath the gilt calligraphy on the Monument. A few soldiers in the brown khaki of the Chinese Army stood a couple of yards apart along the route, at ease, slightly chocolate-box. Otherwise there was no sign of military precaution. The feeling was light and expectant, the chatter of the crowds buzzing all around.

With many other correspondents I stood on the pavement in front of the moat, and watched. No one had told me what it was like. No one had told me that half a million people were so many, or that all of them would be laughing and waving more paper flowers than exist in all the world. They came on, and on, shouting, laughing, waving their flowers and flags, fifty to one hundred deep in their contingents, pouring across the echoing square, a staunchless technicolor river of the life of China. The pale sun shining in the dust-laden air was the only unexcited thing of the morning.

Somehow all these people had been organized to trot before us in their hundreds of thousands. There was not a gap, not one hiatus in the river; but there

163

was nothing military, nothing of drill or pomp either. Just people and people and more people, teeming past like all the football crowds in the world. And there was colour: mauves, lilacs, pinks, blues, nile-greens, red reds, a mutation of colour fluttering by all the time. The workers with their slogans, the peasants, the housewives carrying babies on their shoulders, children yelling as only children can yell, floats with scenes from the plays running in the town, Buddhist priests in saffron and Taoists in black, Christians in sober suits, students having a rag, floats with miniature engines and machines, minority people in their wild national costumes, Tibetans in homburg hats and sheepskin coats. Fierce paper dragons a hundred feet long coiled and snaked about above the heads of the boys who rushed with them, and the circus actors rode one-wheel bicycles and clowned. The football and basketball teams marched with the only precision in the day, in immaculate shorts and pale green jerseys, and hundreds of girls in short skirts made patterns out of scarves like a gigantic chorus from a Hollywood film. There were hundreds of woolly doves of peace like flying sheep, and shopkeepers, with just an air of the bourgoisie in new shoes, stumbled along ringed in smiles.

For three whole hours the flood poured past, exhausting to watch, dazing the eye with its colours, deafening you with its cries. Mao Tu Hsi! Wan Hsuei! Good Old Mao! Thousand Years! And Mao stood watching, waving his hand most of the time, very tiny above his preposterous portraits craning his neck to follow the clouds of coloured balloons as they rose from the hands of the people like hundreds-of-thousands taken wing.

It wasn't a procession. It was a free running of the Chinese people before the architect of the new China. It is more than thirty years since he began to make all this, and only seven since it came about. No single man has ever been looked on with such affection by so many people as Mao at the culmination of the first stage of fulfilment. And none in his position has been so unassuming. The old Poet, as the same Frenchman called him, is easy to like.

Chairman Mao strolling outside his official residence, 1957.

The May Day celebration parade, Tien An Men, 1957.

Young people waving flowers towards Tiananmen where Chairman Mao and foreign dignitaries stand during May Day parade, Beijing, 1957.

WORKERS OF THE WORLD

V. G. Wilcox

Vic Wilcox was General Secretary of the New Zealand Communist Party from 1951 to 1977. The New Zealand party's decision to oppose the 'revisionist' line of the Soviet Union meant that its leadership were welcome guests in China over the period of the Sino-Soviet split. The following remarks are taken from a speech which Mr Wilcox gave to the Chinese Communist Party School in Canton (Guangzhou) in February 1964.

Comrades,

It is a great pleasure and honour to speak to you today. An honour not only for myself personally, but for the Communist Party of New Zealand of which I am General Secretary, a party that in the capitalist world is endeavouring to the best of its abilities to uphold the banners of Marxism-Leninism and prepare the way by correct policy and practice for the future advance to a socialist New Zealand. That we face many difficulties you will realise. We have made some gains and we have made some mistakes, the experience of which we have tried to study in order to eliminate them from our theory and practice in the future. In our own way, based on our own experiences and understanding, we have tried to apply the theories of Marxism to our country and its conditions. For any Marxist-Leninist party there is no other way because otherwise we take the road of sectarianism, of dogmatism. Therefore our party programme is based on New Zealand conditions while taking the world-wide experience of our movement both before and since the Great October Revolution of 1917 led by Lenin. . . .

Comrades, as the 81 Parties' statement put it we are in the era of the decline of imperialism and the victory of socialism on a world scale. Today it is apparent that this situation has brought about not only gains but also new problems. New difficulties have brought sharp contradictions, struggles within our world movement and within each individual Communist party. We should not discourage any Marxist. Without difficulties, contradictions and struggle we do not advance. If we do not recognise this, first stagnation sets in and then retreat. It is useless in such a situation to remain placid like a cow chewing its cud and hope that time will bring a solution without our help. No—we must fight, we must oppose all who want to emasculate Marxism-Leninism in such a way that ultimately it would survive as but a bourgeois theory. The Communist Party of New Zealand in its congress decision last year recognised this and we are fighting for the principles of Marxism-Leninism. Within our world Marxist-Leninism movement those who today take a stand will emerge victorious and modern revisionism will be defeated.

Today the idea has arisen that because of the strength of the socialist world the way forward has now become easy, that socialism can be won in the main through reliance on the socialist world and not on the organised fighting ability of the masses led by their own Communist Parties. Looking at it in this way the class struggle as the motive force for change in each individual country assumes less and less importance and class collaboration ideas grow, both in internal policy and international affairs. This is but an expression of revisionism, the same revisionism that Lenin fought, the basic idea being the same as that advanced by the Bersteins and the Kautskys. The modern revisionists may express it in different language, they may try to cloak it by talking about the 'new era', but in content it is the same old story. . . .

Where do the revisionists stand on what is for us the basic question of correct strategy and tactics towards social democracy? They confuse the mass working-class base of social democracy in countries such as ours with a mass working-class ideology. In fact they are starting to argue that if a Labour Party has an overwhelming majority of workers in its membership, it must follow that it has a working-class outlook on policy, or at least that correct policy can be achieved without an ideological battle to win the workers to an understanding of the basic principles of Marxism-Leninism and of the necessity for a Communist Party. In fact they persist in ignoring the historical fact that social democracy nowhere in the world has led the working people and their allies to the achievement of state power and the creation of a socialist society. It is only where a strong and decisive leadership has come from the Party of the working class, the Communist Party, has that been achieved. The modern revisionists, claiming that we are in a new era and that things are different to what they used to be, say that now we can work in a different way, and somehow or other through parliamentary road with little additions here and there achieve a socialist society. In fact they say we can do it without the establishment of the dictatorship of the proletariat. Utter and complete nonsense! They expect to achieve socialism by a Labour party, assisted by a few injections from the present membership of the Communist Party. This leads to the negation of the correct concept of the leading role of a Communist Party and in fact starts it on the road to liquidation. In the mid-fifties the Browder line, advanced for a time in the Communist Party of the U.S.A., suggested organisational steps towards the liquidation of effective communist organisation based on the principles of Marxism-Leninism and many of the present revisionists opposed it then. Today they are taking the Browder road. At the best they treat the Labour Party as a two class Party, but all Marxists know that such a thing is an impossibility. They refuse to learn from Lenin who categorically declared that social democratic political parties, labour parties, are capitalistic parties.

The Communist Party of New Zealand does not view social democracy in this revisionist way. We see the necessity to work and unite on immediate issues of struggle with all sections of the workers including those most strongly influenced by and supporting the Labour Party, we also see the need to conduct side by side with such united front work a continuing educational ideological battle to win the workers to Marxism-Leninism and to an understanding of why no social-democratic party ever leads them to socialism, but in fact merely strengthens the stranglehold of capitalism. We unite in action with these sections but we do not unite ideologically. On the contrary we bring out strongly the leading role of our Communist Party, the reasons why it must be strengthened and its influence widened if we are to effectively lead the struggle for a socialist New Zealand.

FOR THE RECORD

New markets are rapidly springing up in the Pacific, in South America and California and in China and Continental India, which promise to become, at no distant period, sources of considerable profit for New Zealand produce.
  —W. Tyrone Power, *Recollections of A Three Years' Residence in China,* 1853.

The day will come, perhaps sooner than most of us imagine, when, if the Chinese wish to come to New Zealand, not £100 tax nor 100 English words nor even 100 English Dreadnoughts will hinder them.
  —Alexander Don, letter to the *Otago Daily Times,* 23 December 1907.

The average New Zealander has not begun to realise that the future of his country is in any serious way bound up with the happenings in China. China is awake. Is New Zealand asleep?
  —Rev G. H. McNeur, 'An Awakening China and the Pacific', 1926.

It is unlikely that the future of the Pacific, crossed now by aircraft as well as by ocean liner, will be surrendered to the supremacy of any one Power, with others there by suffrance. Nor is it likely that the great nation of China will consent to become the vassal of any other nation.
  —*Evening Post* editorial, 4 March 1939.

China will, under any Government, be more interested in New Zealand than we are in China.
  —External Affairs file note, 9 March 1950.

LETTER TO A CHINESE POET

Ruth Dallas

Po Chü-i, AD 772-846

Days, moons, go beyond, pass away
Futile to mourn, to grieve.
—Old Chinese Poem

1. On Reading your Poems

Chuang Tzu, when his wife died
Shocked his friends by playing upon a drum.

You, when your brother had been dead a year,
Wrote him a letter full of family news.

In the eleven hundred years since your death
Has anyone, I wonder, written to you?

2. The Written Word

Not one of the ten pine-trees in your courtyard,
In whose fresh company you felt ashamed,
Sound and stillness lulling the air of spring,
Symbol of calm in the stir of the world's noise,
Not the tallest pine-tree, nor the youngest,
Shaped a cone that carried seed as far
As the box you made of cypress for your poems.

Seeds of a thousand autumns have drifted over
The terrace of sand, the waste and the green land;
And still within your poems the pines breathe,
Symbol for me as once they were for you,
Speaking in lands unrumoured when you were here.

Of the box you fashioned and knew so well
The inscription stands, preserving your doubtful sigh.

3. The Rose

To learn the several thousand characters
So many years with a brush and a steady hand!
And in the streets the people endlessly passing,
Hurrying to see a procession, or just idling along.
Reading your poems translated into English
Is like conning
The names of roses in a catalogue;
Where are the words to convey what a rose is,
Or tell the transforming difference in shape or shade?
But once the rose has grown by the path at home,
Or is brought from the garden of a loved friend,
The name, a hint of the scent, and all is known,
From bud to final petal-fall.

Rosa chinensis,
Enriching roses in a foreign garden,
Fragrance in the air.

4. Clouds on the Sea

I walk among men with tall bones,
With shoes of leather, and pink faces;
I meet no man holding a begging bowl;
All have their dwelling places.

In my country
Every child is taught to read and write,
Every child has shoes and a warm coat,
Every child must eat his dinner,
No one must grow any thinner;
It is considered remarkable and not nice
To meet bed-bugs or lice.
Oh we live like the rich
With music at the touch of a switch,
Light in the middle of the night,
Water in the house as from a spring,
Hot, if you wish, or cold, anything
For the comfort of the flesh,
In my country. Fragment
Of new skin at the edge of the world's ulcer.

For the question
That troubled you as you watched the reapers
And a poor woman following,
Gleaning the ears on the ground,
Why should I have grain and this woman none?
No satisfactory answer has been found.

5. Overheard

Easy, easy, sleeps the head
On a soft bed.
Not mine, the mutter
In a hard gutter.

Besides, they are so far,
These people, they are,
Really, what can one do?
They have such large families, too.

These thoughts are not nice
Either, if one spills rice,
Or burns bread,
Or is feeling over-fed.

Let us go to the races
At Easter—and other places.
Why should you bother?
Leave it to some other . . .

. . . indistinguishable.

Conversation in the bush.

6. The Green Earth

I could show you mountains fair,
Rocks like men with frosted hair,
Forest-tops afloat in air,
Unguessed when you were here.

Then as now the trees were deep
In centuries of unguarded sleep;

The same torrents round them leap;
Mosses over their branches creep.

Sweet water rises from a stone,
Paths in a day are overgrown,
The lakes mirror a freshness known
To the first man who dwelt alone.

So temple-quiet are the long
Corridors he wandered among
The ear expects a bell, or gong;
Is startled by the bell of birdsong.

No monastery is built in air;
You would not find a pilgrim stair,
Hermit sage, or man of prayer,
But voices of the earth there.

7. The Shells

I do not think you would like my appearance,
My fair European skin and large bones
Descended from Scottish, Swedish, English,
Adventure-loving ancestors,
Who crossed the world lightly;
Suppleness and strength
Fashioned for the sea and the sea shore,
And to withstand
Unutterable loss
Always in the wash of the waves.

For me the bone is a shell at the sea's edge,
Inhabited for a season,
Delicate conveyance, most wonderfully alive,
Empty house of the dead,
Sand and dust blown on the wind of time.
I cannot tell from sand or the wind's tone
If this man's skin was yellow, this man's brown;
But I hear through a thousand years
The heart singing in an old poem
Near as over the width of the earth
A clock in London strikes within one's room.

'BANNED BY TIDES . . .'

New Zealand in the Asian Century

Keith Buchanan

My theme in this paper is New Zealand's awareness of Asia as we move into the latter stages of what one historian has termed 'the Asian century'. Inevitably, I confront this theme from the angle of my own chosen discipline—that of geography; I confront it, moreover, not as a New Zealand geographer but as a geographer trained in the ancient, more crowded, lands of the Old World— in Europe, Africa and Asia. These personal details are not irrelevant for they may help in part to explain my sensitiveness, perhaps my oversensitiveness, to New Zealand's isolation; because of this isolation the joys, the aspirations, the sorrows of the great majority of mankind reach us as but distant murmurs, as the muted echoes of 'old, unhappy, far-off things . . .' We are, as Keith Sinclair has perceptively said, 'banned by tides from the sorrows of continents . . .'

This quality of remoteness is a quality which made a lasting impact on me when, somewhat over a decade ago, I sailed from Britain to New Zealand by way of Panama. Quoting from a letter I wrote on the voyage:

> Days flow into one another in an eventless timeless sequence—each day identical with the next—brilliant hot sunshine and all around us the endless blue emptiness of the South Pacific. Not a speck of land, not even a ship, since we left Panama . . . the world of broken hills and rolling plains, of wheat fields and cities and villages, takes on an insubstantial dream-like quality—a deep subconscious memory from an earlier terrestrial existence . . . . We wander Noah-like upon a waste of waters and only the white seabird winging past the ship reassures us that a world of rocks and soil and birds and people exists somewhere beyond the horizon . . .

This physical remoteness attenuates our awareness of the wider world and this attenuation persists, even in an age of jet travel, as a kind of historical hangover; we do not find it easy, perhaps because we do not feel it necessary, to confront the reality of Asia.

We are isolated from the great majority of mankind in another way—for our affluence and our Western-centred vision combine to alienate us from the impoverished one and a half billion people who live on the southern and eastern fringes of Eurasia, from the great diversity of non-Western peoples who are our nearest neighbours and with whom, whether we like it or not, our future must increasingly be shared. The one and a half billion who in a generation will be four

Great circle azimuths (or bearings) and distances
from Wellington to all parts of the World.

Azimuthal Equidistant Projection

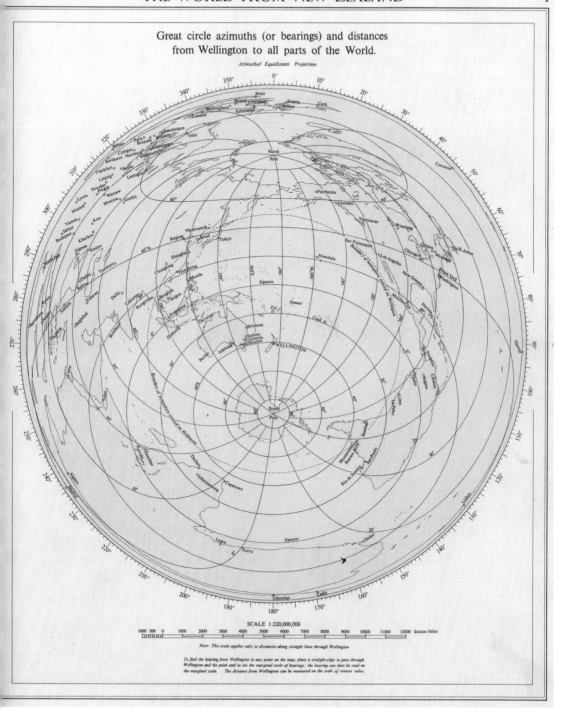

SCALE 1:220,000,000

1000 500 0   1000   2000   3000   4000   5000   6000   7000   8000   9000   10000   11000   12000 Statute Miles

Note: This scale applies only to distances along straight lines through Wellington

To find the bearing from Wellington to any point on the map, place a straight-edge to pass through
Wellington and the point and to cut the marginal scale of bearings: the bearing can then be read on
the marginal scale.   The distance from Wellington can be measured on the scale of statute miles.

billion and who increasingly are going not only to *share* but to *shape* our future or our children's future . . .

By a simple process of non-recognition, by employing the fabled head-in-the-sand technique of the ostrich (the virus which causes this pattern of behaviour was probably brought over by some of those rugby-playing boys from the Transvaal), we almost succeed in halving Asia's population. 'Free Asia', which includes such improbable countries as South Korea, South Vietnam and Thailand, contains just over 800 million people; the remaining 750 or so million belong to countries our New Zealand government does not recognize—750 million people floating presumably in some sort of curious Limbo, way out beyond the Long White Cloud. These people, the people of North Vietnam, of North Korea, of the Chinese People's Republic, are not very OK—except as customers for our wool and such commodities. We thus find ourselves in a Lewis Carroll sort of world; all the foreign trade of China is carried on by government organizations and these organizations of a government whose existence we do not recognize buy from us £1.3 million worth of goods (as against the £0.9 million purchased by India); I presume they pay and I presume many a station-owner (and staunch Nationalist) buys his new car, or even subscribes to National Party funds, from the Red gold earned by the sale of his wool to China; the wool is probably made into good thick People's Army uniforms for all those Chinese we hear about in South Vietnam (and Zanzibar, and Brazil, etc., etc.).

But this is not just a lunatic situation, to be dismissed frivolously; it is also a damnably hypocritical situation and we attempt to justify the hypocrisy by slanted reporting or downright lies. We do not recognize China because she has, our politicians complain, a record of aggressive acts of which the culmination was her attack on India in 1962—or so we were told. But General Maxwell D. Taylor, who was Chairman of the U.S. Joint Chiefs of Staff, gives us a different picture of this culminating 'aggression'. To the question put to him during a Congressional hearing, 'Did the Indians actually start this military operation?' he replied: 'They were edging forward in the disputed area, yes, sir'. At this point the testimony was censored out of the public transcript. The entire tissue of excuses we in New Zealand put forward to explain why we withhold recognition of the Asian communist regimes has the same flimsy, transparent sheerness; it has a gossamer nylon quality—though what it is supposed to hide is not exactly delectable. . . .

Almost half the population of Asia, then, lives in states we refuse to recognize, states which—and let us make no mistake about this—are the only states on the Asian mainland to have begun the long and bitter uphill climb from stagnation to decency, states which are going to dominate the latter half of this century. They are states governed by men who, as Premier Edgar Faure observed, have 'their feet plunged in memories', whose constant motive force is that of patriotism, who are deeply sensitive because 'they still feel around them a circle of distrust, and because they see their identity obstinately being denied. He adds: 'Contempt is a form of violence, and the hour of talks has come'. We might add: but not for New Zealand—for one of the consequences of satellite status is that our leaders have nothing to say on these things, no thoughts or words of their own when they confront this critical socialist half of Asia, only the hollow echoes of the hostility and the holier-than-thou filibustering which is America's answer to the emergence of a new world in East Asia.

We may contrast with the negativeness and the hollowness of the New Zealand attitude the realism of the French attitude as expressed by General de Gaulle: 'On this continent there can be no peace, nor any war imaginable without Chinese being involved. . . .' He goes on:

> In having ties with that country (i.e. China)—official relations like many other free nations have had previously and like we have had with other countries with similar regimes—France is no more than recognising the world as it is. But it could be, too, that in the actual immense evolution of the world the multiplying of direct contacts of one people with another serves the cause of man, that is, the cause of wisdom, of progress and of peace.
>
> It could be that these contacts contribute to the attenuation, already started, between the contrasts and the dramatic oppositions of the camps which divide the universe.
>
> It could be thus that human souls, wherever they are found on earth, will meet each other a little earlier at the rendezvous that France gave to the universe 175 years ago, that of liberty, equality, and fraternity.'

Such 'direct contacts of one people with another' would not only give *us* a more balanced awareness of what is going on, what people are striving for, in that half of Asia from which we avert our faces; it would also enable the Chinese—and other East Asian peoples too—to assess at their true value the lunatic pronouncements on the condition of New Zealand made by our local communist luminaries in the course of their frequent jaunts between Moscow, Tirana and Peking.

Ultimately, the best basis on which we can judge New Zealand's attitude to Asia is the attitude of New Zealanders to the Asians in our midst, those Asians who for many decades have been an element of the New Zealand population and those who visit us as students. These attitudes contain a strong element of the hypocrisy and self-deception I have already referred to; at the most charitable assessment they are ambivalent. Yet as my colleague T. G. McGee has pointed out: 'New Zealand is no longer just part of the Western world, it is part of Asia also. And if we are to be part of Asia we must correct our attitude to our own Asian immigrant groups before we can ever hope to formulate any satisfactory approach to Asia.'

COURTENAY PLACE

Kerry Ann Lee

Courtenay Place, Wellington, 1952.

I remember the first restaurant started in a gambling house in Haining Street. There were so many people they decided to cook some duck and oh, they went crazy! It was never dreamed then because you couldn't buy chicken or duck ready to eat, you'd have to go to a poultry farm.

Kenneth Chan
Taishan Restaurant,
Bowen Street (est. 1984–91)

The first Chinese restaurant in Wellington to provide Chinese food for the non-Chinese, the Shanghai was famous for its Ching Dynasty decor – all red, green and gold with plastic Chinese lanterns. To suit its European customers it served dinner with a side plate of buttered bread and the tea it served was as strong its Railways-strength cups. It had a menu nearly as long as the Great Wall...

Nigel Murphy
'The Shanghai (Courtenay Place):
end of an era', published in
City Voice (5 February 1997)

The 1950s–1970s was a real golden era. All around Wellington a lot of little restaurants cropped up. Mind you, they weren't just Chinese, they had steak and egg European meals too. Our restaurant was first called Moonlight and then we changed it to Cathay. In those days with 6 o'clock closing, it was packed. They'd all come at once and we'd close at 8 o'clock.

Henry Kwing
Cathay Restaurant,
Courtenay Place (est. 1953–69)

New Zealand Artist Kerry Ann Lee has explored 'the transformation of Cantonese settlers into Chinese New Zealanders' in her work Home Made: Picturing Chinese Settlement in New Zealand *(2008). In 2009, she was selected as the inaugural WARE artist-in-residence to Shanghai and has since continued to explore issues of place and identity across geographical borders.*

It was unusual for us to have a Milk Bar because most Chinese had fruit shops, laundries and restaurants. Dad made all his own milkshake flavours, boiled and bottled them. When we had to drink milk at school it used to upset my stomach so Dad would always give me some to take and put in my milk and all the kids would come around and say, 'Can I have some?!'

Esther Lee
The Favourite Milkbar,
Adelaide Road, Newtown (est.1955–81)

I've lost count of how many burgers we make in a day. On average, maybe about 70? I didn't mind this when I was younger. Now that we're older we're more tired.

Shirley Cho
Rice Bowl Burger Bar,
Adelaide Road, Newtown (est.1973)

25

ESTABLISHING DIPLOMATIC RELATIONS

New Zealand established diplomatic relations with the People's Republic of China on 22 December 1972. In announcing the decision the newly-elected Prime Minister of New Zealand, Hon Norman Kirk, commented that 'China has now re-entered the mainstream of world affairs. It is playing an active part in the United Nations. In Asia and the Pacific its influence is great, and is bound to grow. It is logical and sensible for New Zealand to recognise the People's Republic of China and enter into normal relations with it. There is no point in delaying about such a fundamental issue.'

The establishment of relations was formally effected by the signature of a joint communiqué in New York by New Zealand's Permanent representative to the United Nations, John Scott, and his Chinese counterpart Huang Hua. Huang Hua, later to become China's long-serving Foreign Minister, had been James Bertram's roommate at Yenching University in 1936.

JOINT COMMUNIQUÉ ON THE ESTABLISHMENT OF DIPLOMATIC RELATIONS BETWEEN THE PEOPLE'S REPUBLIC OF CHINA AND NEW ZEALAND

The Government of the People's Republic of China and the Government of New Zealand, in accordance with the principles of mutual respect for sovereignty and territorial integrity, non–interference in each other's internal affairs, and equality and mutual benefit, have decided on mutual recognition and the establishment of diplomatic relations with effect from 22 December 1972. The Chinese Government reaffirms that Taiwan is an inalienable part of the territory of the People's Republic of China and that Taiwan is a province of the People's Republic of China. The New Zealand Government acknowledges this position of the Chinese Government. The New Zealand Government recognizes the Government of the People's Republic of China as the sole legal government of China. The Chinese Government and the New Zealand Government have agreed to exchange ambassadors as early as practicable and mutually to provide all necessary assistance for the establishment and performance of the functions of embassies in their respective capitals on the basis of equality, mutual benefit and friendly consultation and in accordance with international practice.

(signed) Huang Hua, Ambassador Extraordinary and Plenipotentiary, Permanent Representative of the People's Republic of China to the United Nations

(signed) John Vian Scott, Ambassador Extraordinary and Plenipotentiary, Permanent Representative of New Zealand to the United Nations

New York, December 21, 1972

New Zealand's first Ambassador to China, Bryce Harland, presents his credentials to the Acting President of China, Dong Biwu, on 20 September 1973.

In October 1973 Hon Joe Walding visited China for a second time, on this occasion in his capacity as Minister for Overseas Trade. He led a trade mission that included representatives of all New Zealand's main industry and producer groups. Members of the mission visited Inner Mongolia to learn about China's approach to pastoral farming.

It was on this visit that Charles Patrick, then International Manager of the New Zealand Dairy Board (on the extreme left in this photograph), laid the foundation for the trade in dairy products that now dominates New Zealand's exports to China.

Six Chapters from Old School Life

Paul Clark

Paul Clark was one of the first three New Zealand students to travel to China under the exchange agreement between the two governments. He studied in the History Department of Peking University (Beida) in 1975–1976. Paul is now Professor of Chinese at Auckland University.

1.

On a bright morning in September 1975 we sat on the narrow wooden benches in our classroom and looked around at our new classmates. Twenty were worker-peasant-soldier students, including four army men and workers from a range of work units in and around Beijing. The other half of the class were international students, from Canada, Britain, other Western European countries, and New Zealand. I had come from a year at the Peking Languages Institute. We were to spend this year at Beida together studying ancient and modern Chinese history as an advanced study class *(jinxiuban)*. Outside, in front of the then new library building, a statue of Mao Zedong raised his right hand above an unusual sight for Beijing, a grass lawn, divided up like a wet rice checkerboard. As autumn became winter we watched during class breaks as the grass was carefully tended by a group of groundsmen. It survived the cold and grew again in the spring, a green carpet so precious that it was off-limits to all students and staff.

2.

Nineteen seventy-six, a momentous year for China, started for us in a makeshift dormitory in an office building at the Capital Steel Works. We spent two weeks there on 'open-door schooling' to learn from the workers and to be workers ourselves. By day, we learned to pack sand tightly into moulds around wooden models of large machine parts. At night, another shift of workers would remove the wooden pieces and fill the cavities with steel. While this happened, the male classmates enjoyed a communal bath in a workers' bathhouse, soaking away the grit of the workshop in luxurious hot water. One evening the head of my political study group, one of three into which the class was divided, shared stories from a book he had borrowed from the Beida library. It was the biography of Zhu Yuanzhang, the first Ming emperor, written by Wu Han, a former Beida professor. The Cultural Revolution had started over ten years earlier with attacks on Wu Han's Peking opera script, *Hai Rui Dismissed from Office (Hai Rui baguan)*. The next morning we woke to sombre music on the loudspeakers: Premier Zhou Enlai had died. The memorial meeting for Zhou was held in the workshop canteen. Several hundred workers squeezed shoulder-to-shoulder into the empty hall. As the commemorations began, an unfamiliar sound swept from the front of the room across the sea of heads back to us. A low, sobbing wail soon filled the entire hall as tears fell.

185

3.

In early April our teachers suddenly announced a field trip for the class. We all piled onto an ancient Beida bus and bounced our way south past the fields of Haidian. We ended up in the southeast of the city, beyond the railway station, at a handicrafts factory. The usual 'brief introduction' and display of glass and wire pot plants seemed nothing special, adding to the mystery of why we had been taken on this unscheduled trip. On the way to the factory we had driven along West Chang'an Avenue. There groups of people were walking eastwards carrying huge wreaths of paper flowers in memory of Zhou Enlai. In Tian'anmen Square itself, we saw from our speeding bus that the base of the Monument to the People's Heroes was festooned with similar wreaths. Events two days later confirmed that the field trip's purpose was not to see glass flowers but for the class to notice paper flowers. On 4 April my army political-instructor classmate (who was also my roommate) borrowed my Flying Pigeon bicycle for the second time ever and made a, for him, rare journey into the city. Zhang Heng's excitement when he returned that evening, having copied down poems he had seen in the square, was infectious.

4.

More 'open-door schooling' came later that month, when the entire class went to Shangnian Production Brigade in Beixiaoying People's Commune, northeast of the Shunyi county seat. We were billeted in peasant homes. On one end of the *kang* my soldier roommate and I made our beds, at the other the group leader and a German classmate slept. Our host family, grandmother, parents and three children somehow squeezed into the other half of the house. Two weeks in the fields gave us a taste of commune life and was almost enough time to master the balancing act of pushing tall wheelbarrows full of fertiliser. Zhang Heng, himself from a farming family near Tianjin, taught me more. He explained quietly that the somewhat precarious hole in the ground within our host family's compound behind the pig pen should be left for grandmother's use, as she was not very mobile. We should use the open, communal lavatory on the street corner nearby. I still remember the girlish delight with which the mother of the family let me pedal her bicycle with her on the carrier rack back from the little village shop one afternoon. Two old men living on the edge of the village were astonished to learn from me that the sun shone in the northern sky in New Zealand. In their view all houses in the world faced south. They shook their heads: 'Winter must be very cold for New Zealanders.'

5.

As summer arrived, there were occasions to explore the campus. One evening a Canadian classmate invited me to join her in walking north beyond Weiming Lake. Past the old Yanjing buildings, this was unknown territory for international students. A path lead through the trees and we could see water in a pond beyond.

Weak electric lights glimmered in reflection among the lotus plants. But what we heard was more unexpected. From a distant window across the water came the faint sounds of a gramophone. It was Mozart.

6.

Sounds are some of our strongest memories. The squeak of the door on the eastern end of the old campus store by Sanjiaodi has never left my ears. Even in the 1980s and 1990s, when I returned to the campus, that squeak persisted. The store was demolished a few years ago. When ten Chinese classmates and I got together for the thirtieth anniversary of our graduation we recalled the old classroom and store. Building 27, a match to our men's dormitory in Building 26, was torn down while I visited in the summer of 2007. The campus has been transformed and expanded in the three decades since those days. Lasting friendships and memories of shared learning enhance the view.

Classmates from the Beida History Department 1975–1976 Chinese History Advanced Study Class. Zhang Heng and Paul Clark are on the left.

SLEEPING WITH THE PANDA

Bryce Harland

It is established practice for New Zealand ambassadors to address a final report to the Minister of Foreign Affairs at the time they complete their assignment. Such reports commonly reflect upon the substantial progress in the relationship during the term of the incumbent. New Zealand's first Ambassador to China, Bryce Harland, had the advantage of starting from a very low base.

New Zealand Embassy, Peking.

24 November 1975
The Minister of Foreign Affairs,
WELLINGTON.

NEW ZEALAND AND CHINA

It is almost three years since New Zealand recognised the People's Republic of China. Having completed my term as the first New Zealand Ambassador in Peking, I will be leaving here shortly. It may be helpful if before going I give you an assessment of our relations with China—where we have got in the past three years, and where we may expect to go from here.

Purposes
2. To do this, it is necessary first to look back and recall why we recognised the PRC in 1972. The war in Viet Nam had fundamentally changed power relationships in the Pacific area. The United States had already begun to withdraw from Indochina, and at the same time to end its long-standing ostracism of the PRC. China had ceased to be an international outcast. It had at last entered the United Nations, and was playing an increasingly active and important part in international affairs. President Nixon had acknowledged this by coming to Peking himself. In the new situation, it was clear that New Zealand could no longer rely entirely on the United States and its allies. It had to be able to deal directly with all the great powers involved in the Pacific area, including China. We had to be in a position to follow their policies, to present to them our own views, and to get these views heard in the right quarters.

3. One of New Zealand's main foreign policy concerns at that time was peace in Southeast Asia. We had learned from experience that when wars broke out there

it was not easy for us to keep out of them. But, in the case of Viet Nam at least, New Zealand's involvement in the war had divided our own country as no other foreign policy issue had done before. We were anxious to strengthen our ties with the countries we had long been associated with in Southeast Asia, and to help sustain their independence. At the same time, it seemed clear that New Zealand's interest lay in trying to avoid further conflict in Southeast Asia, by helping to reduce tensions in the area and by encouraging reconciliation, especially between China and the ASEAN countries.

4.   Trade was of course another consideration in the decision to recognise the PRC. Some people had long felt that China could be an important market for New Zealand goods, if political relations with it could be improved. Others were sceptical: they pointed out that China's foreign trade was relatively small, and that it did not seem to need many of the things we produce. The official approach was that the possibilities were worth exploring, but the prospects were not particularly bright.

Political
5.   To what extent has the main purpose of our recognition been realised? We have got ourselves into a position where we can deal directly with the Chinese. Embassies were established in both capitals by mid-1973, and they have provided direct channels of communication between the two Governments. Even before that, the Associate Minister of Foreign Affairs had been to Peking, met the Chinese Premier, and had talks with the Ministries of Foreign Affairs and Foreign Trade. These talks gave us a better understanding of Chinese foreign policy, and enabled us to put to the Chinese our views on several important questions. They opened a dialogue which has continued at various levels ever since.

6.   One of the first questions we raised with the Chinese was that of nuclear testing, and it is one on which we have continued to press them. We made it clear that New Zealand was opposed to all nuclear testing, and especially to testing in the atmosphere. The Chinese said they understood our position but felt obliged to go on developing nuclear weapons for their own defence. Whenever we have raised the subject again, they have been willing to discuss it, and they have begun to show more interest in the general question of disarmament. In June 1974 they conducted another atmospheric test. But the only test they have conducted this year (in October) was an underground one—the first in China since 1969. The Chinese have not said that there will be no more atmospheric tests: Foreign Ministry officials have pointed this out to us. It is quite possible that atmospheric testing will be resumed at some stage. But it looks as if the Chinese are now trying to build up their own defences without resorting to this very unpopular expedient.

7.   The other question we raised at the outset was that of China's support for communist insurgents in Southeast Asia. The Chinese told us that their main concern was to prevent the countries of that area from falling under the domination of either of the super-powers. We replied that only by playing on the fear of China could the super-powers achieve domination, so it was up to China to reassure the countries concerned. We have gone on making this point whenever we have had the opportunity. Sometimes the Chinese response has been very hard: the present Foreign Minister once told us flatly that as communists they were obliged to support revolution in other countries, and he refused to exclude the possibility of material support. More recently the First Vice Premier has taken a softer line. In talking to New Zealand journalists recently, he used the phrase 'moral support'—a concession the Foreign Minister had never made, at least to us. What is more important is that in the past two years, and especially in the past six months, China has in fact established diplomatic relations with Malaysia, the Philippines and Thailand, and significantly improved its relations with Singapore and Burma. And in each case the Chinese have publicly acknowledged that no country has the right to interfere in the internal affairs of another. There are also indications that the Chinese have in fact been reducing their support for the insurgents, at least in Burma—though there is little hard evidence on which to base an assessment. Since the withdrawal of the United States from Indochina, the Chinese have become much more concerned about Soviet activities in Southeast Asia. They are now trying harder to improve their relations with the Governments in the area, and, in some cases at least, they may be prepared to pay a price in terms of their relations with the communist parties concerned.

8.   The third main subject of our political dialogue with the Chinese has been the South Pacific. They have never asked us to press the island States to recognise the PRC. Nor have we done so. What we have done is to tell the Chinese something about the South Pacific and its problems, and to suggest that China would be well-advised to tread lightly in seeking relations with the island States. They have in fact done so, and this approach is now beginning to pay off for them. After the establishment of relations with Papua New Guinea, Fiji and Western Samoa, Tonga and Nauru are the only Pacific States that do not recognise the PRC.

9.   On each of the three main political issues we have talked to the Chinese about in the past three years, their policy has moved in the direction we favour. There are of course many reasons for this: the fundamental one is China's fear of the Soviet Union. This fear now dominates China's whole foreign policy, and it provides a basis on which countries like New Zealand can argue with the Chinese about specific problems. We can, and do, point out to the Chinese the implications of what they are doing, and the dangers for China itself, especially in nuclear testing and supporting insurgency in Southeast Asia. Other countries do so too—perhaps

not always as bluntly as we do—and collectively we are beginning to have some impact on Chinese foreign policy.

<u>Trade</u>

10. Trade was not our main reason for establishing diplomatic relations with China, but it has proved to be one of the main benefits. In 1971 New Zealand's exports to China amounted to less than $1 million: in 1974 they rose to almost $20 million. In the same period our imports from China increased from $5 million to nearly $18 million. The total volume of trade thus increased more than six times in three years, and an unfavourable balance of $4 million was converted into a favourable balance of $2 million.

11. What is perhaps more important is that in the past three years, and especially this year, the range of our exports to China has widened significantly. Traditionally wool has been our main export to this country: even in 1973/74 it represented 90% of our total exports to China. Since 1973 however we have been selling substantial quantities of pulp and paper here, as well as a growing quantity of tallow. This year we have for the first time sold semi-processed cow hides and sheep skins, and pine logs, and the Chinese have told us that if the initial shipments are satisfactory they will go on buying on a regular basis. They are even buying some steel products from us. And they have shown interest in buying aluminium and iron ore, though at present we are not in a position to supply either.

12. The international recession has affected China's foreign trade as well as ours. After buying 60,000 bales of wool in 1973/74 season, the Chinese bought none in 1974/75—mainly because they could not sell their woollen textiles. Since the beginning of the current season they have begun buying again, and it looks as if their purchases may exceed 30,000 bales by the end of 1975. But the really encouraging thing is that, despite the sharp decline in our sales of wool, the value of our total exports to China this year seems likely to be comparable with that for 1974. In 1975 wool is unlikely to represent more than 30% of our total exports to China. By diversifying our exports, we have made the trade less volatile, and laid a firm foundation for further expansion.

13. The reason for the rapid increase of our trade with China in the past three years is clear. The Chinese have said repeatedly that the establishment of diplomatic relations created a favourable atmosphere for the expansion of trade, and the figures demonstrate the point conclusively. Foreign trade is important to China, and the Chinese have made it clear that they are bent on developing it— mainly as a means of accelerating their own economic growth. But to them trade with any individual country is only one aspect of an overall relationship, which is essentially political. There is nothing we sell the Chinese that they could not if necessary buy elsewhere. So in our case at least a favourable political atmosphere

is essential for the expansion of trade. This has its disadvantages: any change in our policy towards Taiwan would certainly have an adverse effect on our trade with China. But there are also advantages from our point of view. The main one is that in China the New Zealand Government can do more than it can in almost any other country to promote New Zealand's exports and to develop a long term market.

Bilateral Exchanges
14. Maintaining a favourable atmosphere for the expansion of trade is not a simple matter. It requires first of all that we should strictly observe the terms of the agreement on the establishment of diplomatic relations between New Zealand and the PRC, and respect the Chinese view (also held in Taiwan itself) that Taiwan is part of China. This is essential, but it is not enough. In a country where foreign trade is completely under the control of the Government, expansion requires the goodwill, not only of the officials directly concerned, but also of Ministers and political leaders. And when that country has relations with over a hundred others, with 80–odd foreign Embassies in its own capital, the competition is pretty tough.

15. The most effective way of maintaining the right atmosphere for the expansion of trade is for New Zealand Ministers to visit China at regular intervals. The visits made earlier this year by the Minister of Agriculture and the Minister of Trade and Industry certainly did much, not only to maintain the right atmosphere, but also to make the Chinese aware of New Zealand's concerns, and its capabilities. The progress we have made in diversifying our exports to China this year is largely due to these two visits. A visit by the Prime Minister could do even more to promote our trade with China. The Chinese are intensely status-conscious. They attach great importance to visits by Heads of other Governments and they make concessions to Prime Ministers that they do not make to anyone else. If and when our Prime Minister comes to China, it is important that this point should be borne in mind. We should work out carefully in advance what we most want to get out of the Chinese, in trade as well as in other fields, and seize the opportunity to get it.

16. Exchanges between the two countries at other levels and in other fields are also important from the point of view of trade expansion. They keep New Zealand in the news in China, they bring us into contact with influential people in China whom we would otherwise not meet, and they show the Chinese that we are willing to develop the sort of all round relationship that they call 'friendship'. The increasing number of visits by New Zealand businessmen to China, and also of Chinese trade officials to New Zealand, are of obvious importance. But perhaps the most valuable exchanges we have had so far are those in the cultural field. The National Youth Orchestra in particular made New Zealand better known in China than ever before, and provided a very helpful background for our trade and

political work. Exchanges of doctors, scientists, students, journalists, and especially sports teams have also played useful parts in building up the new relationship with China from which we are drawing significant economic benefits.

17. But the favourable atmosphere that prevails at the present time in our relations with China owes a good deal to private New Zealand citizens. Last year more than 200 of them came to China: this year there have been considerably more, Most of them come on group tours organised either by the New Zealand China Society or by private travel agencies, which are increasingly active in the field. New Zealand visitors to China come from all sections of the community, and all parts of the country. Their outlooks and reactions vary widely. Some go away favourably impressed, others not. But simply by coming here they make the Chinese aware that New Zealanders are interested in China, anxious to see it for themselves, and generally friendly towards it. This helps to achieve our current objectives in China, but perhaps it is even more important for relations between the two countries in the longer term. Not many New Zealanders who come here go away thinking that China is either Heaven on Earth or Hell. By seeing the country and meeting the people themselves, they at least begin to shake off the prejudices that have bedevilled relations between the two countries in the past, and to prepare themselves for facing the realities of the future.

Conclusion
18. What then has New Zealand gained from its new relationship with China?
— The most obvious benefit has been the increase in trade. China still takes less than 1% of our total exports, but within another year or two it could be our second most important market in Asia, and make a useful contribution to the overall diversification of our trade.
— On three political issues of importance to New Zealand, China's policy has moved in the direction we want during the past three years, and our own dealings with the Chinese have contributed to this movement. China is still carrying out nuclear tests, and it is still supporting insurgents in Southeast Asia, but it seems to be cutting down on both, and this is surely a gain from New Zealand's point of view.
— It must also be counted as a gain that many New Zealanders now know China at first hand, and quite a few Chinese have seen something of New Zealand. If understanding between the two countries is still not all it might be, it is at least better than it was.

19. The things we have gained from our new relationship with China are fairly modest. On the other hand, we have not had to make any real sacrifices for them. The Chinese Embassy in Wellington has not, to the best of our knowledge, indulged in any improper activities. China has never attempted to draw us away from the United States or any of our other friends. Nor has it ever pressed us to

support its position on any international issue, even when its policy and ours have been diametrically opposed. If the Chinese have at times pressed us about Taiwan, all they have asked is that we strictly observe the terms of the agreement we made with them in 1972. So, for the first three years at least, we have been able to develop a new and beneficial relationship with China, without sacrificing either our principles or our relations with other countries. Things may get more difficult in the future, especially if hostility between China and the Soviet Union goes on increasing. But there is no basis at present for thinking that New Zealand can only develop its relations with China at the expense of its relations with other countries.

20. Where will our relations with China get us in the long run?

— Two years' experience has shown that we do not have much to learn from the Chinese, except perhaps in some technical fields. China's past history, and its present problems, are totally different from ours, and its experience has little, if any, relevance to our needs. Yet many New Zealanders are interested in China and want to see it for themselves. They now have the opportunity to do so.
— Within a few years China may be taking something like 2% of New Zealand's total exports. That is not a large proportion, but perhaps it is of some significance in the context of our overall trade policy. At least it helps to broaden our base and reduce our dependence on a few big markets.
— What of the Yellow Peril? Two years' first-hand observation gives no ground for believing that China will in the foreseeable future threaten our security, or that of the South Pacific area. China is a big country, with a lot of people. It is developing fairly steadily, and will probably go on doing so. But, as the Chinese themselves say, it is still poor and backward, its rate of development is not very high, and, in relation to the United States and the Soviet Union, it is still very weak.. The main preoccupation of the Chinese is, without doubt, the development of their own country, and it will remain so for a long time to come. So it is not too hard to believe them when they say that China will never become an expansionist super-power.
21. New Zealand is a Pacific country. Our future security and prosperity depend on our ability to come to terms with the other countries in the region— particularly with those that have the capacity to influence developments in the region at large. China is one of these countries. Its actions are bound to affect us, so it is wise for us to know how to deal with it. We have begun to learn how to sleep, if not with an elephant, with a panda. And we have found that it is not so dangerous after all.

Bryce Harland
Ambassador

THIRD YOUNGER UNCLE

Dr James Ng

Medical practitioner turned historian Dr James Ng has taken the lead in seeking out and recording the history of earlier generations of Chinese in New Zealand. His four-volume history, Windows on a Chinese Past, *stands as the starting point for all future inquiry.*

NG SEE THOON (1905–1983)

Ng See Thoon was my father's younger brother. His birth name was Ng Sar Kew, his adult name Ng See Thoon and he was known as Ng Kew by Europeans. He was a kind, gentle man and one of the ordinary New Zealand-Chinese of his generation. I called him *'Thum Sook'* or third younger uncle; third because he was the third child, younger uncle because he was younger than my father. His parents—my paternal grandparents—had five children. The oldest child died in childhood, next was my father, then uncle, followed by a daughter who is living in Houston, USA, and then another daughter whose husband first went to Venezuela. She is now living in New York.

Uncle attended our village's primary school, following which he became a boarder at the secondary school at Sheng Mu, the nearby Ng market town. In those days only boys were given a formal education. The future of my father and uncle was a foregone conclusion. They would go to New Zealand, where my grandfather worked, but first they went to Hong Kong to study English for six months, in order to pass the immigration reading test.

Grandfather had gone overseas as a youth, his initial travelling expenses paid by an uncle, who had returned from the United States. He went first to Thursday Island, the pearl-fishing centre and a stopover port for shipping between China and Australasia, and then to Darwin. We have no information of this period except for two stories; that as a hotel boy on Thursday Island he was sweeping the floor and found and returned a sovereign, thereby earning the affection and trust of the hotel proprietress; and at Darwin, he attended the meetings of the Christian catechist, T. F. Loie. From Darwin he came to Wellington in about 1889 where there were Ng clansmen from our neighbouring village. He worked in a laundry, we think in Tory St, and around 1910 went to Gore where he opened the 'Jou Lee' laundry. In 1910 Alexander Don met my grandfather and wrote well of him—'a fine fellow is Pine Joy'.

Through the good offices of Gore's mayor, Grandfather was naturalised but still had to save the poll-tax £100 for each of his sons to enter New Zealand. Other Chinese in Gore included eight Taishan Cantonese, Chin clansmen, who had a market garden; and two men in a laundry named 'Kuong Chin'. After the market garden was flooded in 1913 Grandfather and three Ng relatives bought it. The market garden, comprising about 4 hectares and situated near the abbatoir, was renamed the 'Jou Lee' garden in keeping with the name of the 'Jou Lee' (later 'Joe Lee') laundry, which my grandfather kept. Other Ng relatives established the 'Sue (Water) Lee' market garden at Saltwater Creek, Timaru (the suffix Lee in Cantonese indicates good fortune). Thus the scene was set for their sons to emigrate from China and work in either laundry or either market garden.

Two first cousins of my father came first, to the Sue Lee garden. Then my father came to Gore in 1918, accompanied by another three first cousins. Before leaving our village my father had married at the age of 17 years. He departed immediately afterwards for Hong Kong, where he studied for the reading test, and on to New Zealand. At disembarkation he had hardly begun the reading test before he was clapped on the shoulder by a smiling customs officer and told he had passed. A friend had a more difficult time; his name approximated to Buck U and the old hands among the immigrants had advised him to shout this very loudly at the examining officers. They had also advised the young migrants, before leaving the ship during the stopover at Sydney; to follow the peculiar Australian custom of walking around with open trouser buttons.

Uncle See Thoon arrived in 1920, aged 15. He was the first of the young arrivals to go to school, to Gore Primary School for three years—an embarrassing episode, because he was so much older than the other pupils. In his last school year he was joined by a first cousin, Ng See Gain (Young King) who was 12 years old when he arrived in 1922. The two became firm friends and when Uncle See Thoon died in 1983, Uncle See Gain—now the last survivor of his Ng generation in New Zealand—wept so at the funeral. Uncle continued learning English privately with Mrs Clara Porter, who taught all the young Chinese arrivals. He loved learning but circumstances were against him and he had to work in the garden and laundry. The customary aim of his time was for the young Chinese to learn at least two trades. In my childhood, I found some of his books which had obviously been read and reread. Only a few family stories remain of this period; of getting up at dawn and working till sunset in the garden; of the one or two occasions when an acerbic uncle insisted on harnessing the young men to the plough instead of horses (so the soil would not be so trampled and compacted, he said); of the uncle who used to swipe at the lads' chopsticks whenever he felt they were held or used improperly; of another who became angry whenever someone lifted the lid off the rice pot (to see the progress of cooking) because he said this let the flavour out. Ng See Gain was sent to the abattoir to buy pigs' liver, heart, trotters and stomach, which were otherwise thrown out: he was instructed to reply 'Dog' whenever the abattoir men asked him what they were wanted for.

One by one the older generation, by then in their fifties, went back for the last time to China. As was usual, the rule among them was that one received income only by active participation in work. If a man went back to China, either temporarily or permanently, his income ceased. Hence those who left sought to replace themselves with a son, or sold their share of the business, or the share was held in abeyance. But the Gore business situation changed in other ways. The market garden was flooded again and a new garden was opened further to the south of Gore. Meanwhile my father had gone, and opened a market garden at Ashburton, and because the climate there was better for growing vegetables, the young men closed the Gore Garden in the early 1920s and left either for Ashburton or the Sue Lee market garden. The laundry, however, was a good business and my grandfather and Uncle See Hoon stayed with it. When Grandfather left for the last time for China my father returned from Ashburton to take his place.

The Ng businesses illustrate the trade competition which existed between Chinese. The details are blurred today but the Chinese laundry 'Kuong Chin' closed down in Gore after my grandfather opened (in my father's time, there was a rival European laundry in Gore, run by a woman). Another Chinese market garden at Timaru and one at Tinwald, Ashburton closed after the Ngs were established in those towns. I believe these other businesses were Panyu in origin. Such business rivalry would not have transgressed the Chinese clan and county loyalties of the time. Thus Chin Fooi, a Lawrence and Dunedin laundryman who had opened a chain of three laundries, thought of expanding to Gore but desisted because he was a fellow Taishanese and a family friend.

My Uncle and father took turns to go back to China; each totalling three trips in all. My father first went in 1920 and Uncle in the mid-1920s. There Uncle married and stayed three years. In Gore itself, life did not appear too hard— or shameful. To my generation, laundrywork is odious but the old Chinese regarded it as a good means to an end and hence did not consider it a humiliating occupation. Several European families in Gore were friendly to Chinese—the Porters, Chamberlains, Grahams, Browns and others now unknown. A half-caste friend, Victor Meechang, took father and uncle eeling and shooting rabbits. They developed an interest in cars; one day, my father ran over and killed a sheep dog which had rushed at his car and the shepherd cried but did not blame him. They took provisions weekly to the last Chinese miner at Waikaia. Chinese relations and friends arrived on visits, especially from Invercargill. But the highlights of their lives were their trips back to China.

The Gore laundry supported an employee whenever one brother was away. My grandfather had earned about £2 weekly and could save about half. An example of his frugality was the saving of cigarette butts, the tobacco of which he rolled into new cigarettes. My father and Uncle earned about £5 weekly once past the Depression years. Occasionally a relative arrived to learn the trade. In this way the old New Zealand–Chinese passed on methods of work, which explains why their market gardens, laundries and fruitshops used to look so similar in each trade. Each trade had its particular skills. The laundries had to impart a shine to starched collars and 'stiff' (starched dress) shirts, and cope with dry cleaning. In the former aspect the Chinese laundries were supreme, and European laundries were to concentrate more and more on the more lucrative, less time-consuming dry cleaning.

In 1929, my father returned from China with my oldest brother, aged seven.

The Catholic Church sponsored him as a student as it did for many other Chinese students and did not charge for his education nor for that of his cousin, Ng Garr Yam (Thomas Ng), who followed him to Gore. They were the first of the next Ng generation to come to this country. Both are now deceased; both returned to Christianity when they grew older; one as a Catholic.

In 1939, the New Zealand immigration laws were relaxed for Chinese wives and young children to come as war refugees. Many Panyu and Zengcheng families were already refugees, their territory invaded by the Japanese. Some had fled to Hong Kong, Macau and Zhangiang, where they could embark for overseas destinations. Taishan city was not occupied till 1942 and so despite the bombing of the Taishan–Xinhui–Jiangmen railway and Japanese forays, most Taishan families stayed where they were. Besides, it was further for them to flee to Hong Kong and Macau, the two chief refugee ports. Thus the refugee families who made it to New Zealand In 1939–41 were principally of Panyu and Zengcheng descent. The reunion of Seyip families in New Zealand mainly began after the war.

But mail to Taishan was still possible via circuitous routes from Macau and my father in New Zealand repeatedly urged my mother to leave with my second brother and me. At first she was reluctant to face the unknown, but in 1941 she agreed and took the old migrant route, walking to Guanghai on the coast, where we boarded a junk for Hong Kong. We were in one of the last Chinese refugee parties to come to New Zealand, because Hong Kong fell shortly after we left. Unfortunately, Uncle and Auntie made their moves too late and she and her children missed out on coming. With our impending arrival, Uncle generously handed his share of the Gore laundry over to my father and left to work in a Wellington laundry.

There he witnessed the influx of American servicemen to New Zealand in 1942. This led to the official encouragement of Chinese market gardens to increase vegetable production, to feed the soldiers in their camps near Wellington. Prime Minister P. Fraser himself urged the formation of a Chinese Commercial Growers' Association. The Americans also created a demand for Chinese food, hence the beginnings of the modern growth in Chinese restaurants in New Zealand; before that, there were few Chinese restaurants and Chinese cooking was generally looked down upon in this country. It is said that Joe Ah Chan of Thames at last found a good market for his fortified wines with the American soldiers. Uncle figured that the Americans needed laundry work as well and opened a successful laundry at Paekakariki. Subsequently he shifted back to Wellington and bought the Chan Foon laundry at 5 Marjoribanks St. He built a mezzanine floor for a bedroom in preparation for the arrival of his wife and three sons, who came in 1947. They had survived the terrible Taishan famine of 1942–44.

Uncle's laundry was much like any other, with a tiny foyer for customers, who were served across a bench arranged like a bank teller's space. They were given handwritten or stamped tickets for their parcels; the other half of the ticket was kept for the parcel and its number was written on the clothing labels with indelible ink, a dirty job in itself. Behind the bench was the ironing room, comprising two tables. Flat and electric irons were used, the former for shining starched collars and dinner shirts. Above the tables the wrapped clean clothing was arranged on racks, ready for the customers. A drying room, strung with clothes lines, used two coke-fed Buchanan pot-belly stoves, which also heated the flat irons. The washing room contained tubs, a hot water copper and assorted washing and spin-drying machines. The yard was small in area, and it too was strung with clothes lines. Living quarters included a combined kitchen and dining room, in one corner of which was placed the mangle; this was heated by gas and used for the initial shining of the starched collars. There was one bedroom additional to the mezzanine room and on top of the former was a space for a bed, between the bedroom ceiling and the roof of the building. All the rooms were tiny.

Like many newly-arrived New Zealand-Chinese families Uncle could not afford to rent or buy a separate home. His family lived in the laundry and a fourth son was born and raised there; however, the oldest son and then the second oldest, left when they began work. Uncle closed the Chan Foon laundry in 1981 but left it in its original condition. The mangle, machines, stoves, parcels and such were left as they were on the day of closure. After his death in 1983, Auntie lived alone in the shop until 1986. Because it was the last Chinese laundry in New Zealand the Alexander Turnbull Library photographed it and Television New Zealand filmed the interior before it was gutted and renovated in 1987. The outside shell of the laundry still remains.

My mother and I visited Uncle and Auntie in 1949 and stayed with them. I recall a happy time, including an expedition to catch large crabs for food, using baited cages. We called on other Chinese and I remember numerous Chinese shops in central Wellington. . . . In those days the Maori people had not migrated to the cities in any great number, and the sight of a person with black hair was almost certain to be Chinese. I was instructed to always greet a fellow Chinese politely, and invite them back to tea.

As in many New Zealand-Chinese families, Uncle's two eldest sons had received a Chinese education but were too old to receive much of a formal English one. Hence they went into trades. Uncle's oldest son went to work in a European factory, at that time a relatively new experience for New Zealand-Chinese. Eventually he and his New Zealand-born brother have become a pharmacist and insurance broker respectively.

My uncle was an average New Zealand-Chinese of his generation, and was somewhat overshadowed by my father, who was more outgoing and quicker to act. He was an honest, hardworking man who despite the big number of Chinese in Wellington minded his own business. He was not closely involved in the New Zealand-Chinese Association and indeed he was a retiring person in both the Chinese and European communities. It is ironic therefore, that one of his worst experiences occurred when he went outside his Wellington laundry to take a breather and passing youths bashed him up for 'looking at the girls.' He read extensively and kept up to date with both Chinese and European newspapers. Emphatically he had pride of race and possessed strong moral views. He held wide ranging, interesting discussions with me and earnestly advised me to join the insurance industry, which he believed had good openings for Chinese. He was not a simple man but lived simply. He earned his money by toil and was not rich. He did not smoke, gamble or drink alcohol; he was a self-contained man. When he knew he was dying he faced death head on, stayed home and refused further medical treatment.

The last time I saw him alive, in 1980, was the last time my father and he met also. Both men knew that the other had failing health but greeted each other in the undemonstrative Cantonese way. They clasped hands briefly and Uncle asked Dad to sit and take tea. It was all very simple and dignified.

Recently I met Auntie again, and as always she was quiet and modest. For six years in China she had cared for Grandmother, who had suffered a dense herniplegia. She left China only after Grandmother died. Besides this, she and her children and Grandmother went through fearful privation when contact was lost with New Zealand during the war. In Wellington she brought up her youngest children in the laundry, whilst working in the shop as well. My mind cast back to my own laundry days, of my parents getting up before dawn to stoke up the copper, of the heat of stoves and irons and mangle in summer, of raining days when the clothes had to be dried inside, when better business meant more dirty clothes. All this she bore. She and Uncle epitomise the solid, patient qualities of our forebears, upon which we Chinese–New Zealanders have built our successes today.

Wing Loong village, the Ng's ancestral village, from across its pond.

ODE TO THE EIGHT IMMORTALS
(and remembering one over the eight, Denis Glover)

C. K. Stead

One who could sleep on horseback;
one who, invited to the Court of the Emperor
arrived with two flagons—his 'contribution';
one, a Prime Minister, big spender of public money
especially after the dandelion port;
one—young, rich, handsome, well-dressed—
who had everything to lose
and the determination to waste no time
in losing it;
one, a devout Buddhist who swore off all meats
but kept wine as his path to Enlightenment;
one a thirsty poet whose subtlest haikus
were costed in bottles;
one a calligrapher who, for just half a flagon,
could do you mist, mountains, waterfalls
seen through the branches of a fir tree;
and finally a poor man, a man of no consequence,
whose eloquence in his cups was inebriation's
finest flower—
these the poet Du Fu celebrated
as the Eight Immortal Drinkers
deserving commemoration
and eternal honour.
Let's raise our glasses then, in salute to them all
and not forgetting our own unquenchable Denis
laureate of the grain
Nobel of the grape.

'WITH YOU IN CHARGE . . .'

On 30 April 1976 New Zealand Prime Minister Robert Muldoon met Chairman Mao Zedong, the third last foreign leader to do so before Mao's death. Then Secretary of Foreign Affairs Frank Corner is on Mr Muldoon's left. The occasion was a momentous one for both New Zealand and China, although for rather different reasons. The event has a place in China's history because it was at the conclusion of that meeting (and after the departure of the New Zealand Prime Minister) that Chairman Mao famously endorsed Premier Hua Guofeng as his successor with the words, 'With you in charge, my mind is at ease.'

毛主席亲自接见革命接班人华国峰同志

人民美术出版社　一九七六年　定价：0.16元

HE PAKIAKA

Patricia Tauroa

In May 1984 a Maori Delegation led by the Race Relations Conciliator for New Zealand, Mr Hiwi Tauroa, visited China at the invitation of the Chinese People's Association for Friendship with Foreign Countries. The friendships established at this time led to a plan to create within the New Zealand Embassy a room decorated in the traditional Maori way. With the support and participation of many individuals and tribal groups within New Zealand, the plan was realized in full, and the whare taonga, He Pakiaka, was opened and dedicated on 28 March 1988, in the presence of Rewi Alley and the New Zealand Prime Minister, Rt Hon David Lange.

I nga ra o mua
I te waonui on Tane koe e tuu ana
Kati inaianei,
Ko koe tena, ke Tane whakapiripiri.

In recent days
You stood as part of the Great Forest
But now
You are here drawing people together in warmth and love.

TIME TO GO

Mervyn Cull

New Zealand Herald *journalist Mervyn Cull travelled to China in 1989 to take up a position as a 'polisher', monitoring and correcting the English usage of Chinese journalists. Caught in Beijing at the time of the Tienanmen demonstrations and the brutal armed response of 4 June, he and his wife Ann accepted the Embassy's advice to leave China. Three months later Cull returned to complete his contract.*

Tuesday, 6 June, brought with it a sense of unreality for the foreigners at the Friendship Hotel. Radio Beijing was on the air with an English-language news bulletin at 7 a.m. It was a bizarre collage of items that accorded top priority to the appointment of a new Iranian leader, followed by a report about Pakistan. The third item was a pronouncement by the Chinese Foreign Minister that the country would 'adhere to its policy of economic reform and opening to the outside world'. About the massacre there was nothing.

Then there we were, talking to a party of Australian tourists who had just arrived by bus for lunch. They had flown into Beijing the previous Saturday and had spent Sunday and Monday being guided around tourist attractions on the outskirts of the city. The morning of their arrival at our hotel had been spent visiting the Summer Palace. Now they wanted somewhere to eat. Strangely, it seemed to them, their Chinese driver had had trouble finding one. All the restaurants to which he usually took tourist parties were closed. Only by chance had he reached the Friendship Hotel, where he discovered that the dining rooms were working more or less normally.

For the tourists, the change of itinerary was immaterial. Beijing was new and fascinating to them. The groups of armed soldiers they had passed, and the carcasses of buses and trucks littering the boulevards here and there, were accepted as odd characteristics of life in the Chinese capital.

The massacre had occurred late on the night of their arrival. It was too late to make the television news bulletins, even if the Chinese authorities had wished it to be shown. The *China Daily* did not appear on the Sunday, Monday or Tuesday, and the English-language broadcasts from Radio Beijing would have told them nothing. So they had arrived at the Friendship Hotel in complete ignorance of all that had happened.

Ann enlightened them. An Australian FE had told us at lunch that his embassy was calling all its nationals preparatory to evacuation by a special flight the next day. That was unsettling news for the tourists, but they were grateful for the information, and they assured Ann that they would head straight for the embassy. All around us were signs that other foreigners were leaving the hotel, and China. The fear of some Western analysts was that different armies converging on, or already in, Beijing would line up on different sides, some troops taking up the cause of the students, and others defending the hard-liners. Civil war seemed imminent. At the risk of sounding incredibly selfish, we asked where a civil war would leave us, living as we were in the heart of the university district where all the unrest had begun. The answer that came most easily was 'right in the middle of it'; the Friendship Hotel would almost certainly be part of the battleground. So cars and buses had been arriving at the hotel all morning, and leaving with cargoes of grim-faced residents and hastily packed luggage. The Irish Embassy had sent a special car for David, the only foreigner we knew to be evacuated in such style. But he was the only Irishman there—that is, until he pronounced Barrie, his English colleague at the Thomson school at Xinhua, an honorary Irishman, which meant that he could leave with David. David, as it turned out, was to spend most of that afternoon lying on the floor of the embassy shielding a couple of children for fear of the bullets still flying around that quarter of the city.

The Australians, boarding their bus, asked us, 'Can we give you a lift? We might be able to drop you somewhere near your own embassy.' No thanks. We saw no need to leave just then. We felt confident that *Longmarch* would look after us if the need arose. We would take our chances.

'How about your wife? Would she like to come with us?'

Ann said no, she would stay with me. O God, I thought, this is getting more and more like a corny movie. Next I shall be spitting out a stream of tobacco juice and saying that I'm saving my last bullet for my wife. Them heathen Redskins won't get her.

We went upstairs to the apartment. That bloody helicopter was chuckering overhead again. I tried several times to telephone *Longmarch* for advice, but could rouse no one. The Susie rang to say that she had bought me the Webster's dictionary—for ninety-eight yuan; I could pay her when she brought it round. I wondered where she had raised the money, but presumed that it had come by courtesy of a well-developed system of borrowing and lending that Chinese students seemed to have organised. I determined to pay her back as soon as possible in case we should have to leave abruptly. A ninety-eight yuan debt could leave her in desperate financial straits.

Ann and I walked over to the market across the street from the hotel and stocked up on bread and other items we thought we would need if conditions deteriorated. We returned to the hotel to hear the telephone ringing. It was the New Zealand Embassy, which had been trying to reach us all day. Its advice was, 'Get out, if you can.' All its transport was fully committed and it could not send a car for us. All New Zealanders were being asked to consolidate at the Kunlun Hotel, on the other side of Beijing and much closer to the airport than the Friendship. They would spend the night there and leave for the airport in the morning to join the Qantas evacuation flight with the Australians.

Alex came in; so I passed on the advice and he telephoned *Longmarch* for me. With his command of Chinese, he stood a better chance of finding someone than I did and he managed to rouse Mr Fu Zhen-yuan, the head of the English department. His advice was to stay where we were. He would personally guarantee our safety. All would be resolved 'soon'. We decided to stay.

Five minutes later Mr Fen Yang-jin telephoned. His advice, as a personal friend rather than an employer, was to leave—again with the provision 'if you can'.

It was time to go.

Ann and I had already packed some luggage—a shoulder bag each if we should be restricted to bare essentials, and two or three suitcases graded in importance. If we were lucky and cargo space were no problem, we would take them all. Even so, that would mean leaving behind all the household items and food, some clothes, my typewriter and our two bicycles. At that moment, Doug came in. He had been in Beijing for a month, a New Zealander working on a six-month contract as an English polisher on the *Beijing Review*. He had decided to stay on—he was old and stubborn, he said—and he offered to look after as much as he could for me, pending my return.

We went down to the restaurant for dinner and to say goodbye to friends, but we did not feel hungry. On the way back we looked for a taxi to take us to the Kunlun. The twenty or thirty cars usually stationed in the compound had long since disappeared and our quest seemed hopeless. Kunlun was too far away to reach on foot. But once again Alex came to the rescue. With his web of Chinese contacts, he managed to get a taxi from somewhere. He, his daughter and her infant son, Ann and I piled in, bags and bundles stuffed around us, the boot so full that the lid was left flapping, and we set off for the Kunlun. The streets as we headed east were practically deserted. Burnt-out vehicles were scattered along the way, and in places the road was littered with fist-sized rocks, presumably ammunition that had been used against advancing troops.

The ride to the Kunlun cost us twenty times the normal fare, and we were glad to pay it, for that driver understood exactly how to handle the hazards. He knew where the soldiers were, and how to bypass them; he knew when to turn off the ordinary road and plough down through loose metal to a motorway under construction, its unsealed surface deeply rutted by the wheels of earth-moving equipment; he knew how to remove the barriers erected to keep out unauthorised vehicles, and how to replace them so that our passage left no trace; he knew how not to attract the attention of soldiers standing under the trees along the route as we drew nearer the hotel—'Don't look at them.'

Those days of decision in Beijing stirred my national pride. I know of no embassy that did more to care for its nationals than the New Zealand Embassy, but I have heard of some that did very much less, and of at least one that did nothing at all. Moreover, the New Zealand Ambassador and his staff did everything with an imperturbability that inspired confidence among the evacuees. One could have thought that an evacuation from a foreign capital was an everyday occurrence.

We spent the night at the Kunlun in rooms that the embassy had booked for us, and next morning assembled outside for the transport that was to take us to the airport. On the footpath beside us was the heavy embassy seal, which had been brought in case it were needed to issue documents in a hurry. An embassy minibus, a huge New Zealand flag draped along its side, drew up at the curb. According to one report, which I have never seen confirmed, troops had fired on a Japanese party heading for the airport that morning. At least we would not be mistaken for more Japanese.

We packed ourselves on board, and Rachel, the senior typist at the embassy, took the wheel, with her husband beside her. As she revved the engine and released the clutch, she called to us passengers, 'If we see any soldiers, don't look them in the eye. And if they start shooting, lie on the floor.' It was said in a semi-jocular tone, but we knew she was serious. If we all followed those instructions in that little vehicle, we would have to lie two or three deep, and I wondered how much the thin body panels of the bus would withstand if bullets really started to fly.

The ambassador was standing on the pavement. As we moved off, he shouted to us, 'Good luck!'

Did he sound as though he thought we would need it?

The drive to the airport was uneventful. We never looked a soldier in the eye, although we passed many, and we remained vertical. The airport building was crowded and bustling, but we saw no signs of panic. We New Zealanders stayed together in a loose group, signing papers that undertook to reimburse the Australian Government for our airfares when we reached home. We listened to rumours, never substantiated, that troops had entered Beijing Normal University and shot two hundred students, and that other troops had entered Beida and shot four student leaders.

Rachel was standing in the open, with her back to the wall of the airport building. In her hand was a long French loaf. She was cutting it into three or four segments, and then slicing each lengthwise. She buttered the pieces, then extracted from a box a tin of Watties sweet corn, which she spread over the slices. Meanwhile, her husband was handing round cans of Fanta. Rachel saw me watching her and gave a bright Maori smile.

'Sweet-corn sandwich, Merv?'

It was a dramatic and anxious time for all foreigners, as we moved out hurriedly, most of us leaving friends and possessions behind. We had no idea what was happening in the rest of the city. For all we knew, the army might open fire on the airport at any moment. To Ann and me, standing amid it all, this offering brought new and reassuring meaning to the term 'comfort food'.

'Sweet-corn sandwich, Merv?'

'Yes please,' I replied.

GEOGRAPHICAL FOOTNOTE

The 1989 decision that New Zealand would follow evolving international practice by adopting the usage 'Beijing' rather than 'Peking' did not pass unchallenged by the traditionalists among current and former Embassy staff. Remarkably, the protest took the form of disrespectful and argumentative verses, of which the following is a representative example.

In Xanadu did Kublai Khan
A stately pleasure dome decree
Now Xanadu itself must fall
Or face the charge of cultural
Insensitivity.

Men put their faith in Zhungguo
Forsaking old Cathay
They'll have no truck with Cambaluc
It has a bad fengshui.

Maskee Macartney's dictate
Imperious Elgin's call
Maskee the mighty Mathews
And Wade and Giles and all.

I'm angry at the import
I bridle at Beijing
That can't be proper English
It has a foreign ring.

It's hated in the hutungs
It's banned in the bazaar
Around the earth it raises mirth
From Paree to Moskva.

We'll keep faith with our forebears
From taotai to taipan
The lau bai xing of old Peking
(Or if you're French, Pékin).

WRITER LIU

Mo Zhi Hong

Mo Zhi Hong is a Singapore-born writer now resident in New Zealand. This is an extract from his first novel, The Year of the Shanghai Shark, *published in New Zealand in 2008. The novel is set in Harbin.*

Once, Xiao Wang wanted to know what Writer Liu's favourite movie was.

'Oh, it depends on the category of the movie,' he said.

Xiao Wang scratched his head.

'For example, action, or comedy, or science fiction, etc, etc,' Writer Liu said.

'Well, how about action then?' Xiao Wang asked.

'You have to be more specific,' he said. 'There are many different types of action film. For example, Hong Kong-style Gong Fu, or western style with cars and guns, or old-fashioned police cases. A good example of a typical western-style film would be . . .'

He talked and talked and talked.

And soon we had forgotten all about the question.

It was one thing we quickly learned. Writer Liu loved to talk about films. After the end of every film he would attempt to raise a discussion about what we had just seen. He would say things like, 'What did you think of the characterisation of the minor roles?' or, 'I thought the repeated use of the red theme in every scene was overdone.' And our favourite: 'Did you notice the protagonist's inner struggle?'

There seemed to be a lot of inner struggling in the movies he watched.

And we felt that he expected a little too much from us.

While we were watching a film about a Hong Kong policeman he asked us, 'Did you pay attention to the way the camera remained still for almost the entire fight scene? You don't see that much any more.'

'No,' Po Fan said. 'I was too busy watching the fight.'

Later, Writer Liu began to talk, and Po Fan said, 'The man just beat up twenty other men all by himself. I don't think you should spoil it by talking about how he feels. But since you ask, I say that he feels tired.'

From then on Writer Liu refrained from asking us about the 'inner struggle'.

Writer Liu's apartment was a mess. The floor was covered entirely with movie cases, paper and books. That winter the only occasion I saw it tidy was the time Xiao Wang, Po Fan and I helped him to move in. Looking at his main room, it was hard to believe that all the things in his apartment had originally been packed into those boxes.

He was an untidy man.

And he was very thorough in his untidiness. He was not, for example, one of those people who is untidy but takes good care of their appearance. No, Writer Liu's appearance was as untidy as his apartment. His long hair was greasy, and his clothes were rumpled and worn in a loose, scruffy way. His glasses were always dirty.

Writer Liu was single.

We liked him that way. It meant he had lots of free time.

One Saturday afternoon, Writer Liu fulfilled a promise he had many times made to us. He took us to the cinema to see a movie.

We caught the bus to You Hao Square, and Writer Liu bought four tickets at the big cinema theatre. Only Xiao Wang had been to a cinema theatre before. And though he tried to appear relaxed, we could see the excitement in his wobbling cheeks.

The movie amazed us.

Inside, the theatre was noisy and smoky. People nearby talked and puffed on cigarettes. Hand phones rang frequently. When the Hong Kong actors spoke, laughter rippled through the audience.

But we didn't care about that.

In fact we didn't even pay much attention to the plot.

It was the sight of the enormous images on the screen, moving and talking and fighting, that held us for the two hours the movie ran for. We had seen nothing like it. The outdoor screen at Labour Park was a small and feeble thing by comparison.

We left the movie theatre filled with wonder.

After it had finished, we stood outside the cinema on the pavement. Xiao Wang and Po Fan discussed their favourite scenes, but I couldn't remember any. The only thought in my mind was that I simply had to go again.

Gradually we realised that we were waiting outside the cinema for no reason.

Writer Liu had a keen expression on his face. Several older women began to approach him before noticing us and stopping abruptly. It was cold, but they weren't wearing too much. I could see them shivering slightly.

Writer Liu stared at them intently.

I thought immediately of Worker Chen.

I didn't like to think of Writer Liu as that sort of man. Back at his apartment, I asked as innocently as I could if he had seen the women.

To my relief, he wasn't embarrassed. 'I'm going to write their story,' he said.

'Whose story?' Xiao Wang asked.

'Those women outside the movie theatre,' Writer Liu said.

'What women?' Xiao Wang said.

Po Fan didn't even bother to lift his hand. He just rolled his eyes and shook his head.

'What will you write about them?' I asked.

'I will write about their inner struggle,' he said.

This worried us.

'But how do you know they have one?' We weren't sure that such women had any struggle, outer or inner.

'Everyone has an inner struggle,' he said. And the way he spoke made us think that perhaps an inner struggle was worth having after all. Maybe even worth writing about.

For a while all we saw of Writer Liu was his back. He sat in front of his computer, typing or thinking with his hands on his bowed head. We started letting ourselves in to his apartment and playing movies. He would rarely look up at us.

His apartment attained a previously unknown level of uncleanliness.

He thought and wrote and thought and wrote.

One grey cold afternoon we were in his apartment watching a movie he had left out for us. A young schoolteacher from the countryside had come to the city in search of a missing student.

I thought fondly of Fish and wondered how he was.

The apartment was warm and stuffy. Both Po Fan and Xiao Wang were nodding off.

Suddenly, Writer Liu turned off his computer and sat down on the sofa next to Xiao Wang with a thump. Xiao Wang blinked.

Po Fan yawned. 'What's going on? Have you finished writing about the women?'

Writer Liu nodded.

'Can we read it?' I asked eagerly.

Writer Liu shook his head. His eyes looked very red.

'Why not?' Xiao Wang asked, full of ignorant bravery.

But Writer Liu only sighed.

'Those women have no real story,' he said. 'It's not worth writing anything meaningful about them.' Then he added loftily, 'They are merely small droplets on the surface of a glistening pond of lilies.'

Even Po Fan had to admit that it sounded quite poetic.

'Do you have any big friends?' I asked Writer Liu as he was changing disks. The movie we were watching had come to halfway.

'Yes, I have adult friends,' he said.

'Do you ever visit them?'

'Yes, sometimes,' he said, then considered. 'Actually, not often.'

'Do they ever visit you?'

'Never,' he replied without hesitation.

Writer Liu sat down on the sofa beside us as the second half of the movie began. It was a wonderful fairy tale about a young girl whose baby brother was kidnapped by goblins. In the end the young girl defeated the goblin king, rescued her brother and returned home.

When the movie had finished and we were drinking our bottles of Coca-Cola I asked him, 'Why don't your friends ever visit you?'

'They're too busy, I think. They have jobs, wives, and some even have children,' he said.

'Don't you want a wife and a child too?' Po Fan asked.

'No.'

'Why not?'

'You are a most inquisitive young mind,' he smiled at Po.

Po Fan was not to be put off so easily. 'But why not?' Writer Liu shrugged in an irritated way.

'I have better things to do,' he said.

Writer Liu was always starting to write things but never finishing. In between starts he would read and watch movies, become very excited, then move on to his next piece.

One time he read a story about a gravedigger who gets buried alive, then sat at his computer for a week and grew an odd-looking beard. On another occasion he was inspired by a Japanese movie about a strange building that people go to after they die for a final ritual before heaven.

He consumed vast quantities of instant noodles.

'You could write a story about me,' Xiao Wang told him.

Po Fan and I burst out laughing.

'You're a little young,' Writer Liu said gently. 'Your story hasn't begun yet.'

'Okay. When it begins, you have my permission to write about me,' Xiao Wang said proudly.

Writer Liu smiled.

'Why do you never finish the pieces you start writing?' Po Fan asked one day.

I looked at him with alarm, but he shrugged.

'A . . .' Writer Liu began, then stopped.

There was a pause. Xiao Wang raised his hand to cuff Po Fan but thought better of it.

'Actually,' Writer Liu began again, 'it is to do with freedom.

I have many stories I would like to write, but I don't have the freedom to do so.'

We looked at each other in confusion.

'What does freedom have to do with it?' Po Fan asked. 'Everything,' Writer Liu said solemnly. 'Freedom is the basic ingredient of all artistic endeavour. All artistry comes from the same source—oneself. And to express yourself artistically, you must first be free and unconstrained. Without freedom, my young friends, there is no art.'

It sounded good.

But we still didn't understand why he wasn't free.

'You're too young to comprehend,' Writer Liu told us. 'In the future, when you're older, perhaps I will be able to explain to you.'

'*Ayo,*' Xiao Wang said as we were leaving Writer Liu's apartment, 'maybe Writer Liu has a wife he doesn't tell us about.'

'What?' Po Fan said.

'Well, after my mother makes him stop smoking in the apartment my father always complains that women take away a man's freedom.'

'Don't be silly. If he had a wife we would have seen her by now,' Po Fan said.

'Maybe a girlfriend?' Xiao Wang shrugged.

And we began to wonder.

'If he has a girlfriend I know what she'll have,' Po Fan said, and he smiled wickedly.

We looked at him.

'An inner struggle,' he giggled.

We were watching a frightening film about human robots from the future when Writer Liu announced his next project to us.

'I am going to write a movie screenplay,' he proclaimed.

Xiao Wang and I had our eyes shut at the time. Only Po Fan could watch the most frightening parts of the film without turning away.

'Good idea!' Po Fan said. 'You've seen so many movies you should be able to write one even if you haven't found freedom yet.'

Writer Liu beamed happily.

When the movie finally finished we asked him what his screenplay would be about.

'It should be an action movie,' Po Fan said. 'They're the most popular. And you won't even need to write much. You can just write things like "A big fight happens", or "They chase each other in cars, shooting pistols".'

Writer Liu looked hurt.

'It is going to be about the Cultural Revolution,' he said at last. 'A forbidden love story set during the years of upheaval.'

We looked at him doubtfully. The screenplay sounded boring already.

'To truly represent China, one must go back to the Cultural Revolution,' Writer Liu continued. 'It was both the beginning and the source of what China is today.'

'Really? But who cares what happened back then? No one will go and see your film,' Xiao Wang said.

'Foreigners will,' he said, smiling. 'Foreigners always enjoy watching films about the Cultural Revolution. For example, *Farewell My Concubine*. Foreigners loved that film.'

'They did?' I asked.

'Of course,' he replied.

We looked at each other. None of us had made it through that film awake.

'But why?' we asked.

'It doesn't matter,' he shrugged, 'they just do.'

He was supremely confident.

'Wait wait wait,' Po Fan said. 'Foreigners like watching action films more. Or films about big sinking boats even. I'm sure of it. Listen, I have a great idea for an action film. It's about a young schoolboy with an inner struggle whose parents are kidnapped and . . .'

But Writer Liu was not to be dissuaded.

As Writer Liu progressed on his screenplay we began to notice changes. The curtains in his apartment, once always open, were now permanently closed. After a month, he disconnected his phone. Sometimes he would give us money and ask us to buy food for him.

We bought him instant noodles, ice cream and Coca-Cola.

Once, as we dumped bags and bags of groceries on his cluttered table, he said, 'This is the price you pay, my young friends.'

'The price of instant noodles?' Xiao Wang asked.

'No. The price of freedom,' he said.

'Oh,' Xiao Wang said.

I began to understand.

'Is that why you have your curtains drawn all the time? And your telephone disconnected? So you can be free?' I asked.

'Yes yes yes,' he said. 'There are people who would want to stop me from writing this screenplay if they knew about it. In this way, I am protecting my work.'

'What people?' I asked.

'People,' he said heavily.

'How do you know they would try to stop you?' Po Fan asked.

'They would. Believe me,' he said earnestly.

I looked at Po Fan. He shrugged.

'Don't worry,' Xiao Wang said. 'We believe you. And we won't tell anyone what you're doing.'

Writer Liu smiled. It was a haggard, weak thing.

The next month the weather was warmer. The playground began to get busier and busier.

And we saw less and less of Writer Liu.

The occasions we did drop by were silent and uncomfortable. Writer Liu would spend the entire time staring at the computer screen or pacing in his kitchen; he would always be drinking. Sometimes we would come in to find him watching a movie. But the movies he had taken to watching were all long and boring. Often, he would ignore us completely or mutter angrily at our questions.

His apartment stank.

'He's never going to finish his screenplay,' Po Fan said. 'He should have used my action-movie idea.'

'Shut up. We need to encourage him,' Xiao Wang said angrily.

But none of us really believed he would finish.

We came upon him sitting on his sofa, asleep. At his feet were many tall green bottles of Black Lion beer. They were all empty.

He woke up and looked at us with bleary eyes. He needed a bath.

'Hello Mr Liu,' I said. 'How are you?'

He burped and shook his head ruefully.

'How is the screenplay going?' Xiao Wang asked.

'Not very well, my young friends. The goldfish pond is still half empty.' He shook his head again. 'I need something to inspire me once more. A movie, a book, a single line of poetry . . . anything.'

'None of your movies work?' Po Fan asked.

'Nothing in this worthless pile—'he waved his hand over the mess of movies—'is inspiring me at this moment.'

'You just need more freedom perhaps,' Xiao Wang told him.

'Yes yes yes! That's definitely it!' He sat up, nodding his head and looking at us with excitement. 'More freedom, more freedom, more freedom. Freedom will release my mind and allow me to work. Yes yes yes, certainly. But how to get it, *a?*'

We looked at our shoes.

Writer Liu sank back into his sofa with a black look of frustration.

'I am a fraud,' he said to us. 'I am a trickster, a thief, a nothing. I am no writer.'

He turned and looked at us morosely; his breath made my head feel light.

'I am exactly like that man there.' He pointed at the television screen. We were watching a movie about a short European composer. Writer Liu pointed at the composer's rival.

'Worthless worthless worthless,' he said. All I can do is look and understand and love and nothing more.' He paused. 'It is a terrible thing, young friends,' he continued, waving his hands, 'to be able to feel true art and to be powerless to create it.'

It was a line from the movie.

Before it had finished, Writer Liu was fast asleep and snoring slightly.

We left the apartment to the tragic sound of violins and a classical orchestra.

A few weeks later we went to Writer Liu's apartment after school to see how he was. To our surprise, he was in good spirits.

The apartment had changed dramatically.

The curtains were open once more, the phone reconnected and all of the movies and books were packed away in the big boxes we had originally helped carry into the apartment. The floor and shelves were entirely clear.

Writer Liu was mopping.

'Are you leaving the building?' Xiao Wang asked worriedly.

'No no no,' he replied. 'But I've decided to put all these movies away. They take up far too much space really. And I don't think I've ever cleaned this floor.'

'What about the screenplay?' Po Fan asked.

'A, I'm taking a break from it until I feel inspired again,' he said. 'I'll come back to it eventually, but right now I think it's healthier for me to weigh and consider what will come next.'

Writer Liu put the mop in the bucket and leaned on it.

'Also, I have some news for you boys,' he said. 'I've got a job now. I'm a worker in the stationery section in Walmart supermarket . . . you know the one, right? By Olympic Square.'

We nodded.

'So I won't be able to watch movies in the afternoons with you much any more. This new job will keep me very busy.'

'Does this mean you aren't a writer any more?' I asked. It seemed to me a rather sad end.

'Certainly I am,' he replied. 'As long as I am a free man I can be a writer. I still have it here'—he tapped his heart with his hand—'and here'—he tapped his head. 'Never fear, my young friends. I will still write.'

And he smiled at us with his old confidence.

In the years following we saw Writer Liu only occasionally, but we always kept an eye out for any movie matching his screenplay idea. And now, though I live in a foreign country and feel that perhaps there might be more to a successful screenplay than what Writer Liu originally thought, I still eagerly await the finished product of what he started so long ago.

Perhaps he is working on it even now, or perhaps he still waits for sufficient inspiration.

Or perhaps he is waiting for a time when he truly feels free.

TWO POEMS

Diana Bridge

Pond

1

All winter I have harried the pond
with restless visiting.

As rain heats like drummed lament
on the glass roof and a fan worries

the edge of sight, I remember something
missed. How buds on the Chinese lake

that June rose from leaves like these,
to take on the shape of stupas—each

pleated bulb closed like a cone on hope.

2

The lotuses have flown,
acquired visas and migrated to

the middle of this pool. Here
they huddle, like with like.

Precarious, unrooted; community
is all. Their sons and daughters

rise on curving stems,
turning the plates of their small-featured

faces to the light, as if to music.

Begonia House, Botanical Gardens, Wellington

In a Chinese cemetery

I would structure silence in this way.
A small house set securely in its space,
enclosed by horseshoe walls—arms
rounded, ready to embrace. Lintel and
portico bright with tiled symbol—
happiness red, dream blue—gleaming
with Christmas cracker couplets
more parallel than true.

If you lay in a tomb like one of these
I would call oftener than I do
and sit on the rim of a sun-warmed wall,
a low grey knee, putting behind me
evening, the city gathering in its brooding
dirty air; share your perspective: hills
thrown up in the old volcanic way,
become vistas—spare on line, recession,
spare on everything but time.

Some of the tombs wear crosses, toetoe
wave their spears. Your house fronts,
as it always did, onto a place where children play;
its miniature domain is grassed and planted,
your daughter comes each day. The story
is not yours. Above this pine and cypress track,
this avenue of graves, a fist of cloud opens
and spatters outsize drops of rain.

Dozens of distant little roofs crumble
like the shells of poems, glimpsed, arranged
and given up on. You are as absent now as god
and all my metaphors have changed.
Hinted at opposite on the ravine, the profile
of some Buddha come to share the fullness and
the nothingness of silence, limbs eroded,
smile serene, paws folded.

A PARTICULAR OCCASION

John Needham

John Needham taught for many years in the English Department of Massey University in Palmerston North. This excerpt is taken from a compilation of writing based on journeys, in which Needham sets out to test theoretical ideas in the light of his suspicion that 'travel brings the theorist down to earth'.

At the top of the steps we lean against the cool stone of the battlements and look back. The Great Wall tumbles and climbs its way over the mountain ridges, just as it does in all the pictures, disappearing at last into the blue distance. Down on the plain to the south we can make out a tiny patchwork of fields and the dots of houses. The plain to the north is just a silvery-green blur glimpsed here and there beyond further hills. The breeze is cool but the sun is warm, and on the slopes below us the plum trees are white with blossom. And of course the real lines of defence are now elsewhere—in remote compounds, with high perimeter fences and missiles in buried silos. The amiable clown who wanders the battlements in Manchu warrior garb, crying 'boo' and waving his sword to startle the tourists, is theme-park 'tradition' at its emptiest.

But the Wall remains none the less a potent image of war. We can still imagine the ancient stir of fear and excitement here on the steps when puffs of smoke from some distant watchtower signalled the approach of the enemy—Tamburlaine, perhaps, or Genghis. My son—his mother is Chinese—has just recalled that this is the only human construct visible from the moon. Sad mark of a divided world. One's particular perception—of these stones, these blossoms, these jagged mountains—seems to figure the whole history of humankind.

But thoughts about this unfashionable cluster of terms—the idea and the image, the general and the particular, the natural and the new; all those pairs that Coleridge saw as unified by the imagination—have been flitting in and out of my mind for some time. Yesterday was my elder daughter's wedding—the reason for my being in Beijing—and it was of course a very particular occasion, an affair of family and friends. In the garden of the embassy where she works, we danced till morning with no historic consequence at all, but tomorrow I shall be meeting some Chinese writers whose lives seem inextricable from great events—Mao's victory, the persecution of the Rightists, the terrors of the Cultural Revolution, Deng's economic reforms.

Since I'm standing on one of the world's few surviving tracts of socialist soil, I naturally think of those like Professor Eagleton who reject the whole idea of 'individual consciousness, set in its small circle of relationships'; for them we are all locked into the march of history; 'particularity' is a 'humanist illusion'.

I remember my first visit to China, in 1978. The Cultural Revolution was over, and Mao's widow, Chiang Ching, was cooling her radical zeal in prison, but she was still admired by the feminists of Paris, and Beijing's Friendship Hotel still housed not only innocuous persons like myself (I was looking into I. A. Richards's use of Basic English in China) but diverse Arabs, Africans and Latin Americans whose activities were of interest to 'western' governments. It was in short still the heyday of revolution regarded as an intrinsic good, and Beijing was its powerhouse.

It was a drab, polluted city. It often reminded me of Sheffield in the 1940s, though it was of course much sunnier. It's just as sunny now, and the pollution is unabated, but history has marched vigorously on, and all else—one might think—will have changed accordingly. Or has it? One of the writers I am going to meet spent ten years of the Cultural Revolution down a coal-mine, and started university in Beijing in the year I first arrived in the city. I'll talk about history with him tomorrow; today is for the present.

After running the gauntlet of laughing, red-cheeked countrywomen hawking embroidered table-cloths and Great Wall tee-shirts at the bottom of the slope, we board our mini-bus, and drive off for a picnic lunch at the Ming Tombs.

And here of course history soon returns, though not quite on the march; history as tradition rather than development. The great artificial hills of the tombs, set in the middle of a plain encircled in turn by distant mountains, are a reminder that China is Zhong Guo, The Middle Kingdom. How different from my home in New Zealand, where, so far from being centred in space and time, you readily feel yourself on their outer edge; almost any day at all the dawn coming out of the Pacific can seem like the world's first morning, and you feel a lightness of being either unbearable or exhilarating—it's up to you.

But even a history as long as China's can rest on one lightly enough. Our particular tomb, being unrestored, is deserted, and as we spread our picnic-lunch in a sunny corner of the forecourt, with wild violets darkening the grass, and dwarf pine-trees twisting out from cracks in the high enclosing walls, history is felt only as a deeper sense of quiet.

But it is, I am conscious, a history not my own; and this seems to increase its value. After eating, we clamber up a steep and crumbling staircase onto a platform where we find a vault containing an inscribed stone tablet. We look at it with the special respect reserved for an unknown script, then disperse and wander, singly or in groups, about the tumulus—a grassy knoll perhaps a hundred and fifty yards in diameter and completely encircled by the pine-studded retaining wall. It rises up through a grove of conifers, and at its summit is a dome of small stone blocks. The dome, about twenty feet high, with no inscription or any other distinguishing feature, takes you rather by surprise, and in this, as in its suggestion of the unknown, it speaks vividly of death. Half-hidden amongst the trees and almost a continuation of the curve of the hill, its unobtrusive symmetry seems a rather Augustan 'blend of art and nature'. The particular quality of the place, the full image it presents to the senses, is unlike anything I've seen from eighteenth-century England, but Pope would have responded readily to the idea.

In Confucian China, nature was thought of neither as 'fallen' nor 'unfallen', but simply as something there, to be improved by art. In morals too the aim was to attain neither sainthood nor noble savagery, but to develop 'human heartedness', or 'jen'. And the Augustans too of course were intent on moderating the old Christian conflict between nature and art.

On a sunny May Day some ten years ago, I remember cycling with my wife and a group of students to a Roman Catholic Church outside Shanghai. 'Socialist Revolution' was already a thing of the past, but the May holiday was still kept and the countryside was full of people, eating at roadside food-stalls, shopping at the village markets, or just wandering about. The church—an undistinguished pile but impressively large and perched on the brow of a hill commanding the Yangtze plain—was back in use again and a natural focus for the holiday crowd.

On the hillside just below ran a gravelled walk, winding its way amongst rhododendrons and azaleas, and lined with the Stations of the Cross. Our students were all interested in these exotic spiritual forms, and one of them—Liu, a clever, rather dreamy fellow from Sinkiang—was really fascinated. We left him gazing, and when at length he joined us again he announced that he was going to become a Christian. His classmates generally saw him as a country boy and they mostly responded now with sidelong smiles. But one of them, called Shao, fell into a rage. We all knew why. The Cultural Revolution safely over, Shao's wife and in-laws had reverted to their former religion—some form of Protestantism, I gathered. But Shao—himself religious by temperament and patriotic to boot— had become a Taoist. He had found a teacher and was practising 'chi gung', a discipline for the mastery of 'spirit'. (On the one occasion when I met him, the teacher displayed his power by apparently causing distant objects to move about, and by mastering a remarkable quantity of spirit of the alcoholic variety.) For Shao of course Christianity was both an alien creed and a source of domestic strife.

Liu seemed to ignore his angry scorn, but later, when we started out for home, they began to play the bicycle game. The rules are simple. You overtake your opponent then suddenly brake. If you force him to stop, while you yourself keep balance and pedal on, you win. But if your opponent can swerve aside and throw you off balance, then you're the loser. There are various forms of draw, and every result is disputed. When played in the middle of a cycling crowd the game occasions a general release of high spirits. Conviviality was soon restored, and Liu's impulsiveness shortly found a new outlet—in exhortations not to return tamely to Shanghai, but to keep on riding west, like the scholar-gypsies of old, trusting to the peasants for food and shelter. A nice idea, but of course we cycled home, where Liu at last achieved some degree of self-expression by plunging into the university pool at midnight, singing wild Sinkiang songs. Swimming after dark being an offence against regulations, he was duly fined, but this penance too was obviously part of his plan; perhaps he was one of nature's Catholics after all.

Here at the Ming tombs I'm not quite so carried away as Liu by the exotic religious forms. I have more to compare them with—starting from summer holidays in childhood, when I was dragged round hot London pavements to admire the nation's memorials to its great and good; this engrained a deep dislike of obituary pomp into my aching feet. The graves that mean most to me now are those of my parents, in a Yorkshire village, with headstones straggling amongst the tussocky grass and rooks cawing in the church-yard elms. But this Chinese tomb suggests not so much an exalted assertion against death, as the greatness of death itself, and I can feel my idea of memorial grandeur take a more affirmative shape.

To suggest that an individual soul can thus alight on a congenial idea, will seem a double affront to those who believe in nothing but history. But their view of history just seems absurdly limited. They shut out the whole perspective of biology. A genetic code, to take the obvious instance, is without doubt a product of history—of evolution—but it is none the less unique and its elements are none the less universal to all humankind.

The day before the wedding I went out cycling with some family friends. We followed the old tow-path along the Grand Canal—its handsome stone embankments in good repair, though its channel is a foul industrial sink—until we came at length to a public park. Feeling hungry we left our bikes locked at the gates, and went inside to look for a noodle stall. But, unusually for China, it seemed pure park; just grass and trees and flowers and strolling citizens. Our needs being gastronomic not bucolic we strode purposefully about until at last we came upon a red-striped tent by a lake. There was a fence and a box for the sale of tickets, but this was no deterrent to the hungry. Having paid our fee, we discovered that the tent had an open front looking onto the water, and inside there was a long counter with a plastic top; they were dispensing, however, not bowls of noodles but cans of worms and fishing rods. It seemed like a surreal joke about fast food.

Then we saw the anglers. They lined the shore of the lake, almost side by side, but being Chinese they looked at ease in a crowd, and they were plainly catching fish—we could see them being hauled out. The lake, one supposes, is replenished every night with plate-sized carp.

The New Zealand angler is a more elusive soul. You might catch sight of him at evening, waist-deep in the mouth of some stream where the currents run cold and strong into a roughened iron-grey lake. So different from this sociable Beijing pond. But these Chinese men, eyes fixed on their bobbing quills, poised to strike and feel the struggle of the unseen prey, embody the same idea, the same predatory impulse, and its history far transcends the human scale.

So does the history of death. I take a last look at the discreet Ming dome amongst the trees on top of the tumulus, then turn and make my way back down to the courtyard.

As we clear away our picnic, an embodiment of the idea of a caretaker appears and hovers in the courtyard-entrance, giving the imperial dust an occasional stir with his broom. A tall, pale, slow old man, his baggy trousers, cloth cap and faded blue Chinese jacket, seem symbolic of the old socialist days. He is pleased, we find, to take our empty bottles, from which he can make a few cents, but he accepts them with a gravity befitting the custodian of a royal tomb, and he himself seems almost as remote as the emperors.

Vue Schématique de l'Ensemble d'un Tombeau Impérial

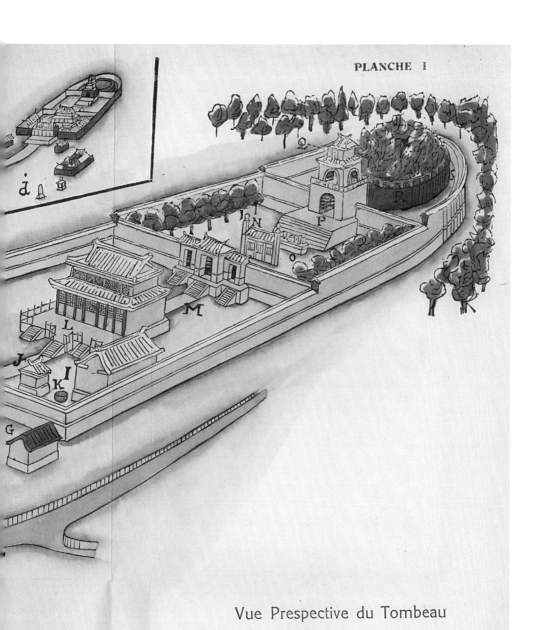

Vue Prespective du Tombeau

AN APOLOGY

Extracts from the Prime Minister's Address to Chinese New Year Celebrations, Parliament House, Wellington, 12 February 2002.

'In the late nineteenth century, the New Zealand Parliament passed discriminatory laws against Chinese seeking to enter New Zealand. The Chinese Immigrants Act of 1881 imposed a poll tax of ten pounds per Chinese person and restricted the numbers able to enter the country to one person per ten tonnes of ship cargo. In 1896 the tax was lifted to one hundred pounds per person and there were further restrictions on the numbers of Chinese able to enter New Zealand.

No other ethnic group was subjected to such restrictions or to a poll tax. Other legislative initiatives also singled out the Chinese.
• In 1908, Chinese people had to put a thumbprint on their Certificates of Registration before leaving the country—no other ethnic group had to leave thumbprints.
• Chinese people were deprived of their right to naturalisation in 1908 and this was not rescinded until 1951. No other ethnic group was deprived of this right.
• A reading test in English was introduced—other immigrants had only a writing test in their own language.
• Even in 1935 when entry permits were introduced after a suspension of 15 years for reunification of family and partners of Chinese people, they were severely restricted. . . .

Many Chinese suffered the indignity of the poll tax and the other restrictions. Arrivals in the port of Wellington between 1888 to 1930 numbered around 2100 people. In total, the estimated number who paid the poll tax between 1882 and 1930 was 4,500. The tax was not abolished until 1944. At that time, the Minister of Finance, Walter Nash referred to the 'removing of the blot on our legislation' and affirmed that the government would not in future countenance any discrimination against Chinese people in New Zealand. . . .

I wish to announce today that the government has decided to make a formal apology to those Chinese people who paid the poll tax and suffered other discrimination imposed by statute and to their descendants.

With respect to the poll tax we recognise the considerable hardship it imposed and that the cost of it and the impact of other discriminatory immigration practices split families apart.

Today we also express our sorrow and regret that such practices were once considered appropriate. While the governments which passed these laws acted in a manner which was lawful at the time, their actions are seen by us today as unacceptable. We believe this act of reconciliation is required to ensure that full closure can be reached on this chapter in our nation's history.'

Rt Hon Helen Clark
Prime Minister of New Zealand

ONE MAN'S MEAT

Mervyn Cull

A year after he completed his first assignment in China, Mervyn Cull returned for a further term, this time under happier circumstances.

'Dabanjing,' I said, and held up three fingers.

'Dabanjing?' the girl queried, hesitantly. Her pronunciation of the word was somewhat different from mine, but she seemed to understand, I nodded, and she disappeared into the kitchen, from which clouds of wood smoke issued periodically, enriching the smell of food that permeated the tiny restaurant. My daughter and son-in-law were visiting me from New Zealand. The three of us were sitting on stools arranged on one side of a table. On the other side sat a young Chinese couple and two male students. The woman was spooning from an enormous bowl of thick noodle soup. Her husband was deftly twisting long noodles around his chopsticks and thrusting them into his mouth. The two students had plates piled high with short noodles, which they were eating with stubby Chinese spoons.

The girl bustled back from the kitchen with a kettle of tea and three bowls. She poured us each a bowl of the almost colourless liquid. By raising two fingers and saying 'Pijiu', I asked for a couple of beers.

'What are we having?' Tim asked.

I pointed to the plate of long noodles that the man opposite was eating.

'Did you tell her I didn't want meat with mine?'

I had forgotten that Tim was a vegetarian.

'Not bloody likely,' I replied. 'The only words I know that they understand here are 'hui mien' for soup, 'somian' for short noodles and 'dabanjing' for long noodles. And 'pijiu' for beer, of course. And I'm not too sure of those, either. I got them from an Australian FE I met here a few weeks ago. He seemed to make himself understood all right.'

Catherine said, 'Well, perhaps one of the Chinese here understands English and can translate for us.'

'You'll be lucky! The people who run this place are Uighurs, and they have their own language. When I was in here with Susie last week even she couldn't make herself understood.'

The Uighurs are a Moslem minority people of Turkic origin from the Xinjiang Autonomous Region in north-west China. The people running the noodles restaurant—in a back alley not far from the Friendship Hotel—certainly looked more Turkish than Chinese. When I had first visited the place I ordered a meal by pointing to what a woman at the next table was eating. It looked appetising, and when my food arrived it was exactly that—long noodles with a meat sauce, all highly seasoned with chillis. Magnificent.

I don't think the menu of the restaurant extended beyond the three dishes that the Australian gave me the words for. I never ate anything else there, anyway. But they were the tastiest dishes I ever had in China, and also the cheapest. The restaurant had no pretensions. It was small, smoky, dirty and abominably unhygienic by Western standards. The scraggy meat and the vegetables were chopped up on a board in the dining room and then whisked into a tiny, dark kitchen, where they were cooked in a wok glowing red over a wood fire. It must have been all that heat used in the cooking that saved us Westerners from the gastro-intestinal upsets we would ordinarily expect from meals prepared and served in those conditions. But perhaps pure good luck protected us from bugs on the bowls from which we drank our tea and the plastic tumblers from which we drank our beer. I doubted whether they ever had more than a cursory dunking in cold water. The chopsticks were of the disposable kind and were always handed out in their original wrappers, so we had few fears on that score.

'You want noodles without meat?' I said to Tim. 'Fine. You order noodles without meat. Personally, I think you'd do better to take the noodles with the meat and leave the meat on the side of your plate.'

Fortunately, a young Chinese woman paying her bill to the gipsy-looking proprietress, whose cash register was her handbag lying on the table in front of her, seemed to recognise our predicament. 'I tell,' she said, and entered into a long conversation with the waitress who had served us. The girl asked a question or two, seemed to understand, and again disappeared into the kitchen.

Tim looked smug. 'There you go. All that's needed is to know what you want and be firm about getting it.'

And know the language, I thought to myself. Some people have a remarkable facility for picking up foreign languages. Dump them in some exotic place where only the natives know the tongue, and by the next morning they are ordering their eggs lightly fried in vegetable oil, their bacon crisp and ever so lightly anointed with chilli sauce, their toast pale brown with the crusts removed, and their coffee topped with cream and shaken, not stirred, all in the language of the host country. And not a Berlitz in sight.

But not me. In Mandarin I never progressed much beyond 'Xie-xie ni' ('Thank you'), and even when I said that to the office driver he seemed puzzled. At first he used to repeat the phrase slowly, word by word. 'Aw, xie-xie ni,' and laugh good-naturedly. Then gradually, as our acquaintanceship developed, his laughter turned into mild hysteria. I think it was my pronunciation. Anyway, after a couple of weeks or so I began saying just 'Umph, umph' and nodding.

But initially I did try, I learned one or two other phrases—for instance, 'You wo-de xin ma', meaning 'Is there any mail for me?' but when I used it on the hotel receptionist she looked bewildered and muttered something incomprehensible. Whatever she was saying stumped me, so I shoved my Berlitz to the back of my drawer and forgot it. If you can't understand the answer, I reasoned, don't ask the question.

From that point on I used gestures for most of my communication with non-English-speaking Chinese, and I became quite good at it. If at the market I wanted, say, some chicken drumsticks, I would flap my arms and make a noise like a chicken. The vendor would pat her chest, asking whether I wanted breast meat, and I would slap my thigh. It could all be done so quickly that Western bystanders would gape in amazement.

Where language was concerned, I admit with embarrassment, the Chinese put me to shame. They were always willing to give English a go. For instance, only a few days before our visit to the Uighur restaurant, I had been waiting at Beijing Airport for Catherine and Tim to arrive. Filling in time in the coffee shop, I noticed displayed on each table little cards canvassing patrons' opinions of the service. Eight categories of service were listed, to be rated as good, adequate or poor. They were 'Active and warm attitude', 'Smile service', 'Adopt civilised words', 'Regular service process', 'Orderly, comfortable environment', 'Delicious dish', 'Speed of serving dish', and 'Clean dining tool', If I had been asked to polish the English on those cards, I think I would have declined. The language as it stood was quaint, but it was fairly comprehensible, and it was far more charming than the end result of any of my efforts would have been.

My Canadian friend Wayne once asked a Chinese journalist what he had found most difficult when studying the English language. After a moment or two of reflection, he replied, 'Passing the examinations.' He had my profound sympathy, for not only is the English language difficult in itself, but it also comes in an extraordinarily large range of accents, A dish at a Chinese banquet I attended once consisted of a couple of dozen deep-fried quail. I say quail but, for all I could tell, they might just as easily have been sparrows—pathetic little carcasses, golden brown, all with their tiny legs pointing skywards. An American friend sitting next to our Chinese woman interpreter handed me the plate with the light-hearted enquiry, 'Care for a leg?'

The legs were about the size of emaciated matchsticks, so I replied, 'No, thanks, but I'll have the giblets if you can get them for me.'

At which the interpreter, bright-eyed and keen, asked, 'Gipsy? Gipsy? You want a gipsy lady with nice legs?'

One of the greatest complexities of Mandarin is the four tones, Every syllable of the language has one—high, rising, falling-rising or falling, and such is their importance that use of the wrong tone can give a word a completely different meaning. The difference can be critical. The word 'mai', for example, means buy when pronounced with the falling-rising tone and sell when delivered with a falling tone.

But different ways of delivering English can mean a great deal, too, One weekend, Ann, my English friend Chris and I made a day trip to Tianjin. A young Chinese student, who had chosen Marlene as her European name, came with us as interpreter. On the way back to Beijing the woman guard came round the carriage to clean up. She wanted to sweep under our feet and, with all the authority of a regimental sergeant-major, ordered me to 'Stand up!' When she had finished, she commanded, 'Sit down—please.' Her instructions were delivered in such a peremptory manner that it would have been easy to take offence, but we were more amused than miffed. A few minutes later she returned and started a genial conversation in Chinese with Marlene during which she asked, 'How was my English? I've been practising hard.' We assured her that her English was excellent.

Instructions that Chinese translate into written English can also convey an unfortunate impression. An invitation I received to a reception at the Great Hall of the People carried the footnote, 'Valid for one person, and no bringing bags.'

So when Tim ordered noodles without meat in the Uighur restaurant he was not, perhaps, as aware of all the possible pitfalls as I. But the Chinese woman who had transmitted all his requirements to the Uighur waitress seemed to be satisfied that she had got the message across all right, so we sat back, poured ourselves some more tea and waited for our meals to arrive.

Five minutes later the waitress appeared with four steaming plates, which she set down on the plastic table cloth in front of us. Three of them were piled high with noodles and meat. The fourth was heaped with meat alone.

I turned to Tim and said, 'There you go, then. All that's needed is to know what you want and be firm about getting it.'

XIA YU

Tze Ming Mok

all the people in puddles
came down with
out their dialects. we
look at each other in english.
tears crash everywhere.

'My room is too small
this must mean it's time
to leave again.' may rain
can't help but be
simultaneous
descending with its talk

colouring the background in
a million relief lines pointing
down, down. 'I'm out of here
soon too it's too cold
out here soon.' may rain
divides a million brief puns

into backroom talk
descending around, around.
'I'm out of room may I
may I rain soon.' no pause
in the fall of the multilingual undress
babbling through its ears: xia yu! xia yu!
rain fall; down with
language

hear the crash everywhere
shaping the silence
of a lover who asks
without moving his mouth:
'What did you put on your skin?
My tongue's gone numb.'

FIRST PASS UNDER HEAVEN

Nathan Hoturoa Gray

In October 2000, Wellington-born Nathan Hoturoa Gray set out from Jiaguguan to walk the length of the Great Wall. 256 days later he ended his journey where the wall meets the sea at Shanhaiguan. In the course of the trek, companions such as the annoying Paolo came and went.

Day 105, 8 April 2001

Ka hinga atu—he tetekura. Ka hara-mai he tetekura.
When the fern frond drops, another rises to take its place.

Threatening clouds sweep across the plains towards the mountain I'm hiking. With no tent, I have to find shelter quickly. I continue along the Wall, passing watchtower after watchtower, but none provide me with a home. All are filled with mud and clay. The clouds congregate at the base of the mountain.

With no one else to follow, the Wall is all I know. It takes me towards the summit just as the elements close in for the kill. I crouch low to avoid the howls of the wind and look back in the direction I have come from. A spectrum of golden

sunlight peers through the clouds, making a diagonal line towards the next peak. It shines on a small cave. There it is.

Paolo has set up his green tent at the mountain's base, sheltered from the wind. I don't have the nerve to go back down to ask if I can sleep. Not after the fight that morning. He has been playing games with me all day, walking ahead of me and then hiding on the other side of the Wall so that I walk past and he reappears behind. One is in more control from behind.

Darkness inks the sky. I push aside my misery and leap into the journey ahead. Each brick becomes my focus: step by manageable step. Diego was right about how much more intense it is to walk the Wall on your own. It's when your relationship with the Wall-builders becomes so much more alive. I walk for an hour before the cave entrance appears. It's a brick stable. I relax upon sighting it, but trip immediately, almost twisting my ankle again. I have to stay alert.

The stable is dark and damp, wet mud and rocks are strewn all over the ground. There is one dry spot just big enough to fit one person. The journey is catering to my needs. I climb into my sleeping bag and lie on top of my grimy, yellow pack-cover and three black plastic bags. I light a candle in an old prayer shrine protected from incoming gusts of wind. As the storm rages outside, the candle flickers resiliently.

'I can do this,' I say to the candle, savouring a handful of salted peanuts and a gulp of water.

The candle burns steadily.

I can do this.

Day 106

I watch the sunrise from my sleeping bag. The mountain I have climbed is clear through the stable arch, surrounded by a horizon of dry fields. Venus shines and gives me comfort. I crawl to the entrance and peer down the slope. I can't see Paolo's tent. He could be anywhere. Without his alarm clock, and one another to egg the other on, my head slumps back to my t-shirt pillow. The concrete ground is surprisingly comfortable, and I fall straight back to sleep.

I awake again, more refreshed. There are no stars now. The wind sings, the Wall's ancestors calling me on. Hunger and the prospect of facing the increasing heat are now the daily motivators. I pack up my small home and move on along the Wall. Surely the next few miles will diminish the problems plaguing my mind.

'What am I really doing here in China?' The separation with Paolo has left me feeling adrift. It's like I've lost a part of myself and I'm not sure who I really am. I've always been a 'we' on this journey.

I walk on and see a shepherd. He is old, and sits looking out over his sheep grazing on the hillside. I spend my time sitting with him, watching the world through his patient eyes. I feel like I can give myself more time to take in China rather than be pushed along by someone else's schedule. The sheep don't do much, so I press on and see Paolo meditating on the next peak. I look again. It's just a rock. I've got to eat.

The Wall heads down to a small village at the base of the range. A dog barks wildly, angered by my foreign scent, as a man in a blue Mao suit looks up from hoeing vegetables in his back garden. I gesture to my empty water bottle. He smiles and invites me into his small brick home.

We enter and are greeted by his wife. She looks loving and sweet—her eye wrinkles point upwards when she laughs. Her daughter smiles, too. She has hair to her waist, a smooth white face, and alert oval eyes. I find her soft serenity a soothing relief after the harsh beauty of the Wall.

The mother passes me a handful of apple slices. I giggle nervously, but have never felt so grateful. It's like I've been sentenced for the crime of self-centredness to a year of strolling amongst some of the planet's most generous people. My hunger compels me to stay. It's been a day and a half since last I properly ate, and I'm sure the mother knows I'm on the verge of tears.

The mother and daughter start to cook bread, noodles, potatoes and tofu. Mixing the water and flour into dough, it is mixed with herbs and spring onions before being moulded into round balls and twisted bread rolls. The process takes most of the day—a significant part of their lives revolving around this meal. The mother likes me filming her work, she laughs happily as I film. Her performance is flawless and I'm going to be invited to eat. I relax properly for the first time since being on my own. We sit cross-legged around the *kang,* gobbling up noodles and bread. Nurturing the body with good food, the soul with community and laughter, these people are giving me the strength to continue.

A dog barks outside and I wonder whether it is Paolo coming past. The daughter is now knitting, pulling the wool from an old jersey to be used for a new one. She has a contented smile as her work slowly grows. It is her meditation. I don't really want to leave these people's home, but reality pesters and I must continue with my project.

I fluster about, readying to leave.

'Man zou,' the man says in a firm, compassionate voice, providing a focus for my glazed-over eyes: Go slow. He places his hand upon my shoulders. 'The journey is the reward.'

My heart soars at this family's kindness. The prospect of tackling the next 1,700 kilometres suddenly isn't quite so daunting. I look up at the Great Wall, thick and brown, contesting its next range. I look forward to what lies ahead.

Outside the village I see Paolo sitting down beside a brick wall in the ploughed fields. My instincts say to just keep on walking, but foolishly I don't.

'I'm just digesting my meal. Want to buy the sleeping mat off me? I'll sell it to you for $30.'

'Thirty dollars American? Jesus, that's more than they cost brand new.'

'Thirty dollars.'

He knows I need it, so there is no point in bargaining any further. I give him all the US dollars I have left, and watch him walk off, wanting nothing more to do with him.

The Wall meanders along another mountain range and heads into a plateau flanked by two villages. Paolo, still well ahead, takes a quiet back-street to find accommodation. I head instead up the main street. A host of local kids follow me excitedly. I enter a shop to buy some supplies for the next day's walk.

'*Binggan doushao qian?*' How much for a packet of biscuits?

'*Ba kuai*' the shopkeeper replies hesitantly. Eight yuan.

'*Bu shi, liang kuai qian.*' No, no only 2 *kuai*, a young child states earnestly. The kids give me their richest attention, but their smiles fade when I'm tapped on the shoulder.

'*Jinlai, laowai.*' Come with me, foreigner. A fat policeman stands behind me in a dark blue uniform. He has thick, black-rimmed glasses. '*Lai, woman qu gong'an ju dengji.*' Let's take a visit to the police barracks.

'But this villager has offered me a place to sleep in his home.' I look to the peasant hopefully. He lowers his head, quickly retracting his earlier offer. We walk through the main street, turn left and enter the police compound. There are four men inside.

'What are you doing in our village?' a plain-clothes cop with a poxy face asks. 'Are you a spy?'

'No,' I respond icily. 'I wouldn't have had any interest in visiting your village if the Wall didn't trail through here.'

'Are you alone?'

'Uummmmm . . . Yes.'

'Can we see your passport?'

'Yes, of course.'

A bespectacled officer flicks through the pages curiously. He is skinnier than the rest. He looks up.

'You've travelled a lot.'

'Yes.'

'*Meiguo ren?*' You American? He points to my Arabian visa from Jordan.

'No, New Zealander.' I'm glad they can't read my US study visa. There's been quite a lot of anti-American sentiment going on ever since a Chinese military jet collided with a US spy plane, killing the Chinese pilot and sending the US plane down into Hainan Island. The US spies were captured and safely returned to the US, but the media had reported that the US plane had purposely rammed the Chinese jet.

'You're not in trouble—we just want to know which lands you have seen.' His glasses reflect the light. He seems to be playing the good-cop role.

I'd dealt with several police and government officials en route. Most of them would test me, first, with their gaze. If I could counter their suspicions with a forceful stare, I would generally be accepted into their clan and invited to partake in a feast. Only a privileged member of the police or government can afford such a multi-tiered affair. Theirs is high-status living.

The second test was the *ganbei*. If I managed to hold my liquor (my university training suddenly becoming invaluable), I would leave the exchange as a fellow comrade blessed for the journey ahead. If not, I guess I'd wake up hungover in some cell. It is fortunate that Caucasians generally have a higher alcohol tolerance than that of Asians. There had been times when I had done a lot of necessary sculling.

'I smell something fishy—you're not telling us something.' The poxy-faced cop grimaces, sensing my inner distress. I can't look him in the eye knowing that Paolo is still in town. It would be very suspicious for him to be found.

'*Ni you shenme gongzuo?*' What is your job?

'*Wo shi lushi.*' I'm a lawyer. The cop's eyebrows rise. Less than one percent of the population are lawyers, only 150,000 admitted to the bar by 2000. They are generally held in high esteem. Indeed, it is a lot safer than saying you're a journalist—twenty-four having been arrested or reported missing according to Reporters Sans Frontiers already this year.

'Look, here's a photo of my family.' I use my second tactic to get them onside, describing each family member enthusiastically to avoid the poxy-faced cop's questions. It isn't working. His dark eyes scan me scathingly, his nose sniffing for a guilty scent. He opens his mouth to ask another question, when suddenly my attention is diverted to a small silver television playing in the corner of the room. It is showing a CCTV 1 news broadcast with an item about the New Zealand Prime Minister, Helen Clark, visiting the Chinese President. They are shaking hands.

'Look, our leaders are making friendship!'

The hard-nosed questioning ceases. I must be the luckiest bastard in the world.

Opposite: Sarah Laing is a fiction writer and graphic designer who lives in Auckland. In 2011 she was invited to China to take part in the annual Beijing and Shanghai international literary festivals.

FURTHER GREEDY ADVENTURES: *Chopsticks*

THE CITY GOD

Paula Morris

Paula Morris is a New Zealand fiction writer of English and Ngati Wai descent. 'The City God' is taken from her first short story collection, Forbidden Cities *(2008).*

He told her that he caught a taxi to work every day. He told her that he caught a taxi home. Taxis in Shanghai were cheap and fast. Nobody had a car, he told her, but everywhere Sylvia went there were thousands of cars, roaring down avenues and around corners, intent on mowing her down. The lights at pedestrian crossings beeped, flashing numbers at her, counting down seconds. If she didn't make it across the road in time, she would be killed. At one intersection, a motorcycle drove onto the footpath and almost ran over her foot. She stepped out of the way, into the path of someone spitting. Everyone spits here, he told her. That's why she had to take her shoes off and leave them just inside the front door. He told her she wasn't to track China into the apartment.

Her son had a lot to tell her. He worked in some sheer gleaming tower in Pudong, the other side of the big river, where just a few years ago it was all rice paddies and hovels. Now everyone lined up on this side of the river to gaze across at this shiny new city. Crowds of gawkers, Chinese and foreign, stood with their backs to the grand old British banks and trading companies lining the Bund. These buildings were restaurants and bars and shops selling luxury goods now Big business had crossed the river, he told her.

'You'll have to come over and see my office,' he said. 'I'm on the fifty-sixth floor. You can catch the train that goes under the river if you like—it goes through this psychedelic tunnel. Maybe Ros can bring you over one day.'

But her daughter-in-law said she never went to Justin's office.

'Never invited,' she told Sylvia. 'If he really wanted you over there, he'd take you himself.'

Ros's idea of a day out was a trip to the huge IKEA or a shopping expedition to the City Market near the Portman Ritz, in search of crème fraiche or organic coffee. She was as tall and polished as the office towers across the river—slender, hard-edged, platinum. When she and Sylvia went out shopping, they always dropped into a Starbuck's for a latte and a slice of dry cake. They always caught a taxi home.

Sylvia preferred going out alone, despite the perils of walking. On her first day out in Shanghai, she learned to respond to noises—the whistles of the crossing guards, the horn of a car turning right on red, the urgent trill of bicycle bells. In a market, she flattened herself against a display of small, snowy cauliflowers at the sound of a moped purring past down the narrow aisle. Walking home in the late afternoon darkness, she listened for bicycles and their bells because none of them, she discovered, had lights.

★ ★ ★

After a week in Shanghai, Sylvia was missing Roy, her husband; since his heart operation, he didn't like travelling such long distances. She wished Justin would come home more often, but she didn't like to say anything to him about it. He was very busy at work, she knew, and when he travelled it was for business. Last weekend, just before Sylvia arrived, he'd been in Hong Kong. Ros hadn't gone with him, though she talked about the shops in Hong Kong as though they were some kind of paradise.

Sylvia spent the day wandering, then returned, feet aching, to the sparsely furnished white apartment. Ros wanted to know what she'd seen, so Sylvia listed a few landmarks. Most clear in her memory were people—the girl in a fur shrug walking her beagle, the dog pulling at its Burberry leash; the tiny woman in rough clothes, prostrating herself on the footpath, her forehead hitting the concrete over and over. And some of the English signs she'd seen were perplexing as well, so she'd written them down. Outside the market, a banner read: 'Construct a consumer environment of rest assured is a common duty of whole society.' On the boards of photographs depicting the history of the Nanjing Road, she'd learned that 'the street is strongly characterized with the fresh concept of a combinational fascination'. The caption for a photograph of the Nanjing Road at night, illuminated and multicoloured, read simply: 'Splendid and Gorgeous'. Splendid and gorgeous, she'd been repeating silently all day.

None of this she told Ros. Instead Sylvia produced the things she'd bought that day: a book of postcards, a small pink tin filled with inedible sweets, a blue-and-white porcelain dish from the bird market, a bag of mandarins. Ros frowned at all these foreign objects and told her the things she should be buying, like fabric and knock-off designer bags.

When Justin got home, later than expected, they sat down for dinner. His job was very, very demanding, he said.

'You seem to have plenty of time for karaoke bars,' Ros said.

'You know that's business.'

'Your mother's barely seen you. She's out wandering the streets while you're drinking whiskey and singing 'Born to be Wild' with some teenage hostess.'

'It's a business thing,' Justin told Sylvia. 'I'm taking Friday afternoon off so we can go around the Old Town together.'

'A half day! You should be honoured, Sylvia.'

Sylvia didn't like the way they spoke to each other. She didn't remember this from Auckland, but she never stayed with them in Auckland. Ros was serving dinner now; Justin was talking about expanding markets. Sylvia's wine glass was empty already, and when Justin leaned over to fill it he kept talking, looking her straight in the eye. She was amazed he didn't spill any. Ros had made pasta for dinner, with a sauce of olives and tomatoes and anchovies. For most of the meal, Justin talked about his Chinese employees and what a problem they were. At school they learned everything by rote and now they couldn't use their initiative. In Chinese companies, the general manager was like a god, and everyone was expected to follow his instructions. They didn't know how to question things, how to innovate. They were too reactive.

'You two don't seem very happy here,' Sylvia suggested. She'd had two glasses of wine. It was the first time all week that she'd expressed a definite opinion.

'What are you talking about, Mum—' Justin seemed angry. He was broad-shouldered like Roy, but otherwise he didn't resemble either of his parents much. Justin looked like her grandfather, stern and dissatisfied. 'We love it here. We love the lifestyle.'

'I've never seen the stars at night,' Ros said, taking another long slug of wine. 'It's smoggy all the time.'

'You can see the stars tonight,' Justin told her. 'Just look out the bloody window!'

'All I can see is scaffolding and cranes.'

'The smog used to be bad,' Justin said to Sylvia. 'But a lot of the factories were pushed out of the city. In Beijing it's much worse. And everyone's really aggressive up there.'

'Because they can't see the sky,' said Ros. 'And they don't know what grass is.'

Sylvia was still wondering about the word 'lifestyle'. In New Zealand, people talked about owning lifestyle blocks, and this seemed to mean having a few acres of land in the country where you could grow some carrots or keep a horse. But Sylvia never gave much thought to her own lifestyle. It involved driving to the supermarket, she supposed, and Sky TV.

'What *is* your lifestyle?' she asked Justin. He gave her a hard look. 'Do you mean catching taxis?'

'I'm here to make my fortune,' he told her quietly. 'We're riding the crest here. Shanghai is the number two port in the world—did you know that? Bigger than Rotterdam and knocking on Singapore's door. Lots of opportunities. Very open-minded, of course.'

'I thought we'd go to Yin for dinner tomorrow night,' said Ros, collecting their bowls and carrying them to the small kitchen. It all looked very flash, but there wasn't an oven, and the stove only had two elements. Ros would leave the dishes piled in the sink for the ayi to wash tomorrow morning. 'They have live jazz there. Unless you'd prefer Indian or Thai or something.'

Sylvia told them she was easy—whatever they wanted. Later, in her little bedroom on the street-side of the apartment, she raised the blind and looked out the window. Ros was right. She couldn't see a single star in the sky.

He told her not to give money to beggars. He told her that if someone approached her saying they'd lost all their money, it was a scam. He told her that the scruffy men on bicycles who clanged heavy school bells were collecting rubbish. They were migrant men, he said, and not to be trusted, though Shanghai was a safe city for foreigners.

For all its crowds, the city did feel safe, and perhaps that was why Sylvia let the girl walk into the building with her. She'd caught a taxi back from the museum, as instructed. Ros had given her a piece of paper with the address written in Chinese characters, and this she'd presented to the taxi driver. He'd understood it, and driven her home quickly through lurching traffic, but getting out of the cab Sylvia felt flustered, as though she was late. This was her last full day here: she and Ros had been out yesterday to the fabric market, and today Justin was coming home early from work to take her around the bazaar in the Old Town. She dropped her package from the museum shop—more postcard books, a T-shirt for her nephew—onto the ground. The girl stepped forward to help her. And then they were walking up the steps together; the security guard was opening the door and they were both inside the marble-floored lobby.

'You live here?' Sylvia asked the girl. She didn't want to be rude, but she hadn't seen any Chinese people in here at all, apart from the guards.

'I'm visiting friend,' said the girl, smiling. She spoke American-inflected English to Sylvia. To the guard she spoke swift sing-song Chinese, pointing at Sylvia and towards the lift. 'Ros Fullerton.'

'You know Ros?' Sylvia was pleased. Ros seemed to have very few friends here, apart from a group of American expatriates she met up with for lunch in Xintiandi once a month. Ros referred to them as The Wives. She told Sylvia that they all sat around complaining about Shanghai.

The girl nodded. She was a pretty thing, slight and rosy cheeked. She wore her long hair loose, the way Ros used to do years ago. Her skirt was very short and the bag hiked onto one shoulder was very large. The spiky heels of her boots clicked across the floor. At the lift she hesitated.

'You Ros's mother?' she asked.

'Mother-in-law,' Sylvia explained.

'Ah!' The girl smiled again, nodding with approval when Sylvia pressed the button for the sixth floor. 'I am Emily.'

'It's nice to meet you, Emily.' Ros hadn't mentioned that a friend was coming to visit her this afternoon. Inside the apartment, while Sylvia slid her shoes off, Ros didn't get up from the dining table, where she sat flicking through the *Shanghai Daily*. She looked over at Emily, and Emily—bag still shouldered, boots still on—looked at her. That was when Sylvia realized they didn't know each other at all.

'Ros,' said Emily. She wasn't smiling now. Her voice shook. 'I am Emily Chin. I am lover of your husband, Justin. We went Hong Kong together last weekend. This not first time.'

Sylvia was still standing on the doormat, its stubby bristles prickling through her stockings. She didn't dare move. Ros was still holding a page of the newspaper, about to turn it. There was no expression on her face—not surprise, not anger. She was looking at Emily the way Sylvia looked at paintings in a gallery, pausing to take everything in, half-conscious of her own reflection.

'I am his girlfriend,' Emily went on, her voice a little louder. 'For six months. He loves me, and wants to tell you, but the time is not right.'

Ros said nothing. Sylvia didn't know what to do. She should never have let Emily walk in with her. She should have asked the security guard to call Ros from reception, except the guard didn't seem to speak English, and maybe Emily would have made her little speech anyway, over the phone.

The front door opened, cracking Sylvia on the elbow. She stepped off the mat, making way for Justin. Now there were four of them in the room, and nobody was speaking. Everyone was expressionless. If this were a soap opera, Sylvia thought, Emily would be trembling and defiant. Ros would be distraught, possibly enraged, clutching the newspaper to her. She, Sylvia, would be aghast, clasping her bosom, or maybe suffering palpitations. Justin would be looking perturbed at the very least, glancing from his wife to his mistress and back. In real life, they were all frozen. It was awkward. Justin looked a little shifty and uncomfortable, the way he looked when he was a child when he'd eaten too many plums, but he didn't move. Ros was still sitting down; everyone else faced her. Nobody knew what to do, Sylvia thought. All the soap operas in the world couldn't prepare you for this.

'I think you should go home,' Justin said quietly and for a moment Sylvia thought he was talking to her. Then Emily's mouth quivered, and she started to cry. He reached out a hand to touch her sleeve. It was a gentle gesture, out of character for Justin—or out of character, at least, for the person he'd become. He cared about this girl.

'You bought me the same bag.' Ros was speaking at last. She didn't sound bitter. She sounded sad, though her face was still neutral, almost dreamy.

'Really,' Justin said to Emily. 'Take a taxi. Have you got enough money for a cab?'

Emily, whimpering, shook her head. Sylvia still had the change from her taxi ride, strange notes stuffed into the pocket of her coat. She reached for the messy bundle and held it out.

'Here,' she said. Justin took the wad of money and handed it to Emily. Ros snorted, half under her breath. Swallowing a sob, Emily clicked out of the apartment and closed the door behind her. The three of them were left, still in place, Sylvia and Justin still in their coats. Sylvia shook her head, trying to waken herself out of the stupor: she had to leave as well. She bent down to pick up her shoes, and the movement seemed loud and theatrical, even though it wasn't; the moment was broken. 'It's your mother's last day,' Ros told Justin. 'You have to take her to the Old Town.'

'No, no,' said Sylvia, struggling to slide on her shoes. 'I'll go out. You two stay here and . . . and talk.'

'I've got nothing to say,' said Ros. She closed the newspaper. 'Have you?'

'Ros,' said Justin. He was an immoveable lump, in the way like a discarded bag of groceries. 'Don't . . . don't *do* anything.'

'Like what?' Ros was brisk, standing up, pushing back her chair. 'Like don't book myself a ticket home on Sylvia's flight tomorrow? Wouldn't that make it easier for you?'

Justin shook his head slowly. He looked as though someone had slapped him across the face.

'Don't go,' he said, so softly Sylvia could barely hear him.

'Take him to the Old Town, please,' Ros said to Sylvia. 'Get him out of here. And one other thing.'

She marched into the big bedroom. Sylvia waited, breath held, listening to sounds of scuffling through the closet. When Ros returned, she was holding a brown shoulder bag, the twin of the bag Emily had carried. She emptied it upside down over the table. The only thing that fell out was half a torn packet of throat lozenges, followed by a fluttering of receipts.

'Throw this out, will you?' Ros thrust the bag at Sylvia. 'Just chuck it out in the street.'

Sylvia took the bag, and told her that she would.

★ ★ ★

He'd told her that Beijing was the place to go for historic buildings and temples, but there was one place in the middle of the bazaar, the Temple of the City God, that sounded promising in the guide book.

They crossed the outer courtyard, hurrying through the smoke of the burning braziers, passing tables piled with packets of incense, and islands of discarded shopping bags and wrapping paper. The stone-flagged corridor linking the temple's courtyards was walled with glass cases housing dozens of small statues. A gaggle of old women, all dressed in bright blue tunics, all so miniscule they made Sylvia feel Amazonian, kowtowed before these cases.

Each ceiling panel depicted a green-winged heron, and Sylvia wanted to ask Justin lots of questions—the significance of the heron, the names of the mini gods, the meaning of the piles of fruit interspersed with the statues. But he'd said almost nothing on the taxi ride here or while they were walking through the thronged cobbled streets of the bazaar. She'd told him again in the taxi that he didn't have to come out with her, but he'd just shaken his head and looked stricken. Sylvia wasn't sure what she was meant to do in a situation like this—commiserate with him or chastise him. Perhaps Ros would leave him; perhaps she wouldn't. Perhaps Justin wanted her to leave him; perhaps he didn't. Perhaps he loved this young girl, Emily; perhaps not. Other people's marriages were their business, too untidy and complicated for anyone else to navigate.

All Sylvia really wanted to do was to go home, where things were easier to understand.

It was quiet here in the temple—that is, quiet until the tiny women crowded into the inner courtyard and began to sing, accompanying their discordant song with small percussive instruments. Sylvia drifted from one English sign to another, trying to make sense of the place, wishing she'd remembered to bring the guide book: she'd left the apartment carrying Ros's unwanted bag, but not her own. From the signs she learned that one room was the Hall of the God of Wealth and that the one opposite was the Hall of the Goddess of Mercy with her delicate blue headdress, platters of brown apples at her feet. A man sat at a rickety desk, playing the flute, a sheaf of music spread out next to his plastic cup. The cup had a lid; it was like something a baby would drink from.

Justin had wandered on to the room of the City God himself, and Sylvia followed him. The City God was small, much smaller than she'd expected. Compared with the giant statue of a general they'd come across in the first room, the City God was almost a disappointment. Everything was red—the fake candles in tall stands, the letters in the 'No Fire in the Hall' signs, the boxes for offerings by each altar, and the broad lacquered face of the City God himself He sat glowering behind his gold curtains like a performer in a puppet show. A young couple kowtowed before him, asking his advice, no doubt. This was why he sat here, she remembered from the guide book: to hear questions on business or personal matters, and dispense some kind of mute advice.

Sylvia stood near the doorway, not wanting to disturb their prayers. In the courtyard, the tiny women in blue had finished singing. Now they were arguing, clutching each other's wrists, pointing in different directions. One of them started singing again in a thin, wavering voice, until the others talked over her, making her stop. They sounded so passionate and so conflicted that Sylvia couldn't help herself: she tapped Justin on the shoulder and asked him, in a whisper, what he thought they were arguing about. He glanced down at her, red-eyed and surprised, as though he'd forgotten that she was there, and told her he didn't know.

Opposite: Kerry Ann Lee, Lilliput.

THE WAY AHEAD

Rt Hon John Key

On 5 September 2012 the New Zealand Prime Minister, the Rt Hon John Key, delivered the opening address at a symposium to mark the 40th anniversary of the establishment of diplomatic relations between New Zealand and the People's Republic of China. Excerpts from the address reflect on New Zealand's China experience thus far, and look towards what is yet to come.

To a New Zealander in 1972, China would have seemed an unknown, mysterious country of close to a billion people. And it's hard to believe New Zealand figured highly in the minds of most Chinese. So much has changed, then, in 40 years.

Since the establishment of diplomatic relations, New Zealand and China have developed a broad and substantial relationship that is now among New Zealand's most important. We have different cultures, different histories, and different political traditions. So we often have a different perspective on things. However, we are able to express our views with openness, honesty and respect. That is an important indicator of our positive intent over 40 years.

Our trade relationship, in particular, has been a huge success, and momentum has grown very quickly in recent years. In part, that is because of China's ever-increasing importance in the global economy. In 1981, when several pioneering New Zealand businesses formed the New Zealand China Trade Association, China accounted for 2.3 per cent of global GDP. By 2011 this had risen to 14.4 per cent. Rapidly rising living standards, increasing urbanisation and a shift to high-protein diets have supported demand for New Zealand products.

Our booming commerce is also due to the fact that New Zealand and China have worked hard to develop our trade relationship over a number of years. New Zealand was the first country to recognise that China had established a market economy, in 2004. We were the first country to agree bilaterally to China becoming a member of the World Trade Organisation. And in 2008, our two countries signed an historic free trade agreement.

Since then, trade between us has grown exponentially. New Zealand's goods exports to China have trebled in only four years, and China is now our second largest export market. Dairy and wood products are the largest export commodities, followed by meat and wool. New Zealand now exports more than ten times the value of product to China every day than we did in the whole of 1972. . . .

People to people links with China are strong too. Chinese tourism to New Zealand only commenced in earnest at the end of the 1990s, but is increasingly significant. Last year Chinese tourist numbers grew by 33 per cent. That number will continue to grow under a new air services agreement that was agreed earlier this year. A lot of young Chinese people also come to New Zealand to study.

Since the 1990s, China has been New Zealand's largest education market. New Zealand is today providing a quality educational experience and pastoral care to around 23,000 Chinese students, and we are aiming to grow that further.

Many Chinese want to stay permanently in New Zealand, rather than just visiting. China is the second largest source of immigrants to New Zealand, behind the United Kingdom. The next census is likely to show a resident population of Chinese in New Zealand of close to 200,000 people. But in relative terms, a greater proportion of New Zealanders actually live in China, rather than vice versa. More than 3,000 New Zealanders are living in China, which is not insignificant compared to our total population of only 4.4 million.

The relationship between New Zealand and China is not just about people to people and trade relations. From time to time, New Zealand hosts military ship visits from China. We work together in regional organisations such as APEC, and on disaster relief. China was one of several countries to send urban search and rescue teams to assist New Zealand in the immediate aftermath of the Christchurch earthquake, and to donate money for reconstruction. We are very grateful for that assistance. New Zealand has also aided China after natural disasters, including the great Sichuan earthquake in 2008. . . .

Looking forward, it is safe to assume that current trends will continue. The centre of global economic activity will keep shifting from the Atlantic to the Asia-Pacific region. Europe will remain a vital outlet for some of our highest value exports, but our biggest growing markets will be around the Pacific basin.

In that environment, New Zealand has a lot to offer. We are a reliable, competitive and high-quality source of food. We have technical knowledge and expertise that can help countries in this region develop, build infrastructure and add value to their natural resources. We can deliver a world class education to the next generation of leaders across Asia and the Pacific. And we are a great place to visit, see wonderful scenery and play a few rounds of golf.

We have lots of things we can sell to other countries, but we also want to see New Zealand businesses forming productive partnerships with Asian and Pacific businesses. There are many new fields of opportunity for New Zealand businesses and people to explore. To operate successfully in this region over coming decades they will need to have a good understanding of China and of Asia in general.

In February, I launched the New Zealand Inc. China Strategy. The strategy is about getting greater efficiency and effectiveness across all government agencies that work in and with China. And it's about developing more targeted and cohesive services to help successful businesses to develop and grow in China. We want to be transparent about our bilateral interests, and get on with advancing them. . . .

One of the immediate outcomes of the Strategy was the formation of the New Zealand China Council. The Council brings together New Zealanders who are engaged in China from across a whole range of fields, including people in the business, academic, science, cultural, and education communities. As the Council's Chair, Sir Don McKinnon, put it, the Council will operate as an umbrella organisation stretching across the breadth of New Zealand's relationship with China, and not leaving anyone in the shade. I think this is a further step in building on what is already a very strong relationship in many areas.

The China Strategy also reinforces the Government's commitment to ministerial engagement, both as hosts and visitors to China, to build important relationships with China's leadership. As Prime Minister, I made my first official visit to China in 2009, where I met President Hu Jintao and Premier Wen Jiabao. And I am hoping to visit China again later this year, to meet the new Chinese leadership.

I also hope to launch the New Zealand China Council's inaugural Partnership Forum in Beijing. I think that would be a fitting way to mark the 40th anniversary of a significant relationship, one which has a proud history and can look forward to an even better future. I am confident that, with the support of you all, we will see New Zealand's relationship with China go from strength to strength over the years ahead.

SOURCES

A New Beginning: Walding statement, typescript in the possession of the editor.

Commissioner Bigge's Report: McNab, Robert (ed.), *Historical Records of New Zealand*, Wellington: John Mackay Government Printer, 1908, Vol. I, pp. 594–595.

Captain William Anglem: Howard, Basil, *Rakiura: A History of Stewart Island, New Zealand*, Dunedin: A. H. & A. W. Reed, 1940, pp. 90–92.

Illustrious Energy: Narby, Leon and Martin Edmond, 'Illustrious Energy', 5th revision, (typescript of screenplay), pp. 10–13.

Stone-horse Village: Don, Alexander, *Under Six Flags*, Dunedin: J. Wilkie & Co., 1898, pp. 87–94

Alison Wong: Two Poems: Wong, Alison, *Cup*, Auckland: Steele Roberts, 2006, pp. 56, 57.

Tents and Huts: Don, Alexander, *Nineteenth Inland Otago Tour*, 1905–1906, Dunedin: New Zealand Presbyterian Chinese Mission, 1906, pp. 1–2.

National Characteristics: Don, Alexander, *The New Zealand Presbyterian*, 31 April 1885, p. 183.

Chinee Johnee: Bracken, Thomas, *Musings in Maoriland*, Dunedin: A. T. Keirle, 1890, p. 352.

Asiatics Restriction Bill: *Proceedings of the House of Representatives*, 23 June 1896.

That Heathen Chinee: 'Search Lights', *The Press*, 25 May 1895.

The Fungus King: 'Compliment to a Chinese', *The Feilding Star, Oroua and Counties Gazette*, 30 January 1911.

The Missionary Explorer: Edgar, J. Huston, *The Land of Mystery, Tibet*, Melbourne: China Inland Mission, 1927, pp. 18–22.

Open Tender: from a letter written in 1872, included in G. L. Meredith, *Adventuring in Maoriland in the Seventies* (1935) and reproduced in J. C. Reid (ed.), *The Kiwi Laughs: An Anthology of New Zealand Prose Humour*, Wellington: A. H. & A. W. Reed, 1961, p. 36.

The Government and the Yellow Peril: Siegfried, André (tr. E. V. Burns), *Democracy in New Zealand*, London: G. Bell and Sons, 1914, pp. 216–228.

Jade Taniwha: Lee, Jenny Bol Jun, *Jade Taniwha: Maori-Chinese Identity and Schooling in Aotearoa*, Auckland: Rautaki Ltd, 2007, p. 17.

Primary Care: Dr H. B. Turbott interviewed by Chris Elder and Michael Green, 16 November 1985 (edited version).

A Chinese Newspaper: Quinn, William, *Wistaria and Jade: An Account of a Southlander's Travels in the Philippine Islands and the Far East*, Invercargill: Southland Times Office, n.d., p. 61.

Where Life is Cheap: 'Where Life Is Cheap', *The Dominion*, 5 August 1931.

Seeking a Name: Wong, Alison, *As the Earth Turns Silver*, Auckland: Penguin Books, 2009, pp. 132–140.

The Factory Inspector: Alley, Rewi, *Yo Banfa!*, Shanghai: China Monthly Review, 1952, pp. 61–66.

The City of Peking: 'The City of Peking', *The Press*, 4 March 1933.

The Twelfth of December: Bertram, James M., *Crisis in China: The Story of the Sian Mutiny*, London: Macmillan and Co, 1937, pp. 1–13.

New Life for China: Shepherd, George, 'News From China', in *North-China Daily News*, 24 March 1936; Alley, *Yo Banfa!*, p. 18.

Chinese Pottery: Sound recording, John Stackhouse interviewed by Anne Kirker, 20 July 1982, MU000466/001/0002. Te Papa Archives, Museum of New Zealand Te Papa Tongarewa, Wellington.

Missionary Zeal: Hall, Kathleen, 'Recollections of the Days of Bitter Struggle', in *The Twenty Years of the China Welfare Institute*, Shanghai: China Welfare Institute, 1958, pp. 92–102.

The Way to Yenan: Bertram, James, *Capes of China Slide Away: A Memoir of Peace and War 1910–1980*, Auckland: Auckland University Press, 1993, pp. 125–128.

A Letter from Shanghai: Hyde, Robin (ed. Gillian Boddy and Jacqueline Matthews), *Disputed Ground: Robin Hyde, Journalist*, Wellington: Victoria University Press, 1991, pp. 363–367.

Robin Hyde: Two Poems: Hyde, Robin (ed. Lydia Wevers), *Selected Poems*, Auckland: Oxford University Press, 1984, pp. 75–76, 79–80. ('What is it Makes the Stranger?' is taken from a longer poem with the same title.)

Shirtsleeves Diplomacy: Confidential Despatch [F 6096/1/10] of 19 June 1939, Viscount Halifax to Sir R. Craigie (Tokyo), on file PM 264/2/7 Vol. 12, held at National Archives; 'Cruel Indignity to New Zealand Agent', *Auckland Star*, 24 June 1939.

Big City Life: Needham, Joseph and Dorothy Needham (ed.), *Science Outpost: Papers of the Sino–British Science Co-operation Office 1942–1946*, London: The Pilot Press Ltd., 1948, pp. 157–159.

The Refugee's Story: Ip, Manying, *Home Away From Home: Life Stories of Chinese Women in New Zealand*, Auckland: New Women's Press, 1990, pp. 86–92.

Chris Tse: Three Poems: Tse, Chris (with Erin Scudder, Harry Jones), *AUP New Poets 4*, Auckland: Auckland University Press, 2011, pp. 3, 11, 14.

Wartime China: Agnes Moncrieff interviewed by Chris Elder and Michael Green, 8 December 1985 (edited version).

A New Zealand Guangyin: Trevelyan, Jill, *Rita Angus: An Artist's Life,* Wellington:, pp. 192–193.

Gee Hong's War: Neale, Imogen, in *New Zealand Listener*, 3 November 2007, pp. 42–43.

Mandarin Summer: Kidman, Fiona, *Mandarin Summer*, Auckland: Heinemann, 1981, pp. 37–42.

More About Keri Keri: 'More About Keri Keri', *North China Daily Mail*, February 1929, clipping in Moore, L. A. L., Turnbull Library MS-Papers-0599-03.

Sheep Can Fly: Morrison, Colin W., 'Report from China 1947: Exploratory Mission February–June by Colin W. Morrison, Dominion Secretary-Treasurer of CORSO (New Zealand Council of Organisations for Relief Services Overseas Incorporated), 1ˢᵗ October, 1947.' (Unpublished typescript), pp. 50–54.

Desert Hospital: Spencer, Barbara, *Desert Hospital in China*, London: Jarrolds, 1954, pp. 86–94.

New Zealand Representation: Morrison, *op. cit.*, p. 276.

Squaring the Circle: McGibbon, Ian (ed), *Undiplomatic Dialogue: Letters between Carl Berendsen and Alister McIntosh 1943–1952,* Auckland: Auckland University Press, 1993, p. 254.

The Village of Nam Hu Chu: Garland, Margaret, *Journey to new China*, Christchurch: The Caxton Press, 1954, pp. 126–130.

The Communist Speaks: Baxter, James K. (ed. J. E. Weir), *Collected Poems*, Wellington: Oxford University Press, 1979, p. 373.

A Pioneer Trader: Ron Howell interviewed by Chris Elder, 28 November 1985 (edited version).

The Chinese Earth: Buchanan, Keith, *Out of Asia: Asian Themes 1958–66*, Sydney: Sydney University Press, 1968, pp. 153–155.

A Cloak for Mao: Newnham, Tom, *New Zealand Women in China*, Auckland: Graphic Publications, 1995, pp. 98–99.

The May Day Celebration: Cameron, Nigel, *The Chinese Smile*, London: Hutchison of London, 1958, pp. 48–50.

Workers of the World: V.G. Wilcox, 'V. G. Wilcox's Speech at Party School in Canton', *Peking Review* No. 12, March 20 1964, pp. 14–17.

Letter to a Chinese Poet: Dallas, Ruth, *The Turning Wheel*, Christchurch: The Caxton Press, 1961, pp. 9–14 (extract from a longer poem).

'Banned by Tides . . .', Buchanan, *op. cit.*, pp. 56–72.

Establishing Diplomatic Relations: *Foreign Affairs Review*, December 1972.

Six Chapters from Old School Life: Clark, Paul, published in Chinese in Li Yansong and Xia Hongwei, eds., *Honglou fei xue: haiwai xiaoyou qingyi Beida (1927–2008)* (Red buildings, flying snow: foreign alumni recall Peking University), Beijing: Beijing daxue chubanshe, 2008, pp. 140–143. Published for the 110th anniversary of Peking University.

New Zealand and China: memorandum from New Zealand Ambassador, Peking, to Minister of Foreign Affairs, 24 November 1975, held on file PM58/264/1, National Archives.

Third Younger Uncle: Dr James Ng, unpublished typescript in the possession of the editor; revised version published as Ng, James, 'Ng Fon and his family in New Zealand', Amity Centre Publishing Project, October 2001, p. 24.

Ode to the Eight Immortals: Stead, C. K., *The Red Tram*, Auckland: Auckland University Press, 2004, p. 56.

Time to Go: Cull, Mervyn, *The Foreign Expert: A New Zealand Journalist in China*, Auckland: Hazard Press, 1997, pp. 98–102.

Geographical Footnote: typescript in the possession of the editor.

Writer Liu: Mo Zhi Hong, *The Year of the Shanghai Shark*, Auckland: Penguin Books, 2008, pp. 97–108.

Diana Bridge: Two Poems: Bridge, Diana, *Porcelain*, Auckland: Auckland University Press, 2001, p.28; *Red Leaves*, Auckland: Auckland University Press, 2005, p. 28.

A Particular Occasion: Needham, John, *The Departure Lounge: Travel and Literature in the Post-Modern World*, Auckland: Auckland University Press, 1999, pp. 90–94.

An Apology: Clark, Rt Hon Helen, Address to Chinese New Year celebrations, Parliament House, 12 February 2002.

One Man's Meat: Cull, *op. cit.*, pp. 138–142.

Xia Yu: Tse Ming Mok, *Sport,* Spring Issue 29, October 2002.

First Pass Under Heaven: Gray, Nathan Hoturoa, *First Pass Under Heaven*, Auckland: Penguin Books, 2006, pp. 181–186.

Chopsticks: Laing, Sarah:'Let Me Be Frank', http://sarahelaing.wordpress.com/tag/china/

The City God: Morris, Paula, *Forbidden Cities*, Auckland: Penguin Books, 2008, pp. 193–205.

The Way Ahead: Key, Rt Hon John, Address to 40th Anniversary China Symposium, 5 September 2012.

ILLUSTRATIONS

SUPPLEMENTARY BIBLIOGRAPHY

Alley, Rewi, *At 90: Memoirs of my China Years*, Beijing: New World Press, 1986.

Alley, Rewi, *Sandan: An Adventure in Creative Education*, Christchurch: The Caxton Press, 1959.

Barton, Henry H., *George Hunter McNeur: A Pioneer Missionary in South China*, Christchurch: Presbyterian Bookroom, 1955.

Bertram James, *North China Front*, London: Macmillan & Co, 1939.

Bertram, James, *Return to China*, London: Heinemann, 1957.

Brake, Brian, *China: The 1950s*, Wellington: Museum of New Zealand Te Papa Tongarewa, 1995.

Chinese People's Association for Friendship with Foreign Countries, *Rewi Alley*, Beijing: China Reconstructs Press, 1988.

Condliffe, J. B., *China Today: Economic*, Boston: World Peace Foundation, 1932.

Cushing, Lincoln and Ann Tompkins, *Chinese Posters: Art from the Great Proletarian Cultural Revolution,* San Francisco: Chronicle Books, 2007.

Dalzell, Matthew, *New Zealanders in Republican China 1912–1949,* The University of Auckland/New Zealand Asia Institute Resource Papers, No.4, 1995.

Don, Alexander, *Memories of the Golden Road: A History of the Presbyterian Church in Central Otago*, Dunedin: A. H. & A. W. Reed, 1936.

Edgar, J. H., *The Marches of the Mantze*, London: China Inland Mission, n.d.

Elder, C. J. and M. F. Green, 'New Zealand and China 1792–1972', in Ann Trotter (ed.), *New Zealand and China: Papers of the Twenty-First Foreign Policy School 1986*, University of Otago, 1986.

Heinz, William F., *Bright Fine Gold: Stories of the New Zealand Goldfields*, Wellington: A. H. & A. W. Reed, 1974.

Hyde, Robin, *Dragon Rampant*, London: Hurst & Blackett, n.d.

Mawson, Rev. William (ed.), *The Story of the Canton Villages Mission of the Presbyterian Church of New Zealand,* Dunedin: Foreign Missions Committee, 1926.

McNeur, Rev. G. H., 'An Awakening China and the Pacific', in *The Report of the New Zealand Missionary Conference, Dunedin,* Dunedin: Conference Committee, 1926.

McNeur, Rev. Geo. H., *The Missionary in Changing China*, Dunedin: Foreign Missions Committee, 1935.

Milner, Ian F. G., *New Zealand's Interests and Policies in the Far East*, New York: Institute of Pacific Relations, 1940.

Newnham, Tom, *He Mingqing: The Life of Kathleen Hall*, Beijing: New World Press, 1992.

Ng, James, *Windows on a Chinese Past*, Dunedin: Otago Heritage Books (4 Vols), Vols 1 and 4 1993, Vol 2 1995, Vol 3 1999.

Power, W. Tyrone, *Recollections of A Three Years' Residence in China, Including Peregrinations in Spain, Morocco, Egypt, India, Australia, and New Zealand,* London: Richard Bentley, 1853.

Tai, Yuen William, *The Origins of China's Awareness of New Zealand 1674–1911,* Auckland: New Zealand Asia Institute, 2005.

Thomson, James C. Jr., *While China Faced West: American Reformers in Nationalist China 1928–1937*, Cambridge Massachusetts: Harvard University Press, 1969.